Ailish Henderson's quirky, deeply personal textile work takes inspiration from her family life and history, creating evocative and meaningful pieces with a combination of vintage fabric, found textiles, sketches and photography. In this fascinating book, Ailish explains her working methods and inspirations, as a guide to help you create your own unique and personal textile art.

Chapter One explains how to start your project, looking at sketchbooks, mood boards and sources of inspiration. Chapter Two shows various ways of collecting and sourcing materials for your pieces, with a focus on memorabilia and found textiles. Chapter Three explores different ways of making, from printing to stitching, sketching or sculpting, always with a focus on cloth and textile. The rest of the book takes you through a series of narratives from Ailish's own life that have shaped and inspired her work, giving helpful tips and prompts along the way. There are also contributions from other leading textile artists who create narrative textiles.

Beautifully illustrated with the author's own work and that of other contributing artists, such as Lise Howie, Caren Garfen and Daisy May Collingridge, this book revels in the stories that can be told through textiles. It is the ideal book for any artist who wants to explore new sources of inspiration and create work that is meaningful to them.

Narrative Textiles

TELL YOUR STORY IN MIXED MEDIA AND STITCH

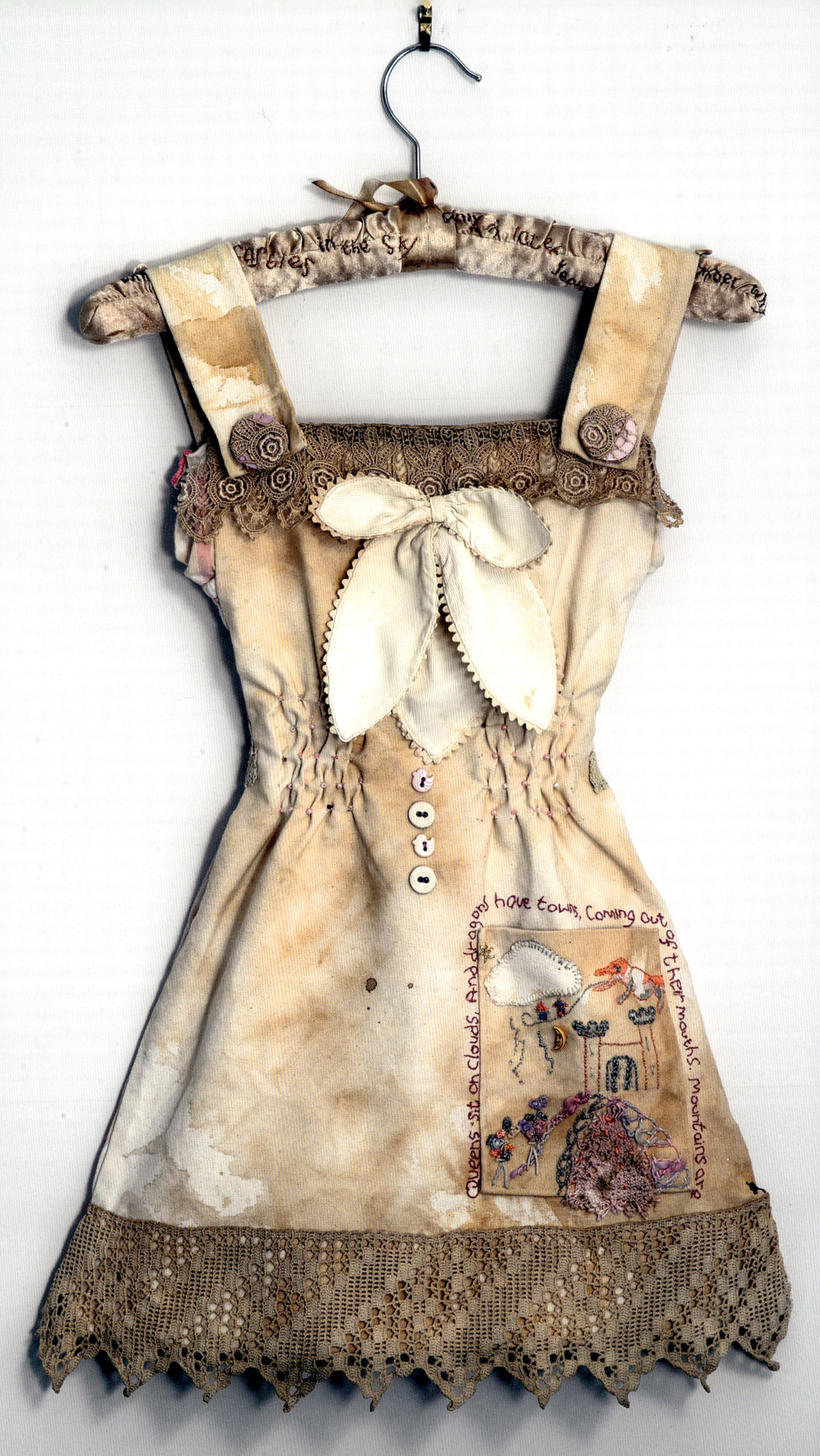
arbles in the Sky
Queens sit on clouds. And dragons have towns, Coming out of their mouths. Mountains are

Narrative Textiles

TELL YOUR STORY IN MIXED MEDIA AND STITCH

Ailish Henderson

BATSFORD

First published in the United Kingdom
in 2024 by
Batsford
43 Great Ormond Street
London
WC1N 3HZ

An imprint of B. T. Batsford Holdings Limited

ISBN 978 1 84994 882 1

A CIP catalogue record for this book is available from the British Library.

10 9 8 7 6 5 4 3 2 1

Reproduction by Rival Colour Ltd, UK
Printed and bound by Toppan Leefung Printing International Ltd, China

This book can be ordered direct from the publisher at www.batsfordbooks.com,
or try your local bookshop.

Dedication

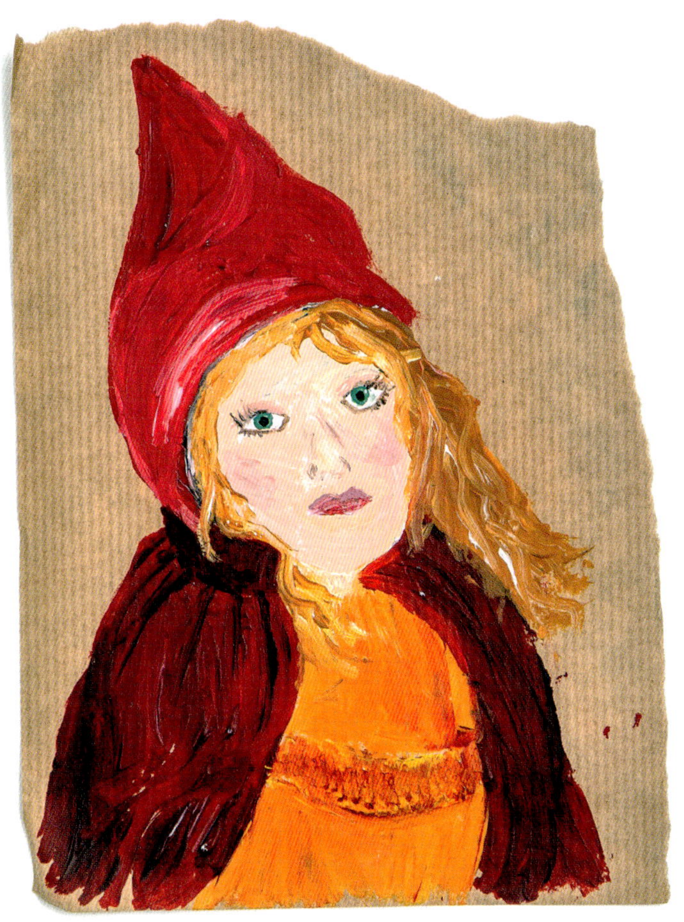

To my grandmother, Narg: you wove the narrative within my soul.

To my grandmother, Lillian: I never met you, yet your fine soul led my pen to paper.

To my mother, who sewed the seed and taught me to read.

To my father, who taught me how to feel life.

Finally, to Barnabus, who led me into love again.

Thank you.

PAGE 2: Castles in the Sky Dress *(Ailish Henderson, 2013). Childhood linen, thread, antique familial lace.*
ABOVE: Red and I *(Ailish Henderson, 2011). Oils, brown packaging.*
RIGHT: *Clasping after the loss of nargdad. My treasure Narg and I (2012).*

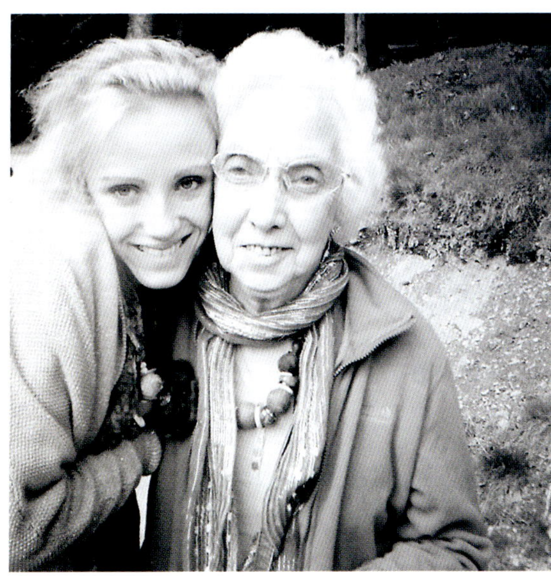

Contents

Once upon a time...

Step into my curious world, the tall and true tales of Ailish.

As a child, I was nurtured, cosseted and nourished in warmth. I led a *Little House on the Prairie*-style life, home-schooled by my dear mother, and I owe her for everything that flows from my head, mouth and hands. We did it all, including nature days and school trips to many a historical location – don't get me started on the graveyard lichen trip or the chemical compounds of the White Cliffs of Dover!

As a young woman, my mother had made all her own clothes, and she endeavoured to pass this trait down to me. Let's just say we differed on this. My weapon of choice would always be my pen and paintbrush – or so I thought. Yet here I am, writing a book about textiles!

My mother is the reason I look around the corner and go the extra step. We walked the curriculum line: every exam taken, no chickening out allowed and 9-to-4 days were mandatory. I thank her now for my ability to stay focused and driven. I thank her for our bedtime story nights, *The Teddy Robber* and glances of voyages across the seas. She may not have taught me the theory of everything, yet row by row my spelling is only in order because of her arduous 'line-giving'.

As an artist, I actively use my own narrative line to build visual textile-based artworks. Almost every area of our lives can be used to create artistic matter. Be it good or bad, life's path will be full of inspiring fuel to create artworks; we just need to comprehend how it can be used. This is where I hope to journey with you. I will walk you through using your own stories as a source of material. From traditional embroidered examples, through mixed-media stitched collage, to using the most subtle colour palette within a sculptural setting, there will be an aspect that captures your own interest.

My own personal pieces are used as illustrations, with suggestions as to how you can repurpose these ideas for your own personal stories.

This book is full of images, using examples from my own practice, from other narrative-focused artists, and from my own past and present students.

As the story-keeper, I will lead you through a variety of possibilities so that ultimately you can create a personal version using your own tales. I will leave you with a 'comma'; you can then finish the sentence – your sentence, your narrative – leading to whatever your 'full stop' might be.

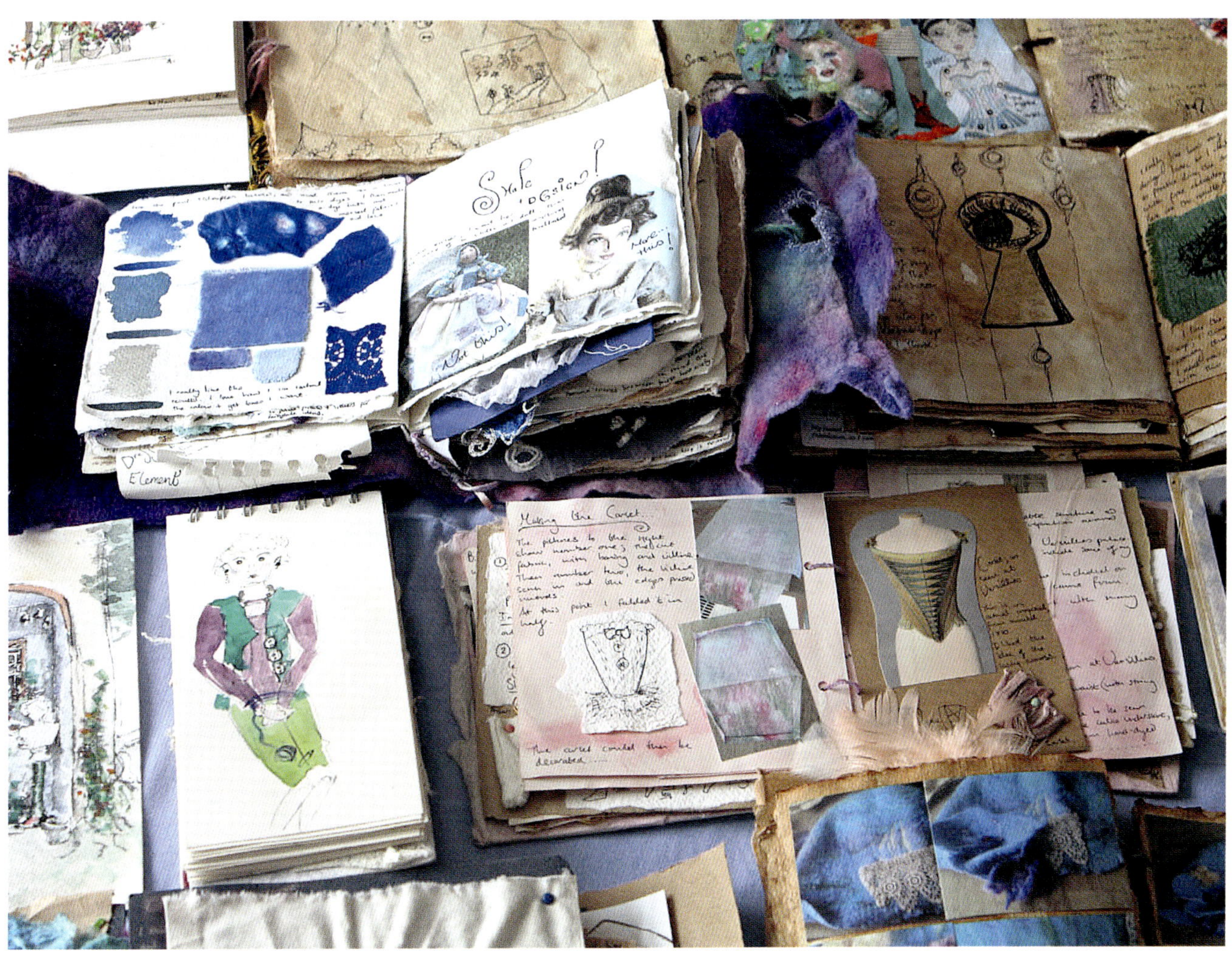

Life can be beautiful, no matter the obstacles along the road. It is up to us to look for the beauty, to capture it and tame it to become a visual storyline: our story.

'I will tell you the story, of Jack and the Glory...if you don't speak in the middle of it.'

I held my breath and waited for my grandad's (henceforth Nargdad's) conspiring twinkle: Silence. Curiosity killed the onward vocals.... I caved, too impatient to wait. Of course, he was never going to tell me the story. He was teaching me a vital life lesson: patience.

My dear Narg, his other half, with knitting always in hand, her stories were always my demand. She never had a book in her hand. Life can be cruel, and only as I grew did I appreciate why she always made her stories up. I thought she did it especially for me, not realising her eyes had ceased to see.

Jack and the Bean Stalk, Red Riding Hood...this duo of grandparents, without knowing it, sowed the narrative deep within my soul. Ask any of my friends: even now I will go around the world and back just to tell the story of my day before I get to the point.

Yet isn't that what makes life beautiful? The ability to see life with more volume than the skeleton narrow view?

This early foray into the world of non-book-led stories created a requirement for me to develop my own stories. This, of course, could have been translated in

ABOVE: *A selection of my handmade sketchbooks.*

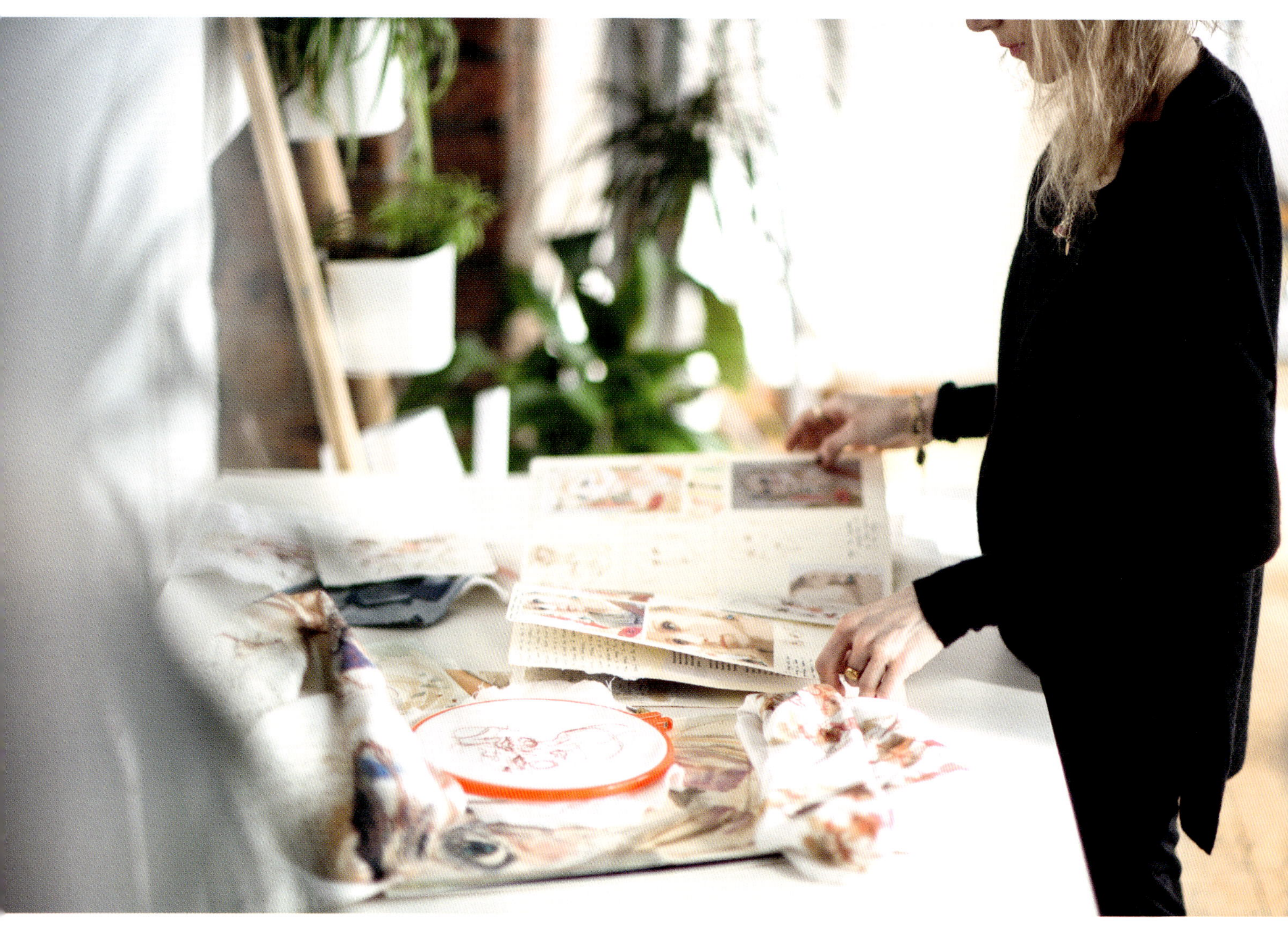

many ways. For me personally, it has found expression in art.

We all have our own life stories, or those we make up for ourselves. How can we use these as the ignition to produce textile art or mixed-media outcomes?

Within this book, I will not prescribe to you any definite course, one that you cannot make your own. I will lead you through a multitude of possibilities and starting points; things to make you think 'what if I...'

Cherish your curiosity; embrace your own history, travels and the things that make you uniquely you, and use them to fuel your textile art projects. It is my hope that my book will give you the strength to follow your own narrative line and develop all those characters that lie in your heart.

'Let's start at the very beginning, a very good place to start'

– Julie Andrews, *The Sound of Music* (1965)

ABOVE: *Artist at work.*

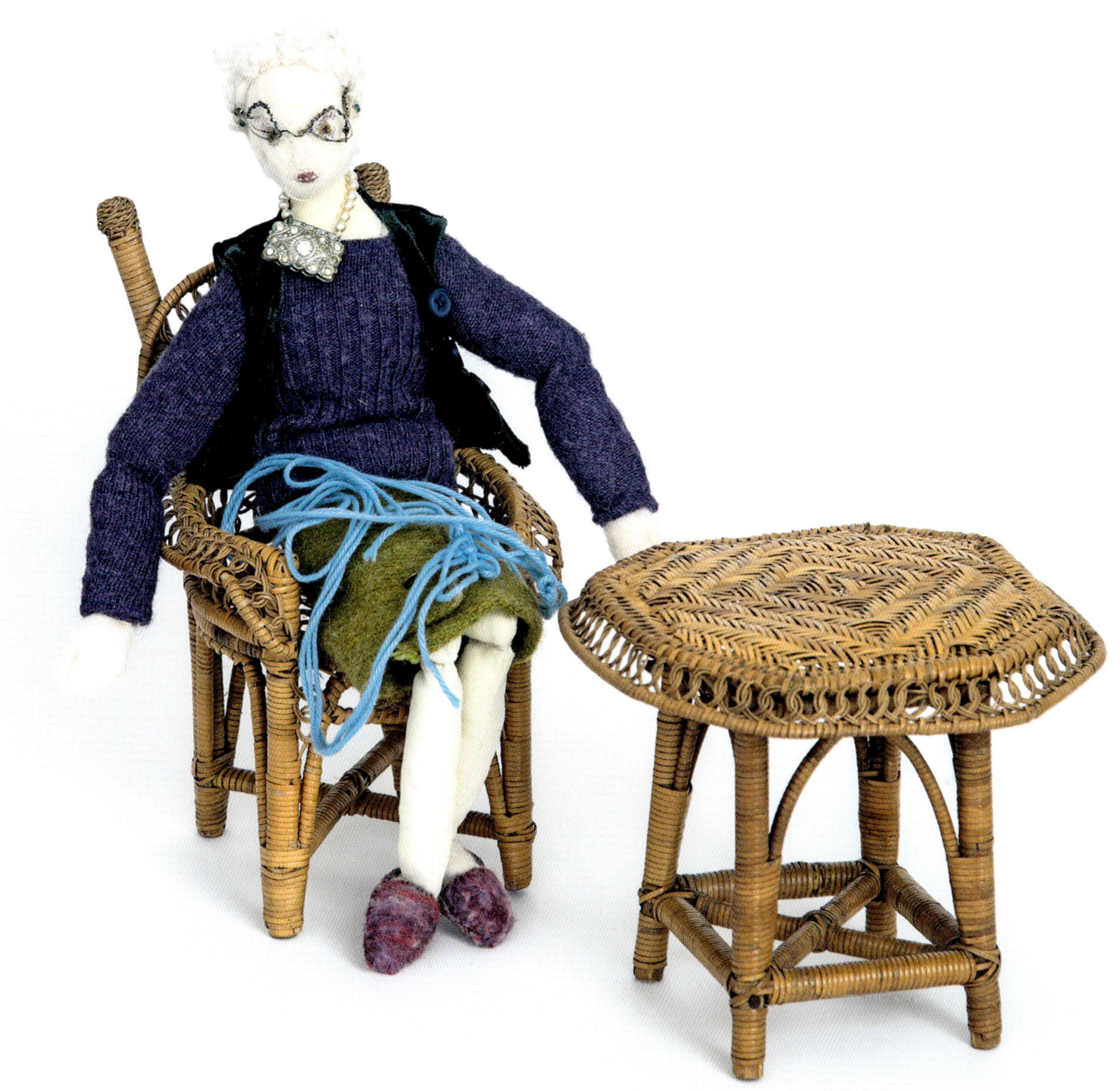

The *narrative* custodian

Moments matter. Do not let them scatter.

As an artist, and indeed simply as a human being, that statement shapes my path, dominating my thinking and practice. I like to question the impact that life's events can have on our ongoing narrative; the things that are set to make us or break us. Strongly entrenched events, experienced in early years may only come to the surface decades later, where they often take on new meanings and can finally be understood and processed.

This focus has led me to specialise in research to connect the repair and restoration of you, the author of works, to the act of making – 'Maker: Mended.' This evidences itself in my work in both the written and practical form.

I wasn't always inclined towards textiles. I began life very much led by pen and paint, pursuing an early education in the so-called Fine Arts. I was a raised in a family with a mother and grandmother who enjoyed cloth-driven practices, while my father's side was very much paint-driven, so maybe I was always destined to bounce between the two. Experience has taught me that I don't have to, I can combine and define a narrative path for myself. It took a happenstance with a certain textile arts tutor to formally introduce me to the material bound. I had met my match! This was love at first sight, and the novelty has never worn off.

As I have developed my practice, I haven't bound myself to any one technique. I enjoy questioning how to marry textiles, sculpture and, yes, paper and pen.

My focus as an arts practitioner is to build evidence and research to provide depth and substance to my belief that, through artistic practices, one can ignite a form of repair for oneself, a 'Maker: Mended,' narrative in real time. The comma (,) at the end denotes the cold fact that there is no one-time fix. However, one can access a form of soothing and constant care through the application of one's hands.

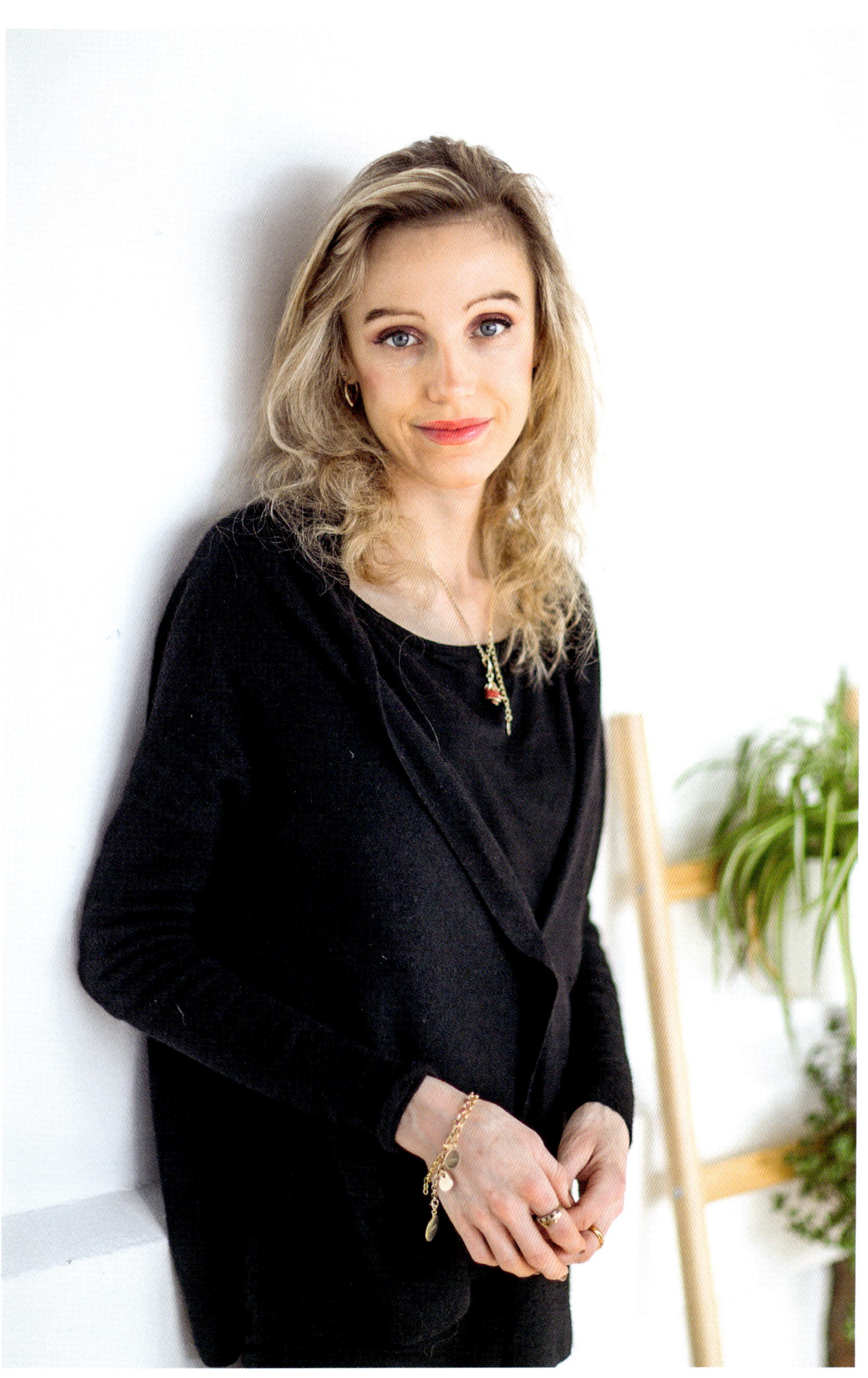

RIGHT: *The author (2019).*

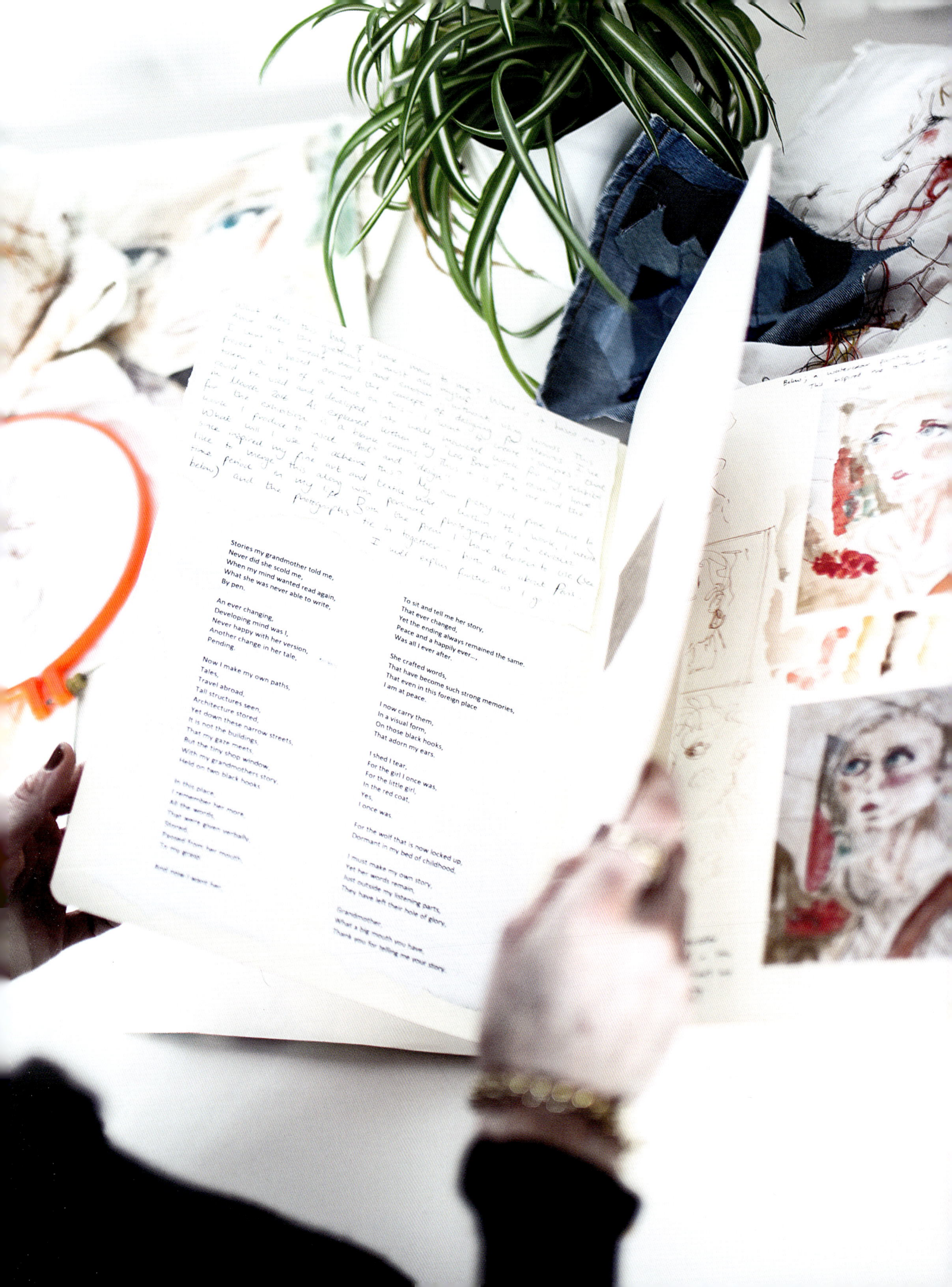

Stories my grandmother told me,
Never did she scold me,
When my mind wanted read again,
What she was never able to write,
By pen.

An ever changing,
Developing mind was I,
Never happy with her version,
Another change in her tale,
Pending.

Now I make my own paths,
Tales,
Travel abroad,
Tall structures seen,
Architecture stored,
Yet down these narrow streets,
It is not the buildings,
That my gaze meets,
But the tiny shop window,
With my grandmothers story,
Held on two black hooks.

In this place,
I remember her more,
All the words,
That were given verbally,
Stored,
Passed from her mouth,
To my group.

And now I know her.

To sit and tell me her story,
That ever changed,
Yet the ending always remained the same.
Peace and a happily ever...,
Was all I ever after.

She crafted words,
That have become such strong memories,
That even in this foreign place
I am at peace.

I now carry them,
In a visual form,
On those black hooks,
That adorn my ears.

I shed I tear,
For the girl I once was,
For the little girl,
In the red coat,
Yes,
I once was

For the wolf that is now locked up,
Dormant in my bed of childhood.

I must make my own story,
Yet her words remain,
Just outside my listening parts,
They have left their hole of glory.

Grandmother,
What a big mouth you have,
Thank you for telling me your story.

How to read this book

Within these pages, I will give you the inspiration, the desire and the inner strength to fly. However, I won't tell you the correct flight path, because there isn't one. It depends on the turbulence, the conditions and the destination: *your* destination. Having said that, I will not leave you high and dry, at a loss as to how to proceed, so that you just don't bother.

As much as possible, I have endeavoured to illustrate visually how you *could* approach things. I always find that a 'could do' list is much more tempting than a 'have to' list, don't you think?

The narratives you will encounter are a juxtaposition of the fabricated and the true. You may identify with some of these narratives, but my goal is for you to locate your own story, thereby building your own personal textile narrative.

OPPOSITE: *Considering odes to one's grandmother in direct connection to textile narratives.*
RIGHT: *Example of a scrapbook exploring ancestral linkage with grandmother.*

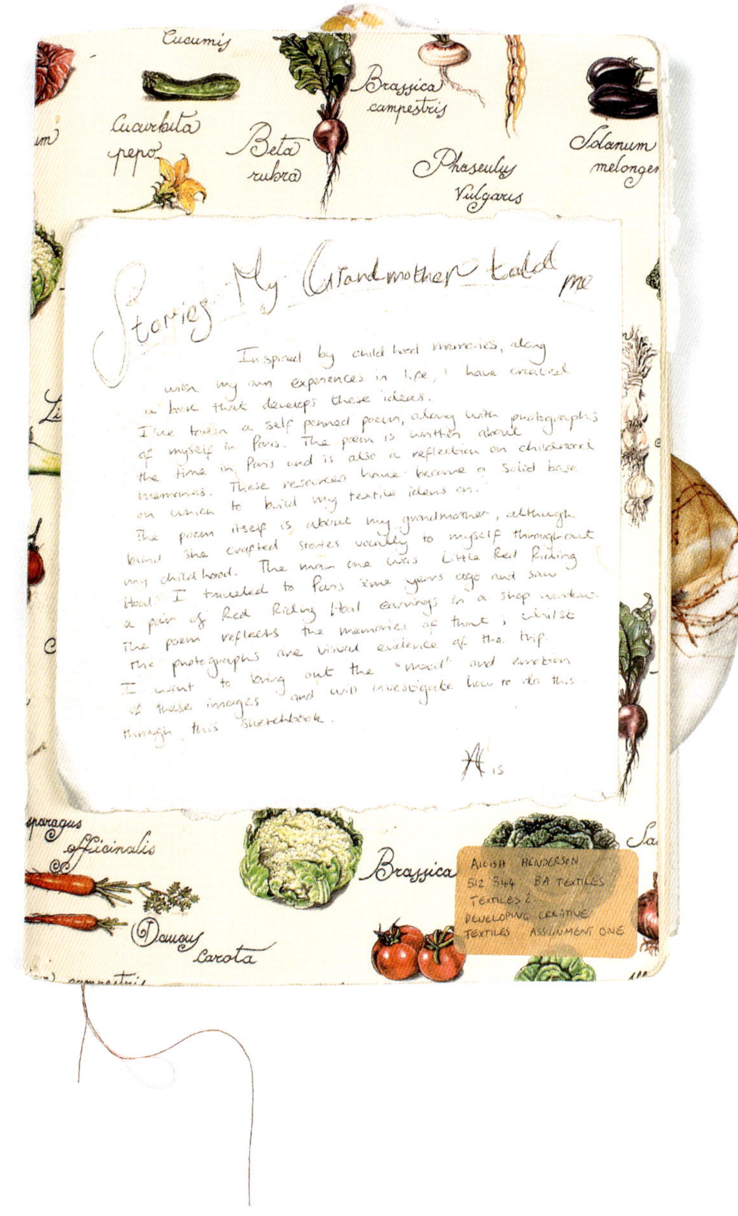

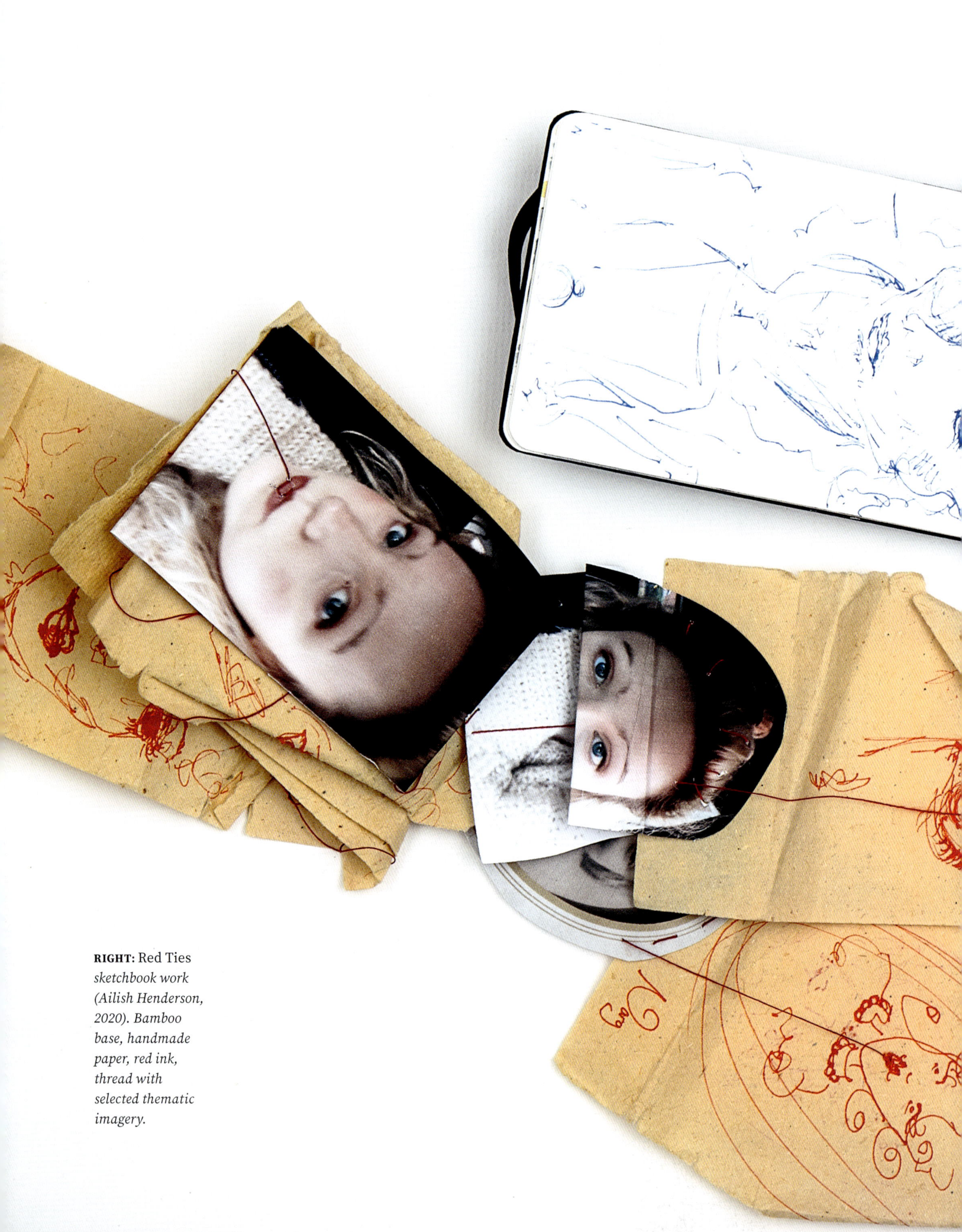

RIGHT: Red Ties *sketchbook work (Ailish Henderson, 2020). Bamboo base, handmade paper, red ink, thread with selected thematic imagery.*

Processes in *motion*

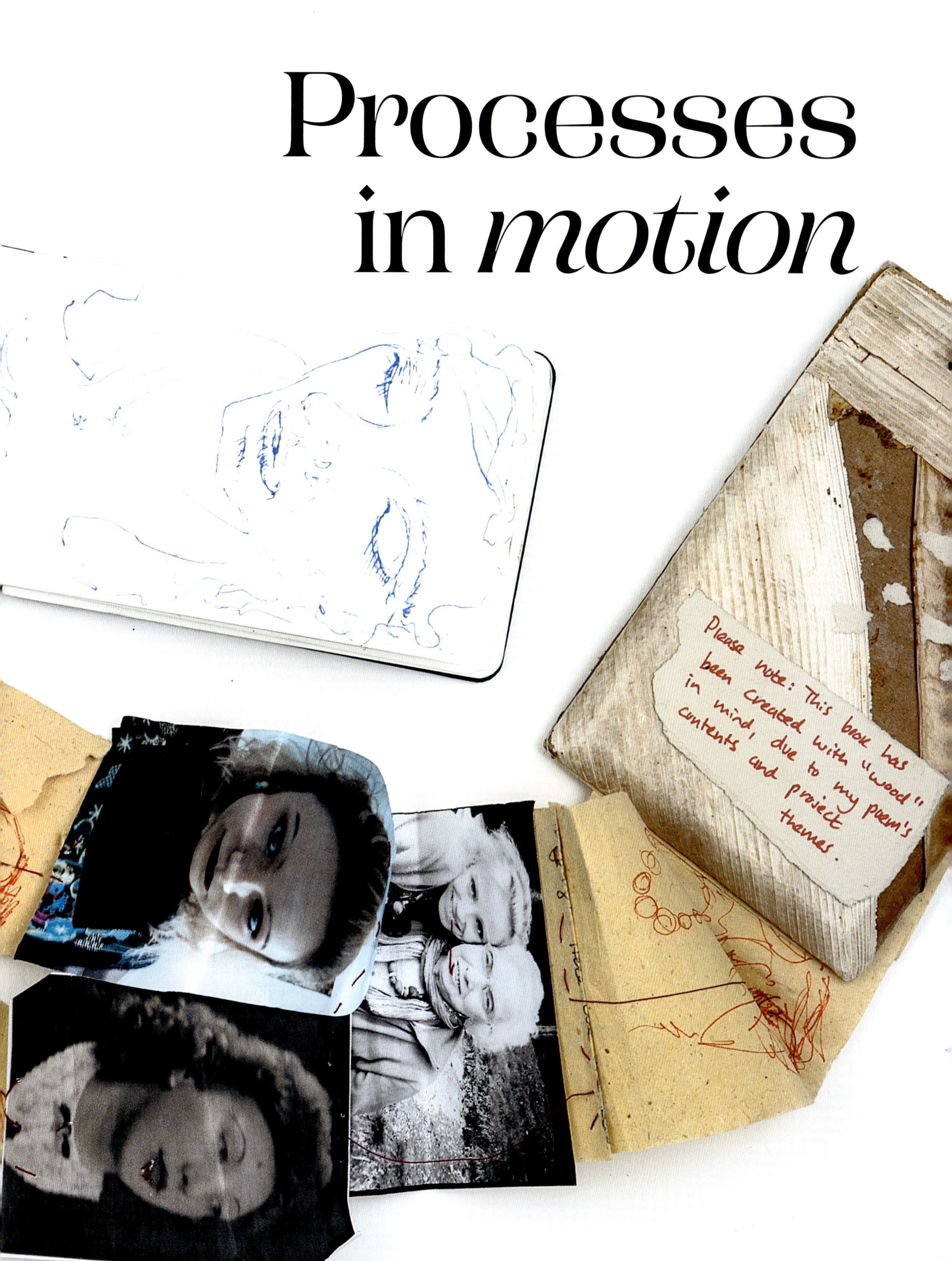

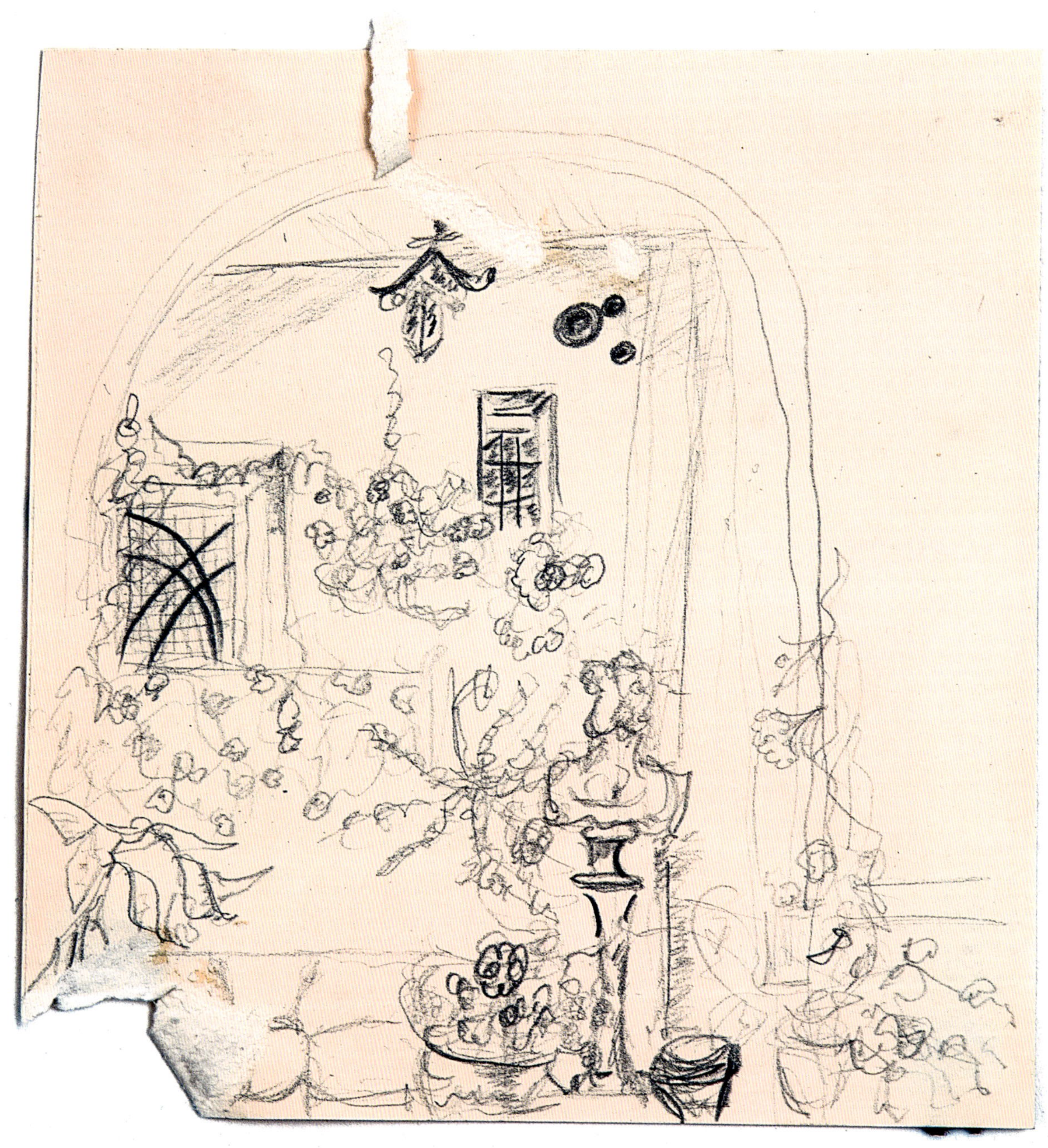

ABOVE: *Initial sketching out of* Gigi's Garden *(Ailish Henderson, 2019).*

This section is divided into three subsections. I hope they become jumpstarts for your own artwork. They are not a prescription, but they are important. In my early learning days, I remember going to an interview with a portfolio of my artwork; all carefully executed watercolour illustrations. The judging committee challenged my inspirational sources.

'Where from?' came the opening gambit.

'My imagination, of course!' I responded.

'Yes, but artwork must have a background,' was their 'checkmate' answer.

Granted, at times it is lovely to just make impromptu artwork, without any prior plan. However, I have learned over the years that the best ideas have a 'walk-before-you-run' aspect. In other words, you must know the basics before tackling the *complex*.

This is where this section comes into its own. If you are like me, on any gallery visit, you tend to be curious about why the artist in question created that scene. What went through their mind? Usually (although this is not a given), there will be a reason or a thought, which turned into a plan, which turned into a visual.

The key is not to get bogged down with doubts about what will appear in your creative hands. That is why I have titled this section 'Processes in motion'; it is about keeping moving and taking the pen for a walk, rather than sitting down and reflecting too much.

Let's look at three key ways of doing this:

1. Mood boards/vision boards
2. Drawing
3. Keeping sketchbooks

Boards of *visual* accumulations

I enjoy creating these boards. I also enjoy having a nose at other people's – either my own students or when visiting events where designers bring along not only their finished work, but also the creative history behind it.

RIGHT: *Stitched collage portraits mood board. (mannequin based).*
OPPOSITE, ABOVE: Red Ties *mood board (2018). Selected paper-based media to plait together own narrative line with grandmother's.*
OPPOSITE, BELOW: *Studio handmade visualisation board, capturing current musings.*

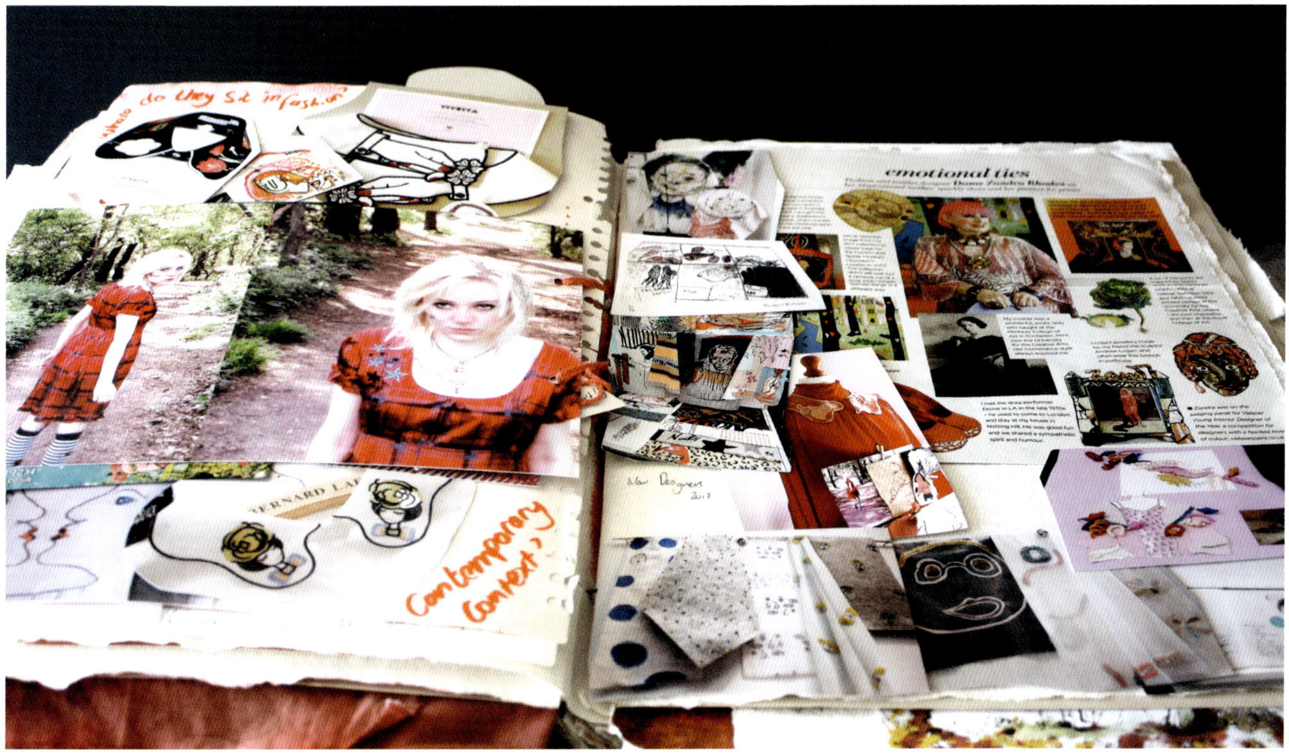

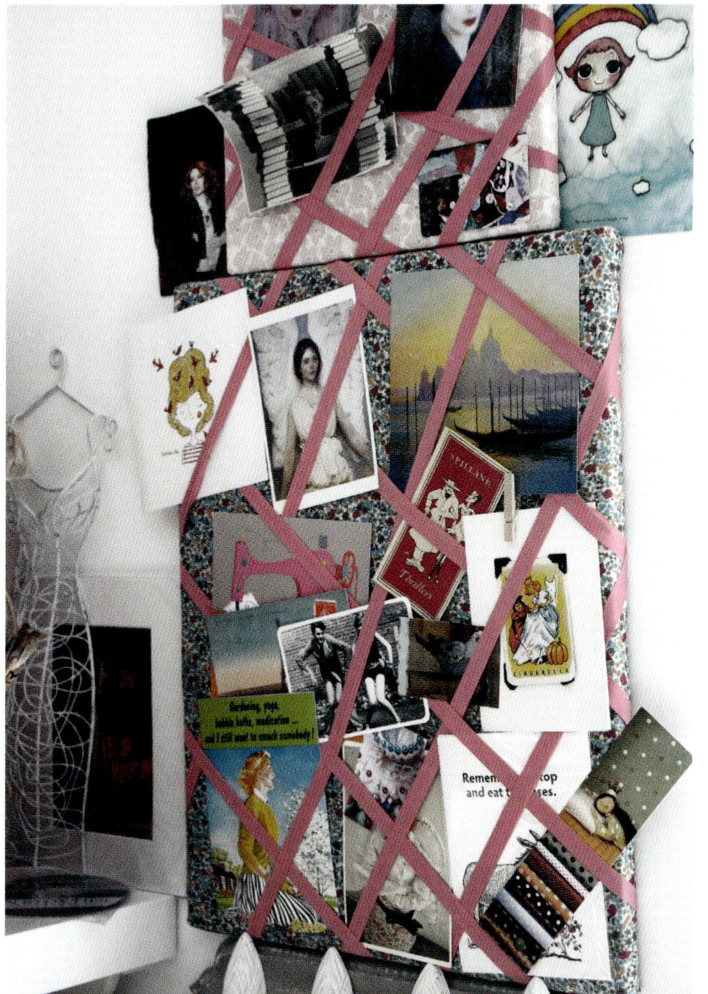

Create your own boards

Where to begin?
Have a theme in mind: faces, for example.

What do I need?
Gather a selection of photos, magazine cuttings and any other visual fuel you wish to put on one page.

What might it look like when I am finished?
Here are a few examples. You may wish to structure yours in a certain order, creating it on a flat table until satisfied, then stick it in place on a large piece of card to give it some structure.

Sample themes?
Nature, family, travel...decide on what suits you personally.

FEATURED ARTIST:
Lise Howie

I had the privilege of spending time with Lise when she came along to one of my masterclasses at The Biscuit Factory, Newcastle. We had previously been in touch over social media – she currently lives in France. I loved her open-hearted nature which I observed through her creations. The works are not frothy, nor flimsy, they have an edge without becoming uncomfortable.

Lise Howie reveals:
'I was auditioning textiles – stitched, botanically dyed and vintage – for a piece called Me, Myself and Eye. *The embroidered flowers, top right, are from a tablecloth stitched by my grandmother, a flower crown metamorphosing into a crown of thorns. The finished piece considered mental health, particularly schizophrenia, from the perspective of its effects on the five senses – auditory, visual, olfactory, gustation and tactile – and how this might manifest in the form of hallucinations, persecution, and delusions.'*

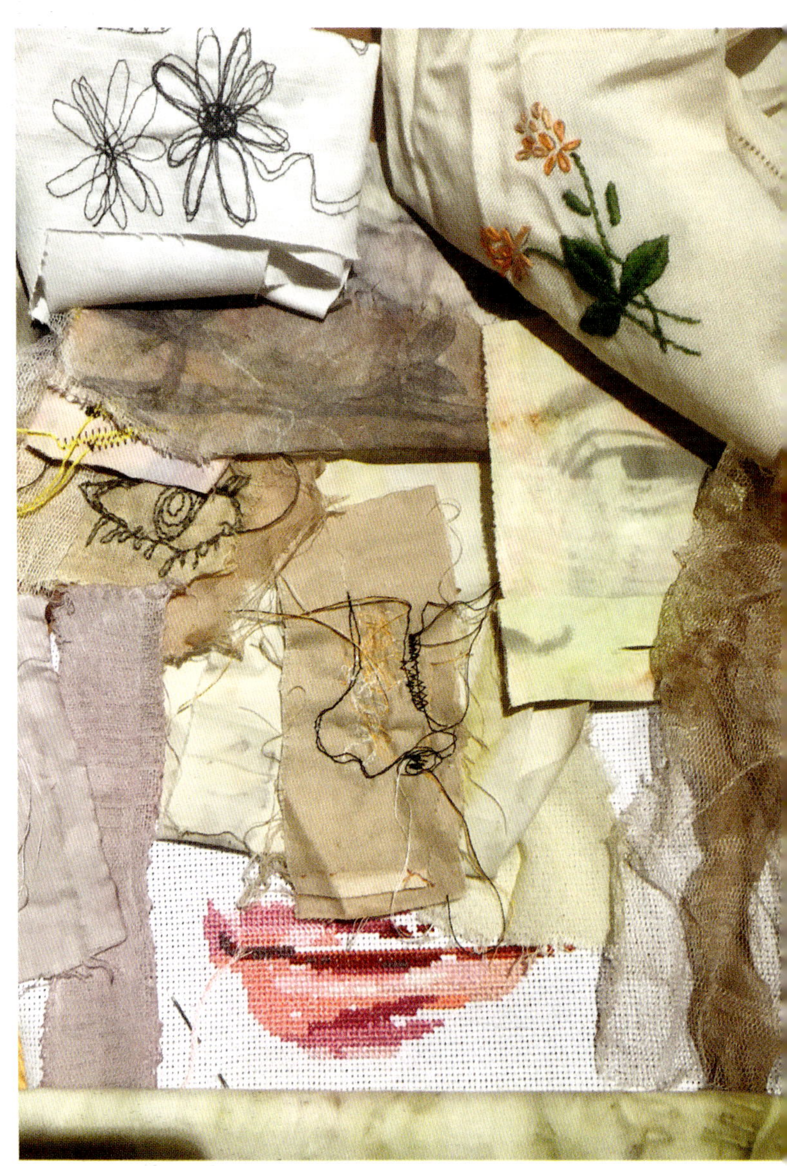

ABOVE: *Visual auditioning for* Me, Myself and Eye *(Lise Howie, 2021). Mixed textiles.*

Drawing it out (from head and heart)

Okay, let's cut the 'I don't know where to start, so I won't bother...'

Believe me, I go there most days of my life. Therefore, to take the heat out of it, I very rarely go out and purchase a spanking brand-new white sketchbook, waiting for me to consummate the first page (yes, I mean, I couldn't just start on page three, could I?!).

Forget that preconception. Thinking of my own work as an example, I live a busy life, and I often buy something like flowers and think 'I need to draw these; I MUST draw these.' But do I? Well, no. I often do not have the time before their petals rust and furl, dropping from their green cages. I do not get the chance to place out all my Van Gogh-like paints and canvases, ready to create a masterpiece.

A few years ago I decided I needed to cut out this way of working. Instead I needed to develop a way to capture the floral moment. So, sitting with my dinner, I took out my white IKEA napkin and found there were two together. I used one for its usual purpose, while the other I placed on the right-hand chair arm and grabbed a pen. Soon I had a left-hand forkful hitting the side of my mouth and a right hand visually telling a tale...yes, using a paper napkin.

This has now become a tried and tested routine. I now even add paint and inks to these napkins. I have also begun to embroider, cut up and embellish these virgin, quarter-folded hidden gems.

There may be many reasons you have not yet developed the skills you feel you need, but it is never too late.

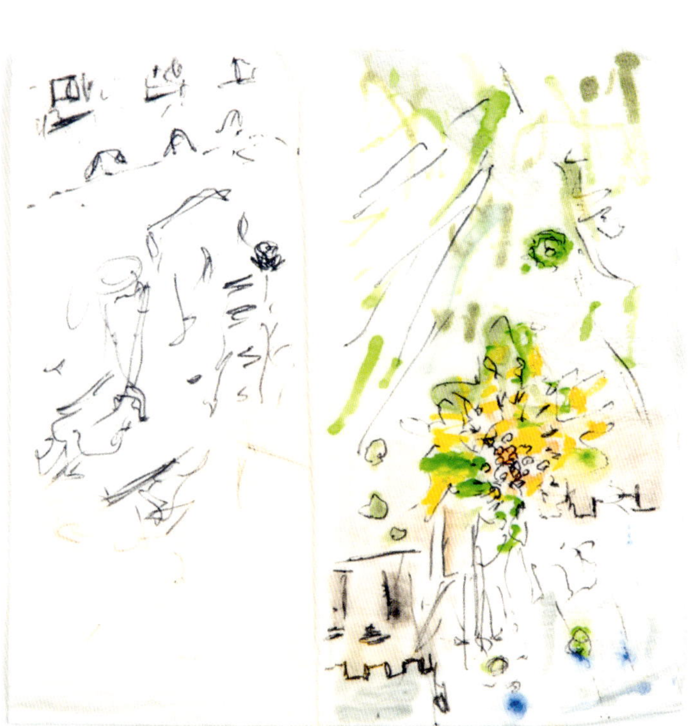

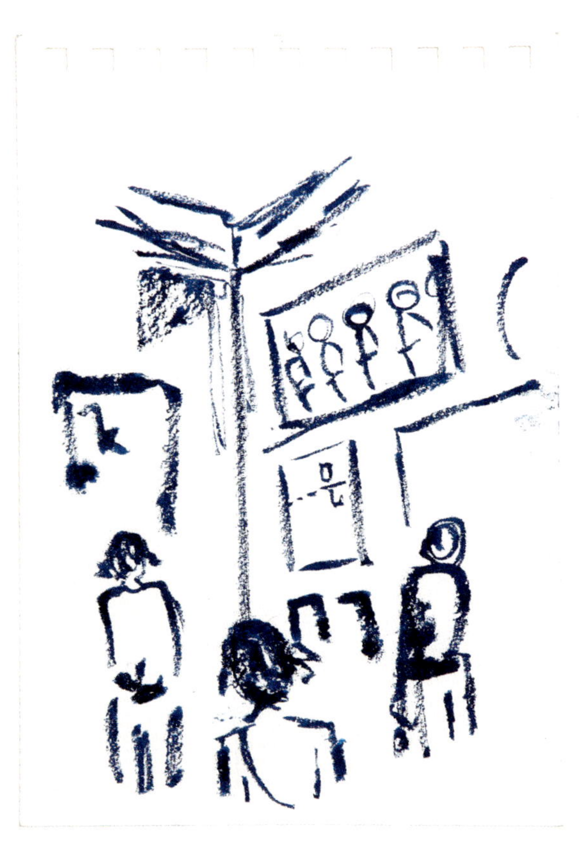

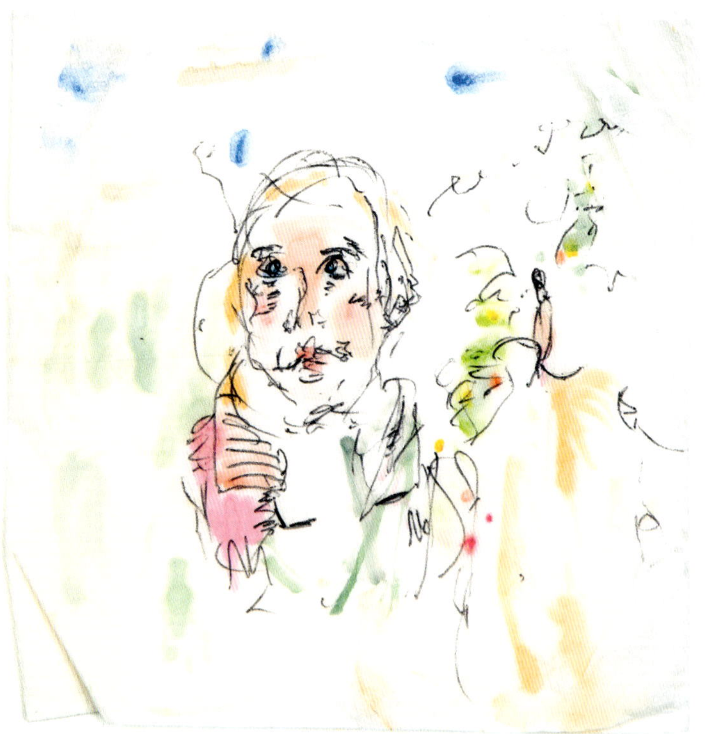

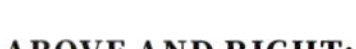

ABOVE AND RIGHT:
A selection of napkin-based drawings, detailing various narratives (Ailish Henderson, 2022). IKEA white napkins, inks.

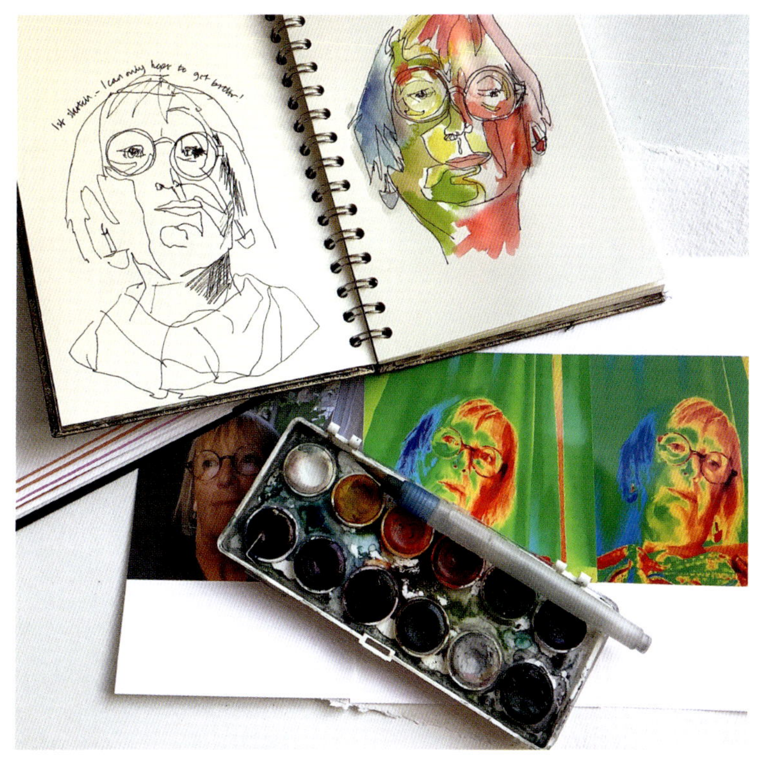

LEFT: *Drawing build-up work for self-portrait (Anne Richards, 2020).*
BELOW: *The use of imagery to build portrait drawings (Vicky Lockwood, 2020).*

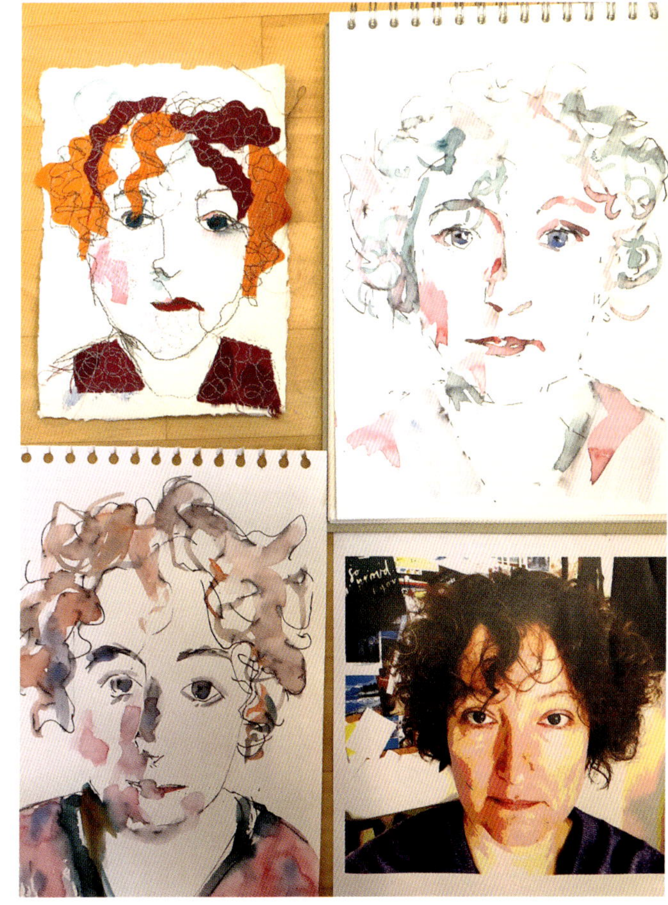

The 'S' word (sketchbooks)

Many people struggle with sketchbooks. Why? Maybe it is the formality of them, or maybe it is the idea of spoiling a clean book, derived from early childhood.

We don't want to make a mistake, do we? So, we never start. And therein lies the problem: FEAR.

RIGHT: *Detail of colour sketchbook page (Ailish Henderson, 2018).*
OPPOSITE, ABOVE: Let's Talk About Yes *(Julia Triston, 2020). Created for the Textile Study Group's* Insights *project.*
OPPOSITE, BELOW: *Sketchbook, research and initial ideas page for further development (Mandy Pattullo, 2022).*

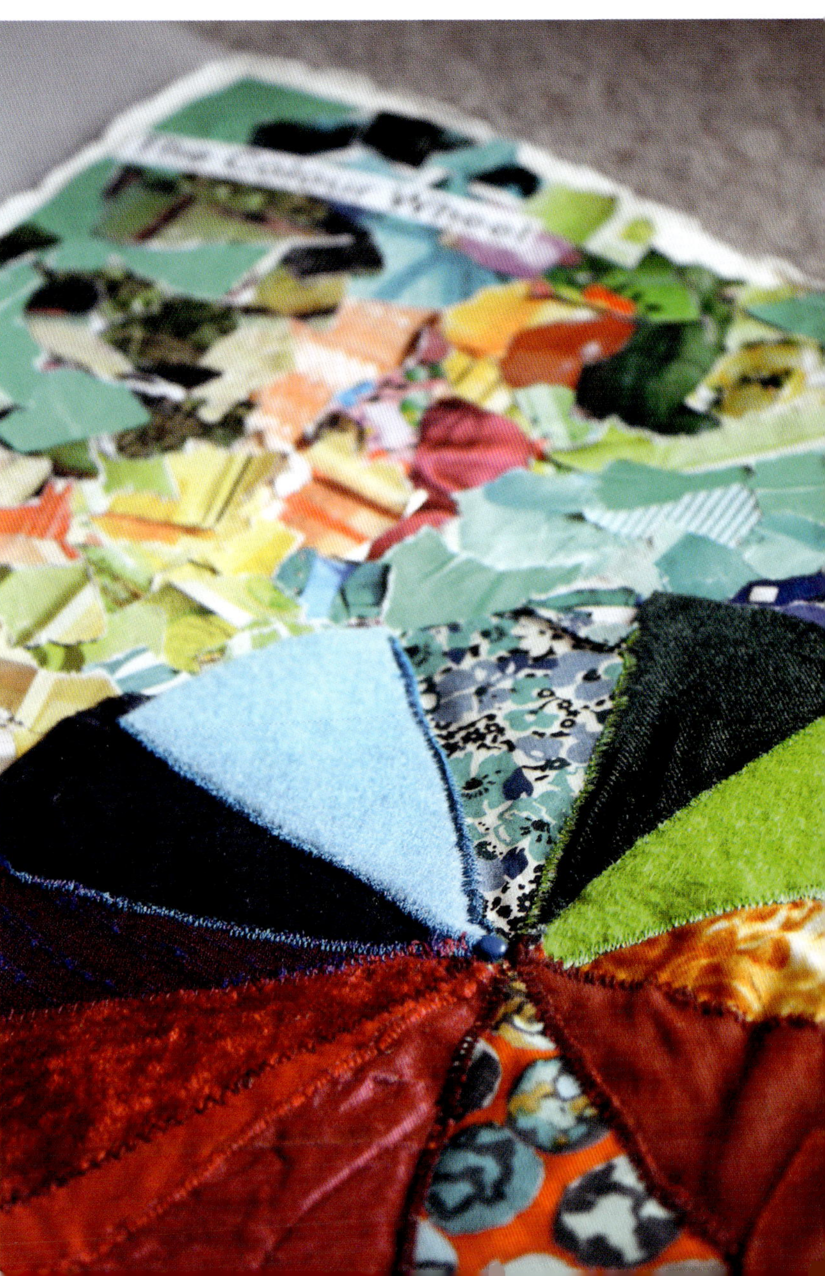

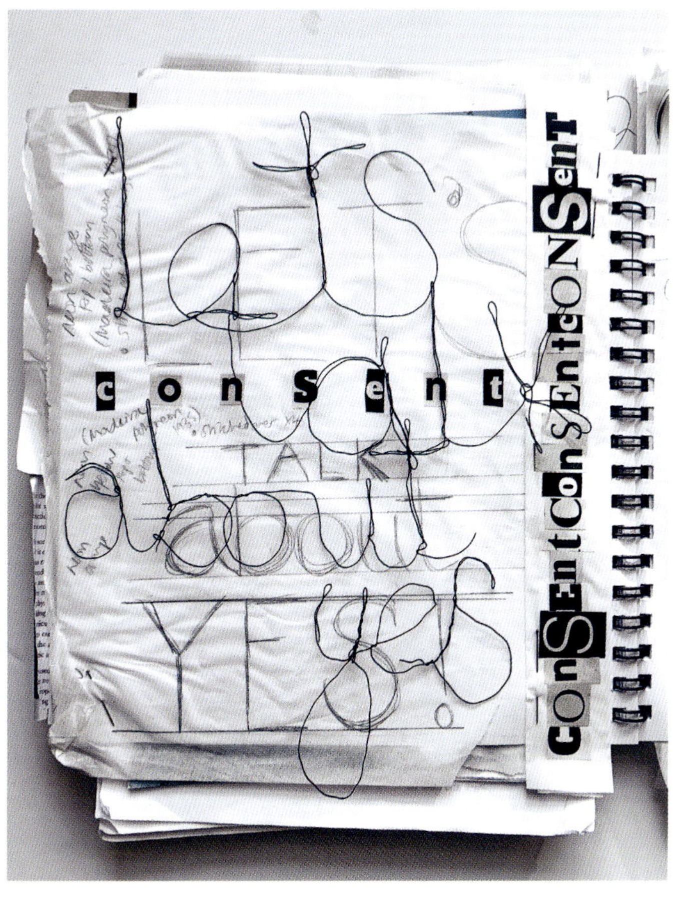

Remember what the definition of a sketchbook is:

- 'A book of sheets of paper for drawing on' *Oxford Advanced Learner's Dictionary*

- A few words are all it takes to define a whole balloon of fear in our minds – so let's pop it! Just lose the 'S' word and call it something else.

- As a visual artist, I tend to use a sketchbook as a diary; it is my way of making sense of whatever I am processing in my head.

- Take the childlike approach – a book of pages is simply a playground of possibilities. My own sketchbooks contain to-do lists, diagrams, notes I don't want to forget, paintings, pressed flowers, more final thoughts, and even some stitching if the paper allows! Maybe 'scrapbook' would be a better word?

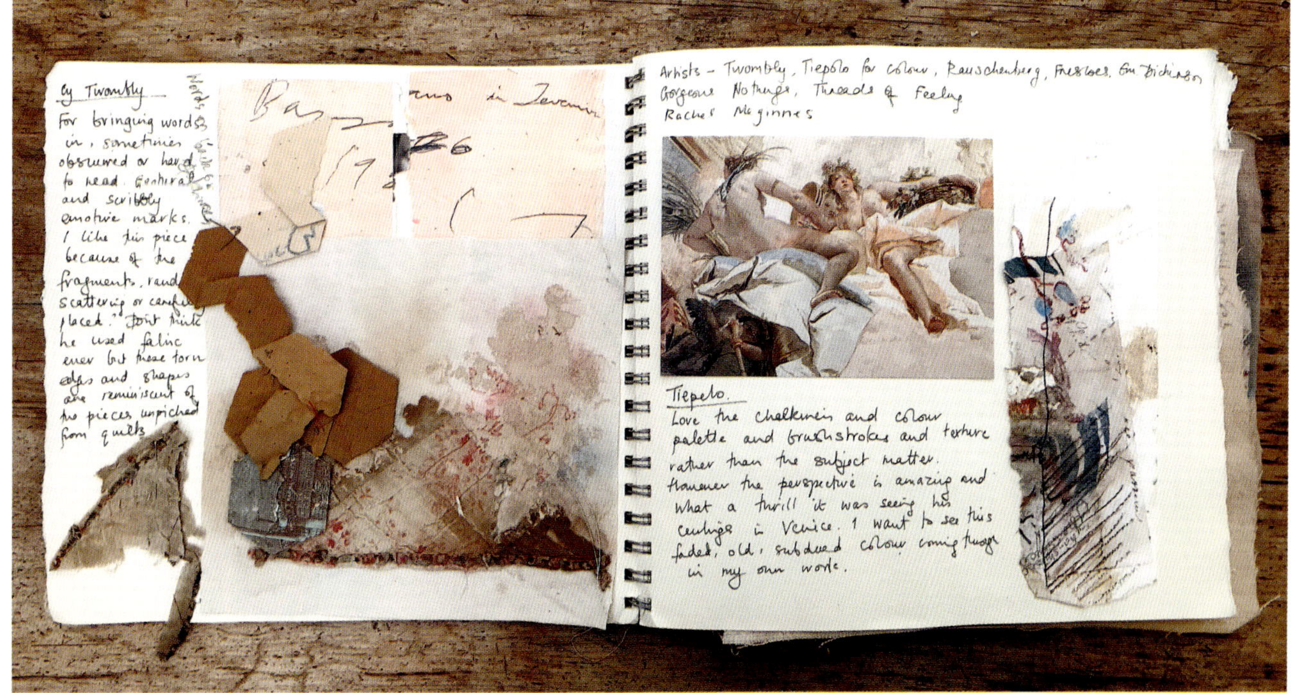

Try these ideas:

One: Take any loose pages you find and use them one at a time. Then put the pages in one pile.

Two: Stitch or link pages together. There are plenty of 'how-to' guides available on this, or you may have your own ideas.

Three: Give yourself a working theme: Colour; Trees; and Shape and Line are just a few I have covered.

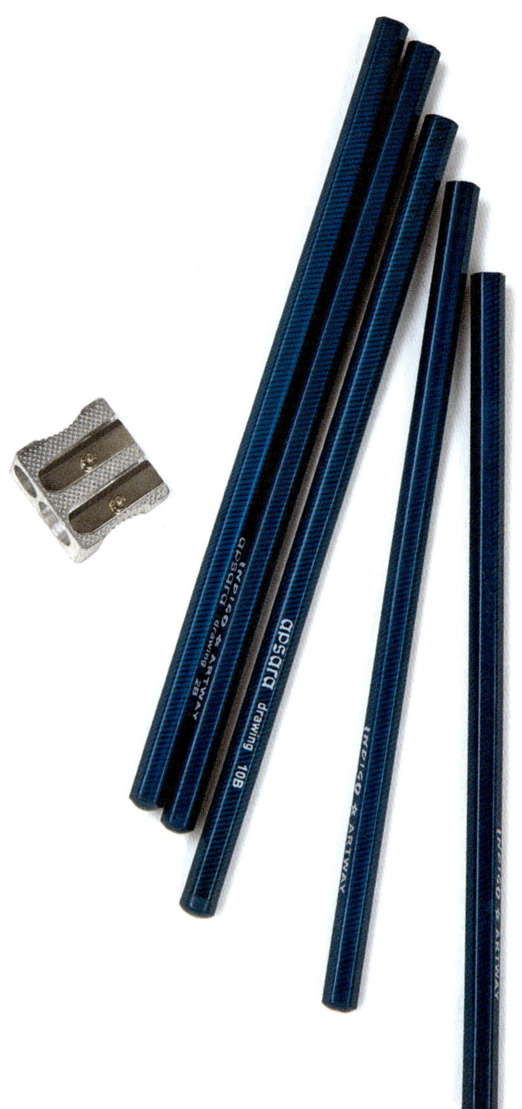

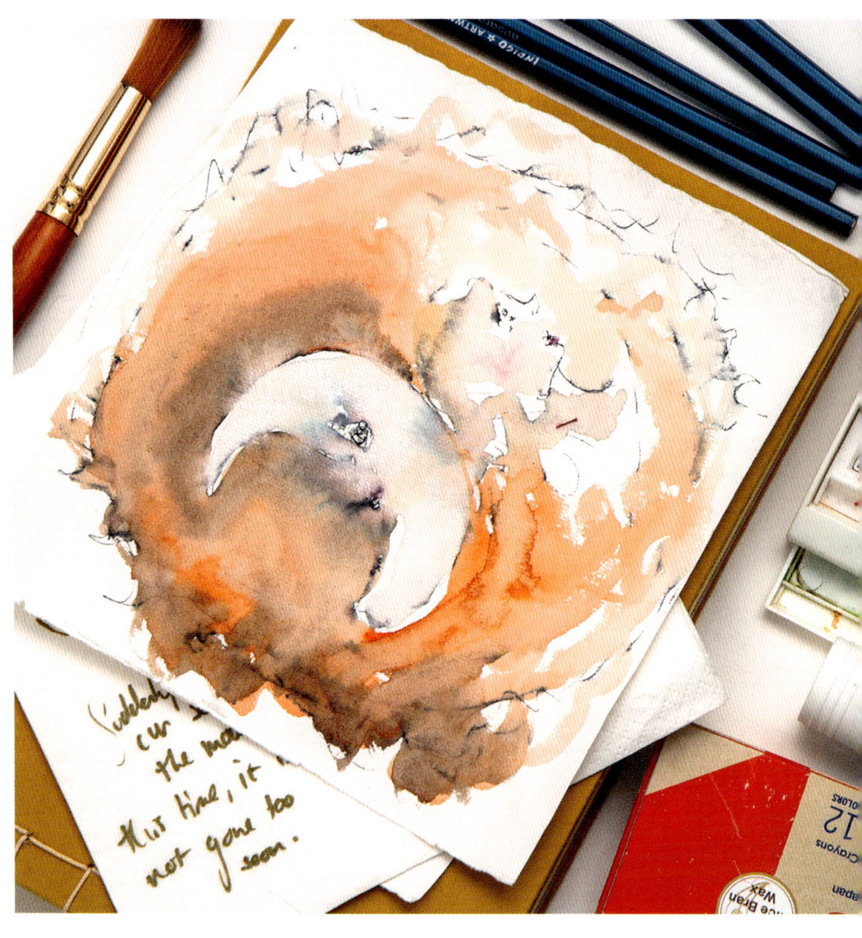

Why we keep sketchbooks:

• To remind us of a place we have visited.

• To remember an art or textiles exhibition that we found inspirational.

• A memory aid, for future use. (Many of my ideas stay in my sketchbook, in written or quick doodle form. Sometimes they are let out to play.)

• A visual and written diary.

• A 'story' that leads us through ideas that we may have on the journey to making a finished piece.

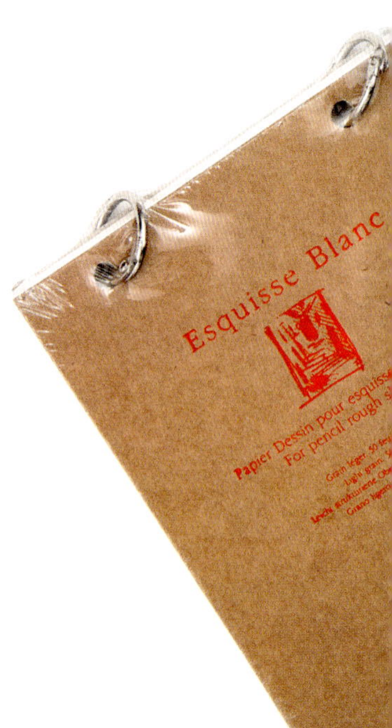

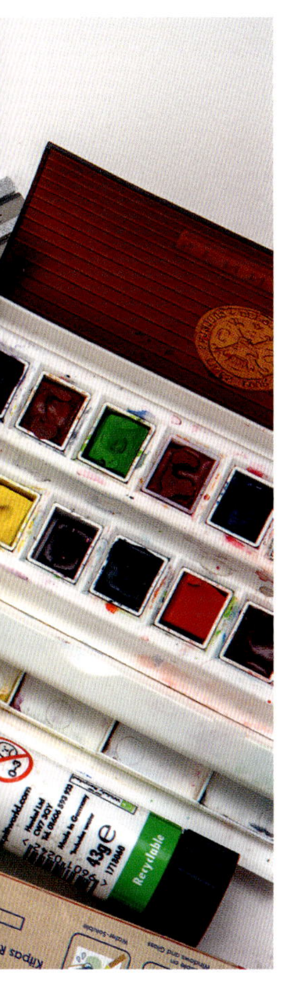

*Here are a few things that keeping
a visual diary can do for us:*

1. They help us explore ideas and sort out thoughts without too much time being wasted.

2. They offer insights about what is going on in our heads.

3. They help us reflect on our ideas without forgetting them. We are then better able to decide if we want to continue with a certain idea.

4. They make our thoughts real. Even if they only stay in our sketchbooks, we have them in store.

5. They encourage deeper thinking on our theme or topic.

6. They promote self-directed learning, rather than waiting for someone else to teach us.

7. They help us focus.

8. They inspire confidence to either make more sketchbooks, or make something else.

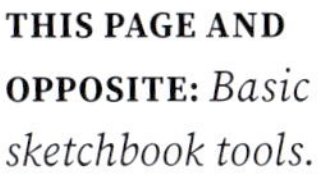

**THIS PAGE AND
OPPOSITE:** *Basic
sketchbook tools.*

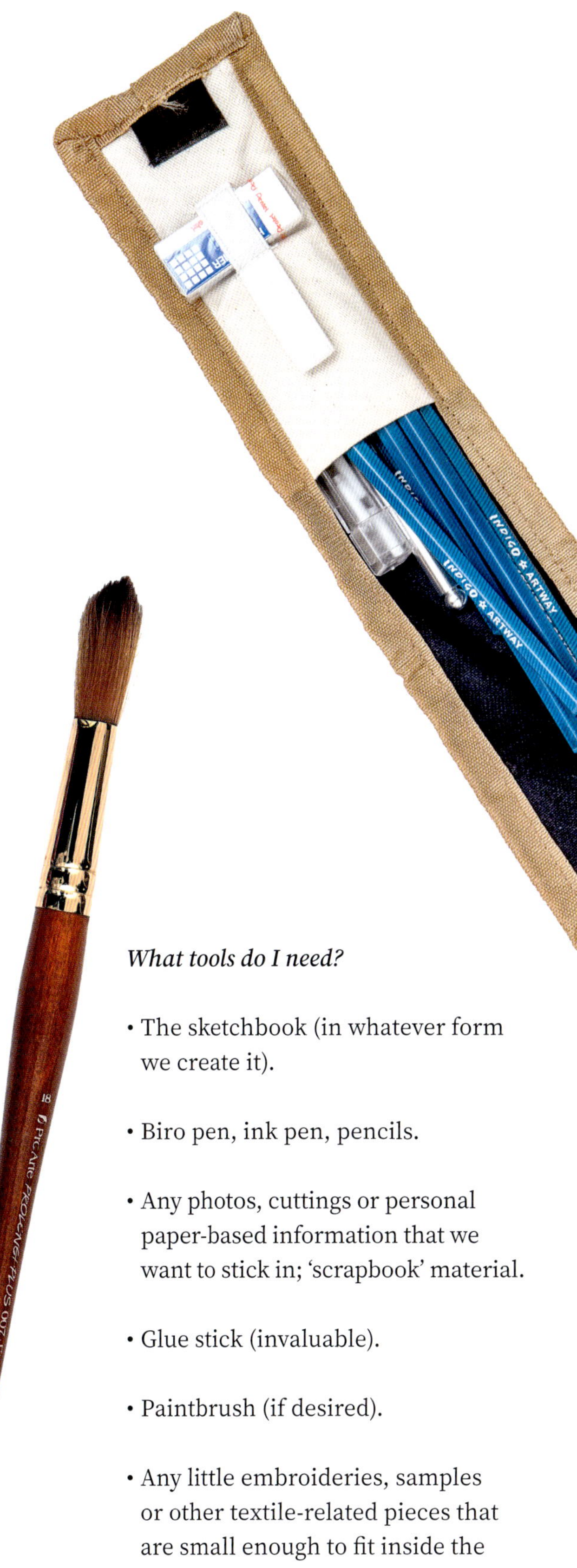

What tools do I need?

• The sketchbook (in whatever form we create it).

• Biro pen, ink pen, pencils.

• Any photos, cuttings or personal paper-based information that we want to stick in; 'scrapbook' material.

• Glue stick (invaluable).

• Paintbrush (if desired).

• Any little embroideries, samples or other textile-related pieces that are small enough to fit inside the sketchbook.

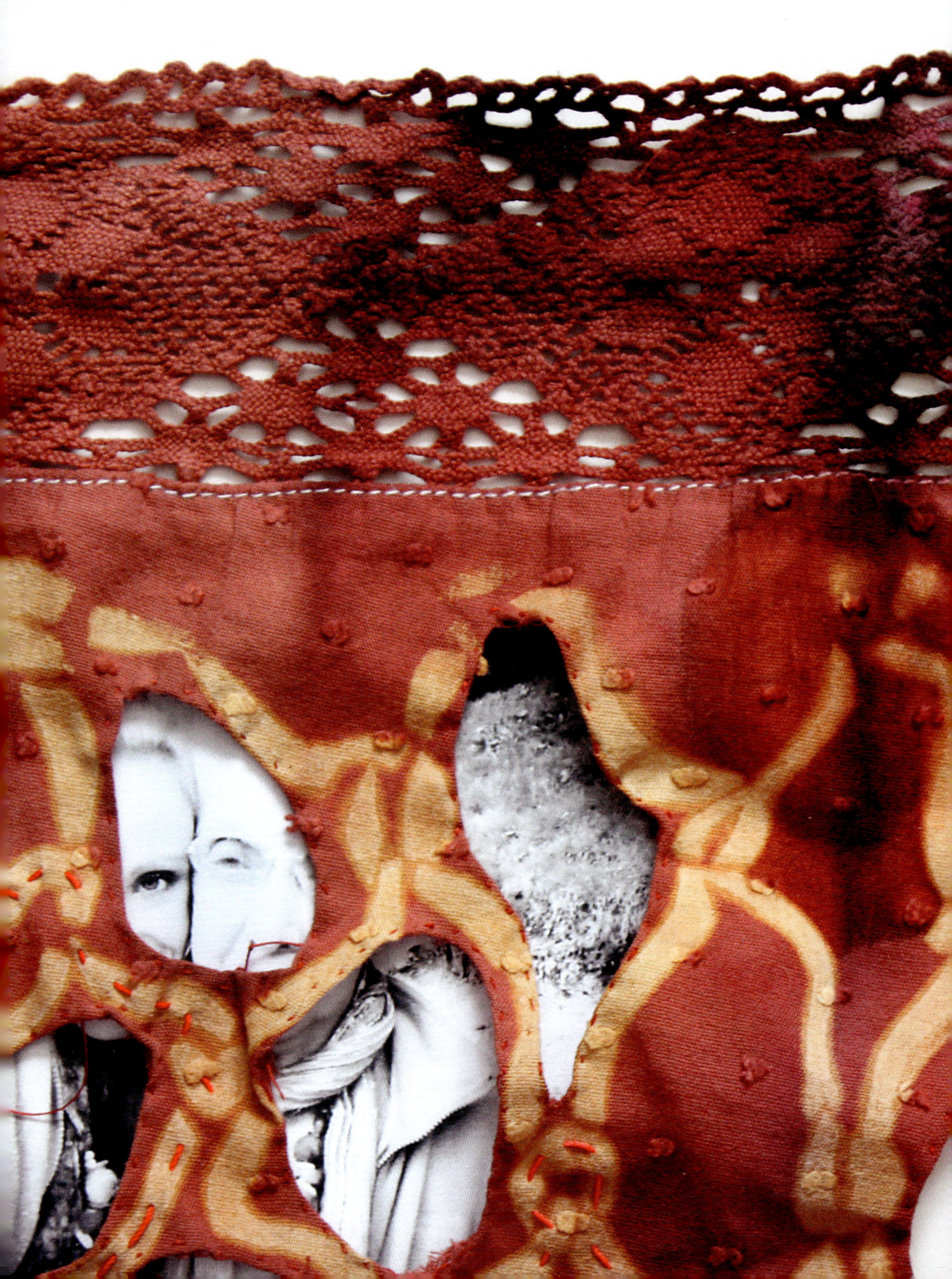

Materials: the rags we see as *riches*

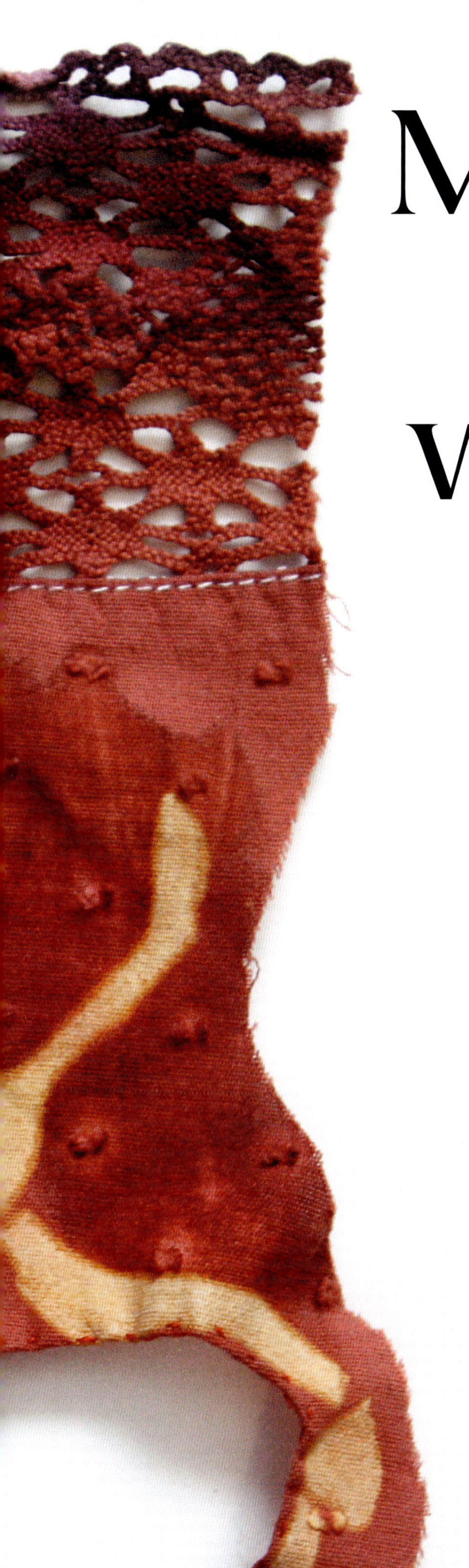

LEFT: Red Ties collection. Hand-painted vintage cloth with decolourant transfused onto cloth via hand-cut stencil/screen-print method. (Ailish Henderson, 2020).

Before we connected with textiles, we may have passed over the chintz, the passed-down family lace, the market stalls littered with fabric possibilities. Now that we have become aware of their potential, I dare you to allow your inner, heart-driven magpie to come out.

In this section, I will highlight three possible sources where you may find your own cloth-based riches.

It could be...

Happenstance (surprise finds and discoveries)

Ancestral (family heirlooms)

Archival (historical, with no direct link back to us)

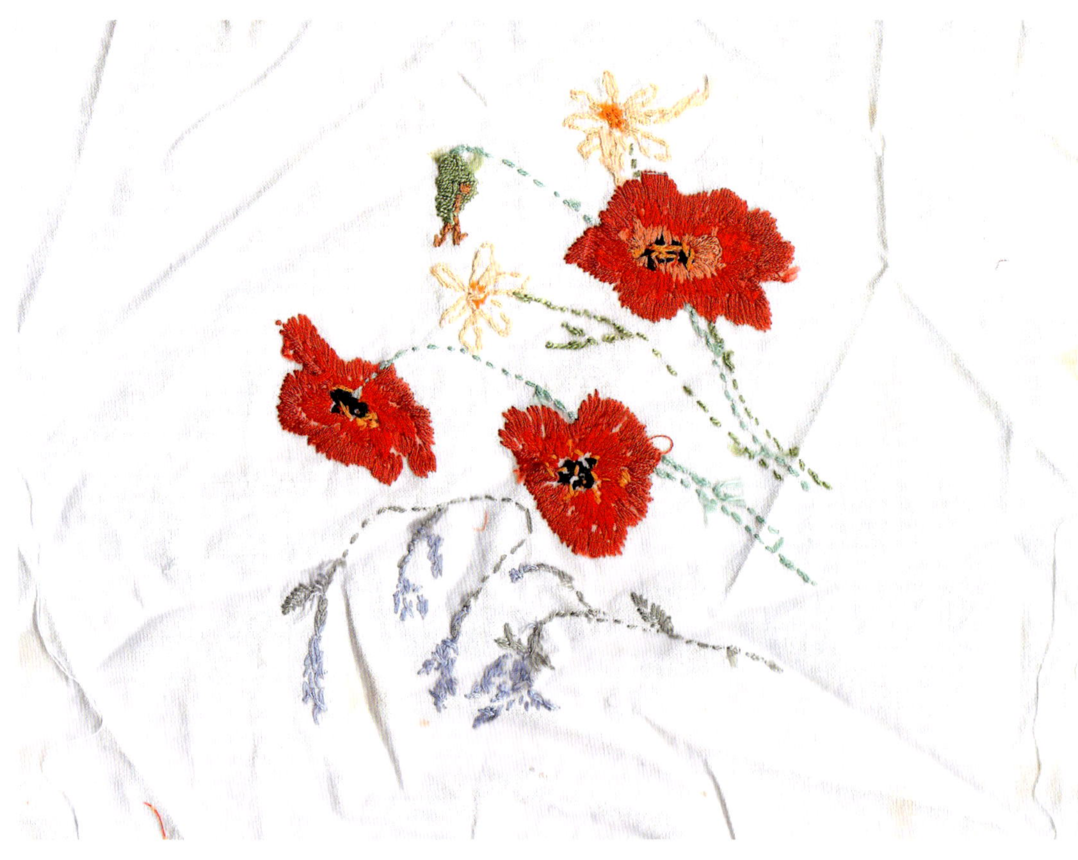

LEFT: *Heirloom hand embroidery by mother's own hand (1980).*

Happenstance

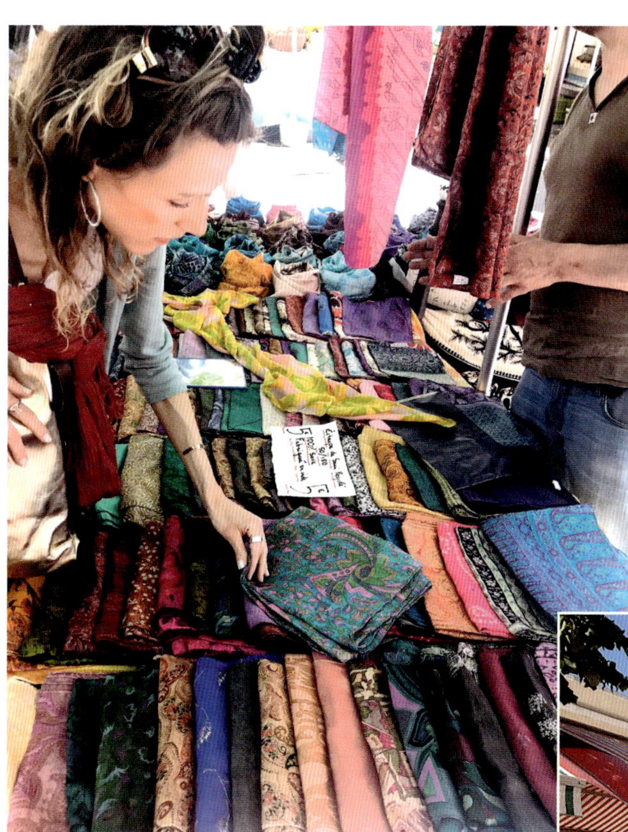

ABOVE: *Paris market, silk stall (2018).*
RIGHT: *Nice travels for treasures (2022).*

Happenstance = being in the right place for surprise finds.

• Market stalls at home or further afield.

• Secondhand shops and online suppliers.

• Walks in nature, where you may collect items, such as leaves, to collage.

• Your own garden, where you may find flowers to press.

Take time now to develop your own ideas.

Ancestral

As an artist, I deliberately look for materials to incorporate into my practice. Often, I am given beautiful clothing, lace or other items by family members. Consequently, there are many memories tied up with the pieces given to me. I store these in drawers or plastic storage boxes in my studio. I stare at them and I get them out just to look at them. Where does it develop from here?

Take time to consider what may be among your own possessions ready to be used:

- Most of us have a napkin or tableware drawer. In mine, I know there's a sentimental mix of table linen passed down from my paternal grandfather's hotelier days.

- Lace. I have gathered items from both sides of my family.

- Clothing. I have a collection of items, ranging from a velvet dress from my paternal grandmother to my dear Narg's lingerie.

- Collage materials such as old letters and wrapping papers from historical gifts with an emotional connection.

Here are a few visual examples of how I have been inspired to use treasured family items.

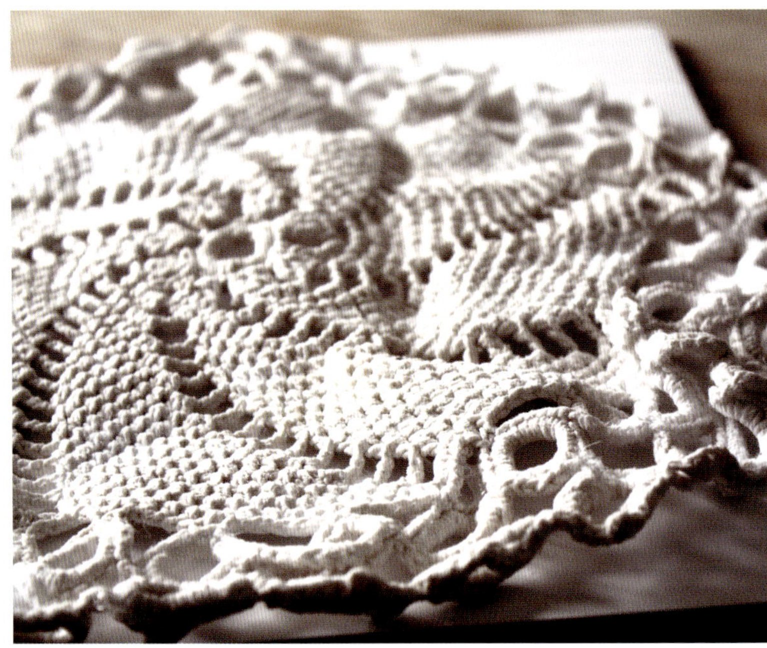

RIGHT: *Jesmonite encased familial lace.*

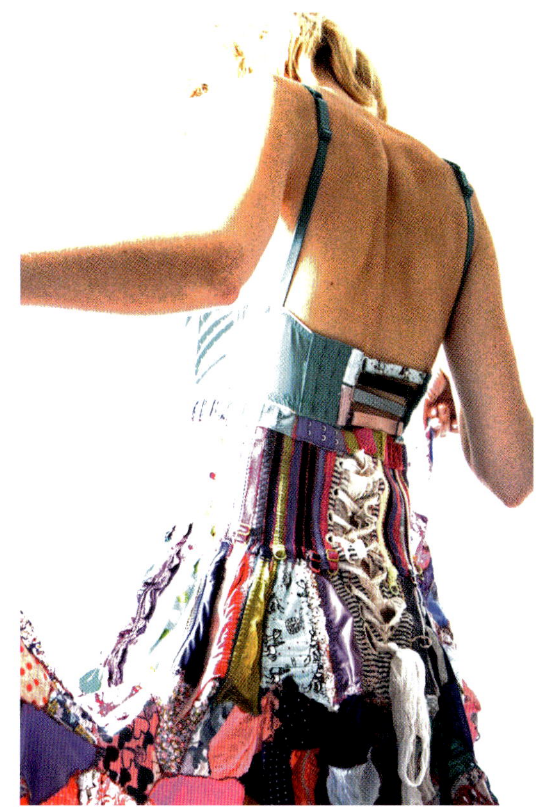

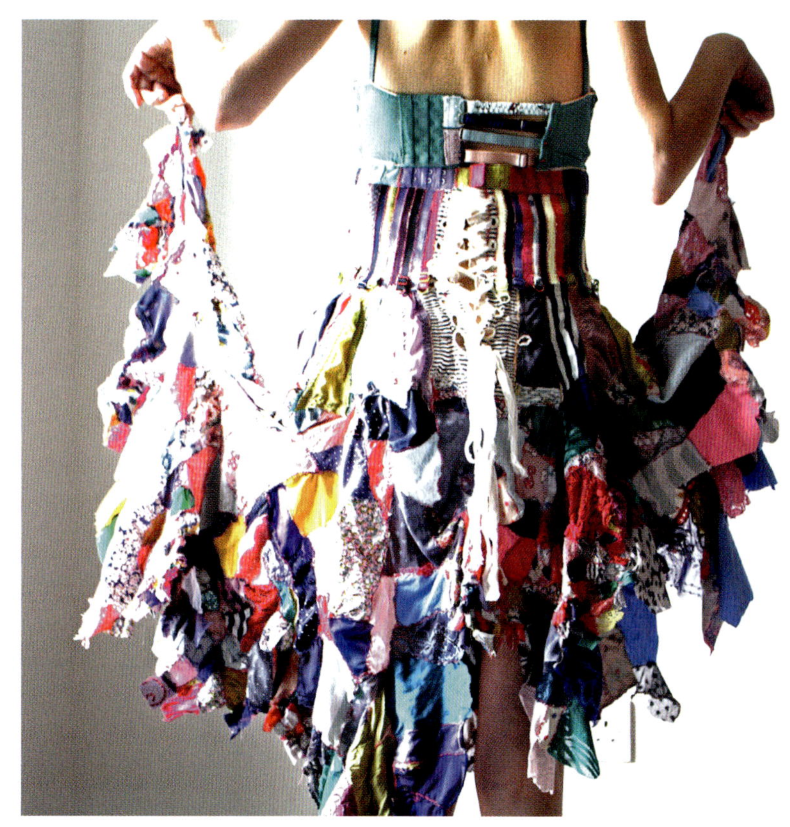

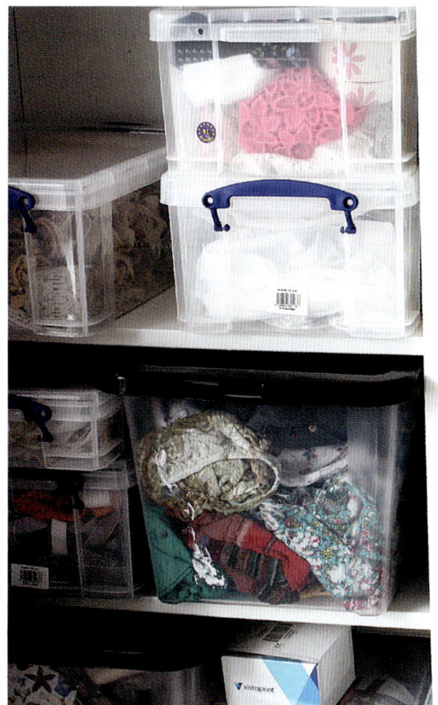

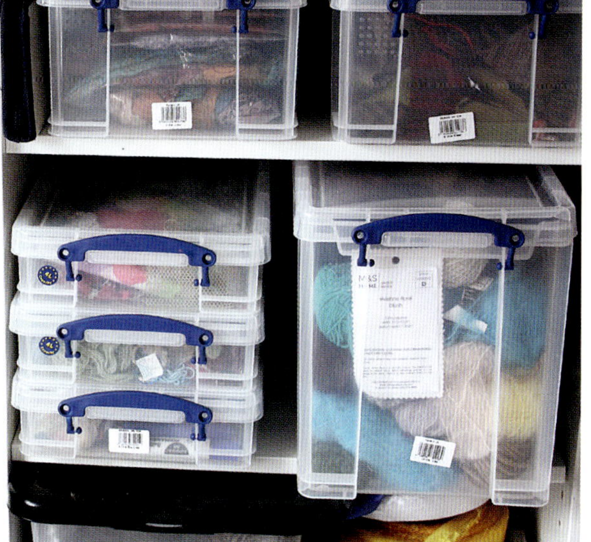

ABOVE, LEFT AND RIGHT: I see no Black *repair dress. A marriage of lingerie and historical items, strung together from a trio of generations, grandmother's bra included (Ailish Henderson, 2016).* **LEFT:** *Ancestral studio boxes.*

Archival

When taking on a role as guest speaker for various organisations, I often receive 'donations' from well-meaning members and friends. At times I think they give me whatever it is they have not finished or couldn't bring themselves to bin as a way to allay their own guilt! We may not know at the time why we have been given something, but it can become future mind-matter: something we return to, maybe lock away and then rediscover years later.

What are you going to get out, cut out and renew today?

Another example of this is the reuse of clothing. We have all witnessed the visible-darning brigade; the cream jumper along with its threadbare holes, rewritten, repaired and given a new value, given a life via the application of a navy thread, thick and holding, soothing its frazzled existence.

I have had plenty of holed wearables, but to be honest I didn't want to jump on the 'repair and stare' bandwagon, although many do it well. Instead, I leave my holes to 'bloom and grow' and turn to other areas of reusing clothing. This came about through the gathering of lingerie and similar treasured items. It wasn't the sexuality surrounding intimate items that attracted me, it was the fact that as humans we adorn ourselves simply *for ourselves*. Lingerie is usually hidden and used as our inner armour. It was this depth of meaning that initiated my collection of three garments, all made by eye (no measuring), to mould and adhere to my own body.

OPPOSITE, ABOVE:
Planning out works using archival materials, including passed down lingerie.
OPPOSITE, BELOW:
Research page from archival sketchbook on father's side.

How I will "butcher" each bra!

← Bra in original state.

Cup!

Back piece

Hook and eye fastening

Straps

Size label

Bows and decorations

Something could be done with these!

Fabric and lace and decoration from each Cup.

I intend to salvage each part and create something new or inventive from each element!!

The bra top may be "developed" as I progress - I have ideas!

Basic bra, remastered to fit me. This will be the starting point to fit everything onto

My "corset" style panel, created with bra straps and hooks. All stitched together and left in a lace up style at the back.

"Bra catch" panel.

Under the skirt of the dress will be a form of wire "umbrella" structure to create desired shape.

The actual skirt material will be created from knicker, bra and other "no longer wearable" clothes particles - all stitched together to not really look too much like their purpose

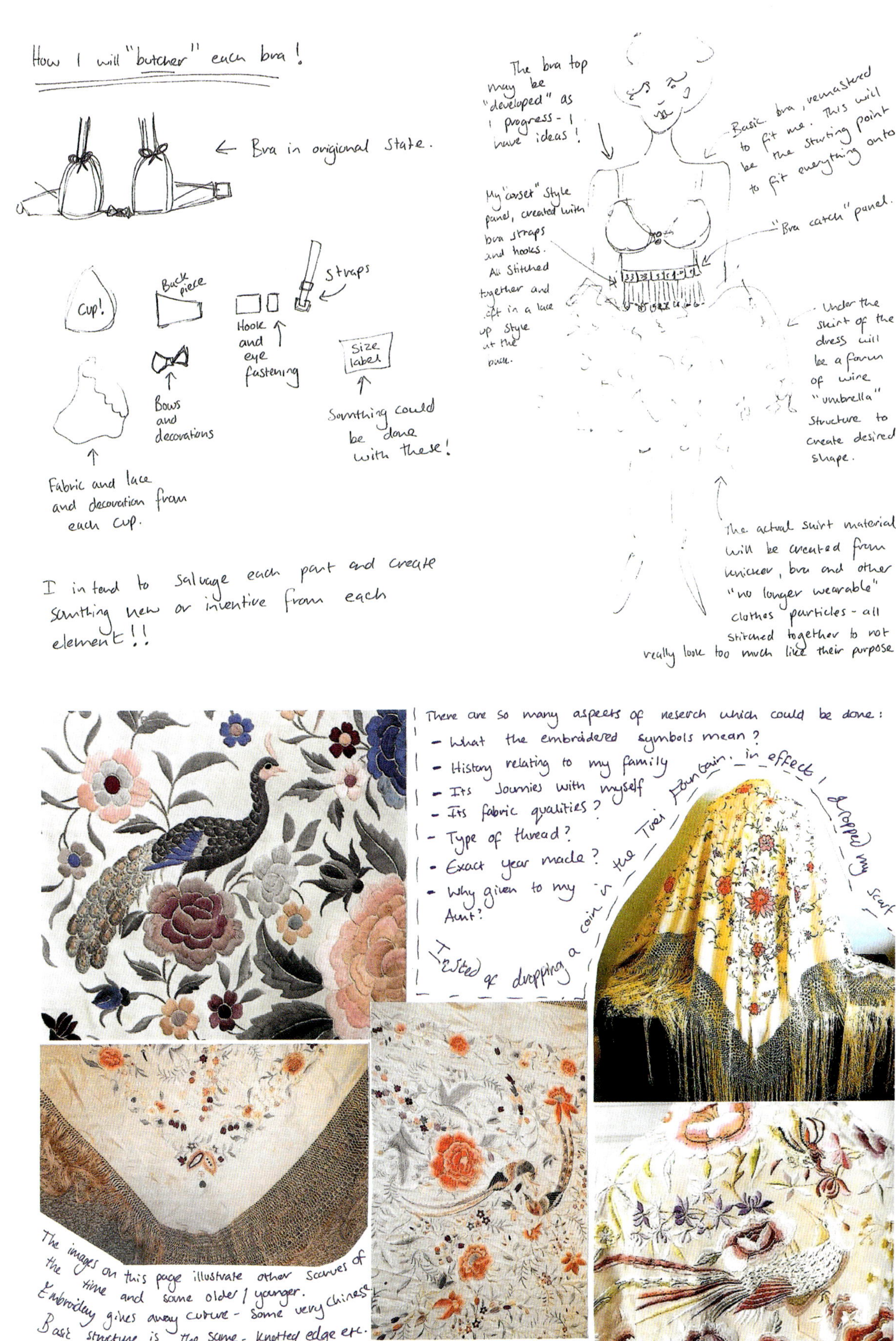

There are so many aspects of research which could be done:
- What the embroidered symbols mean?
- History relating to my family
- Its journies with myself
- Its fabric qualities?
- Type of thread?
- Exact year made?
- Why given to my Aunt?

Tested of dropping a coin in the Trevi fountain - in effect I dropped my scarf

The images on this page illustrate other scarves of the time and some older / younger. Embroidery gives away culture - some very chinese. Basic structure is the same - knotted edge etc.

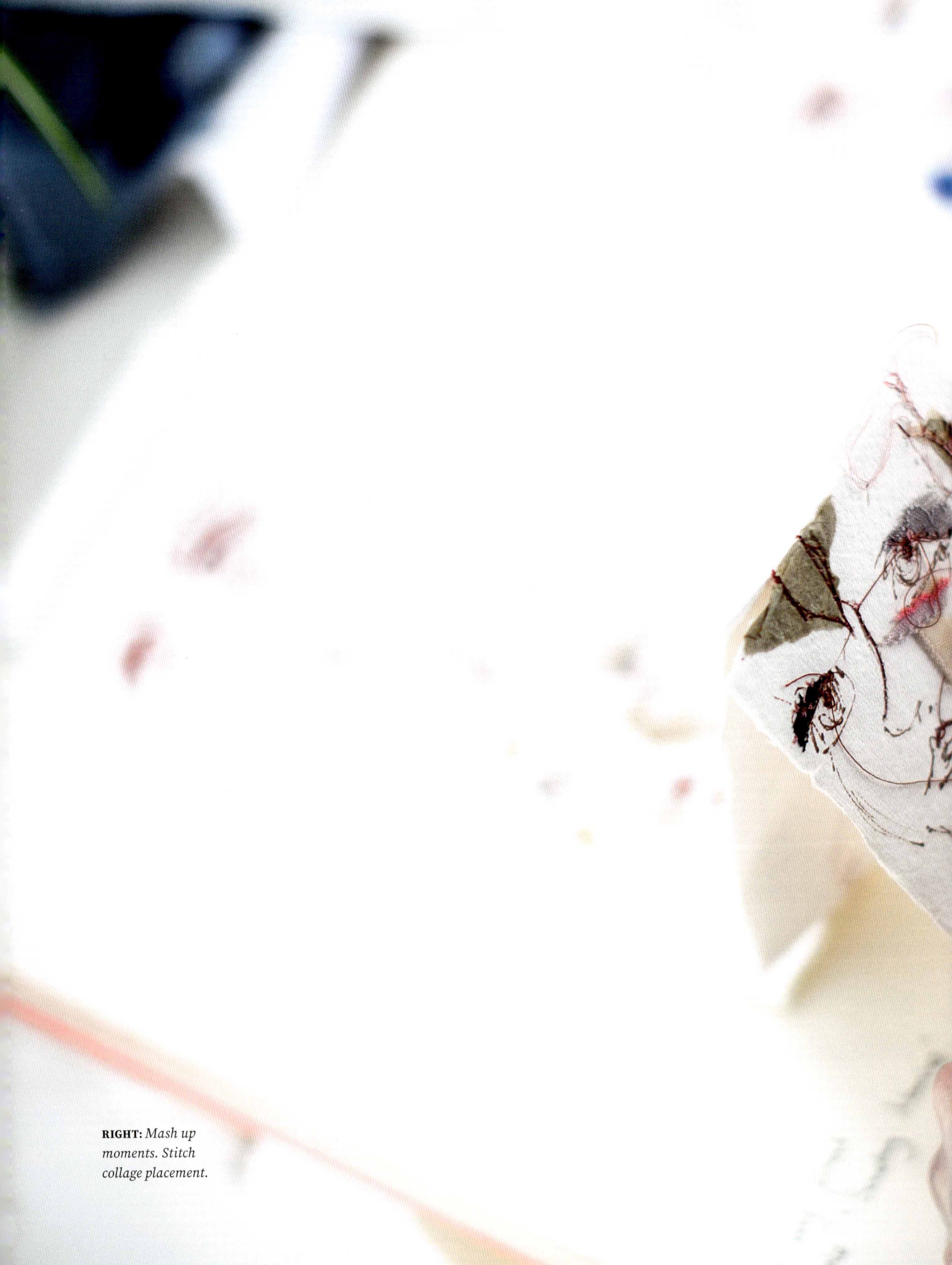

RIGHT: Mash up
moments. Stitch
collage placement.

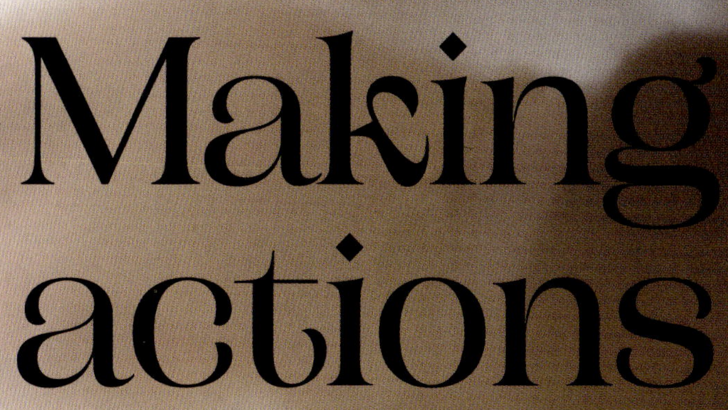

Making actions

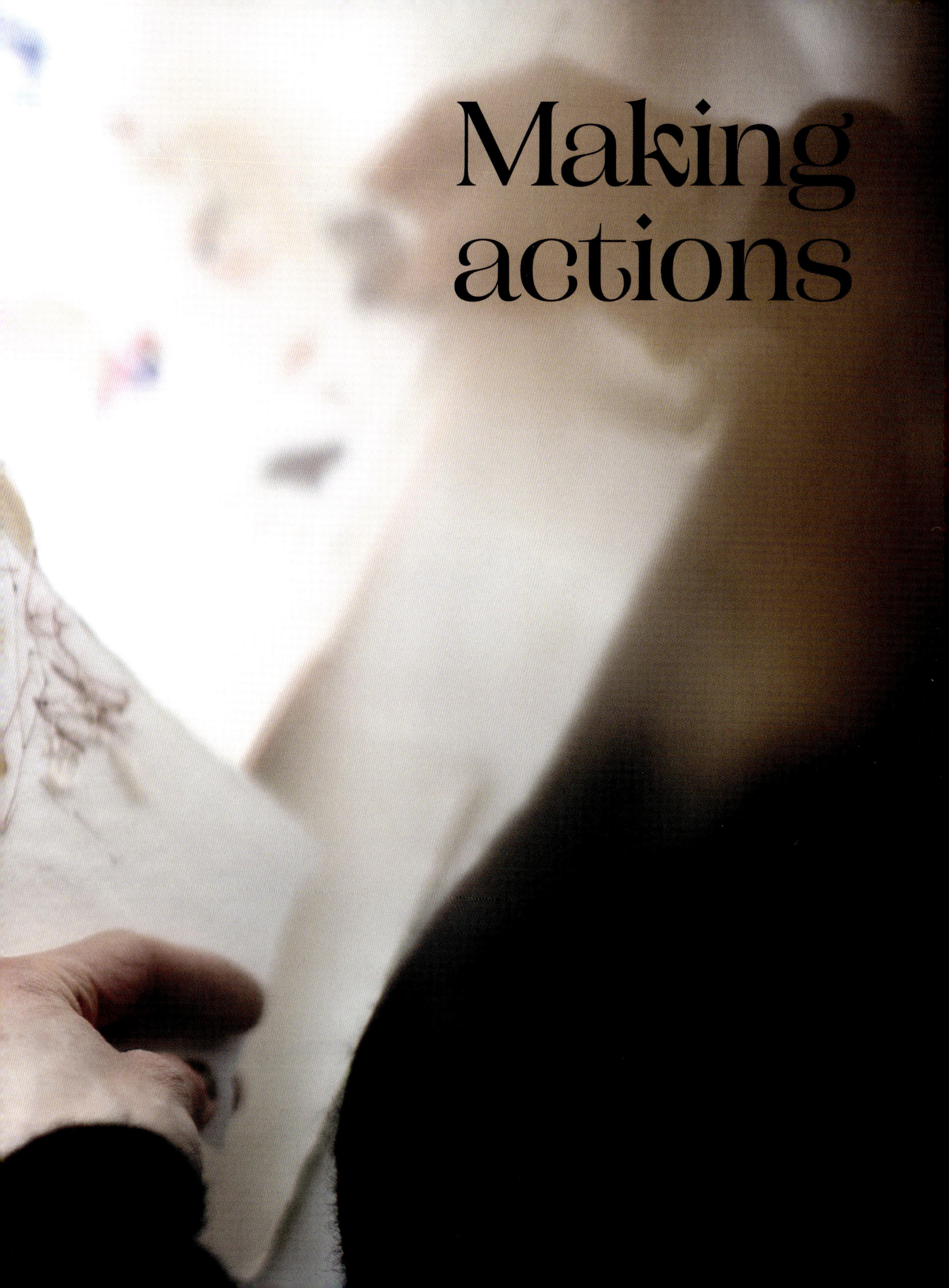

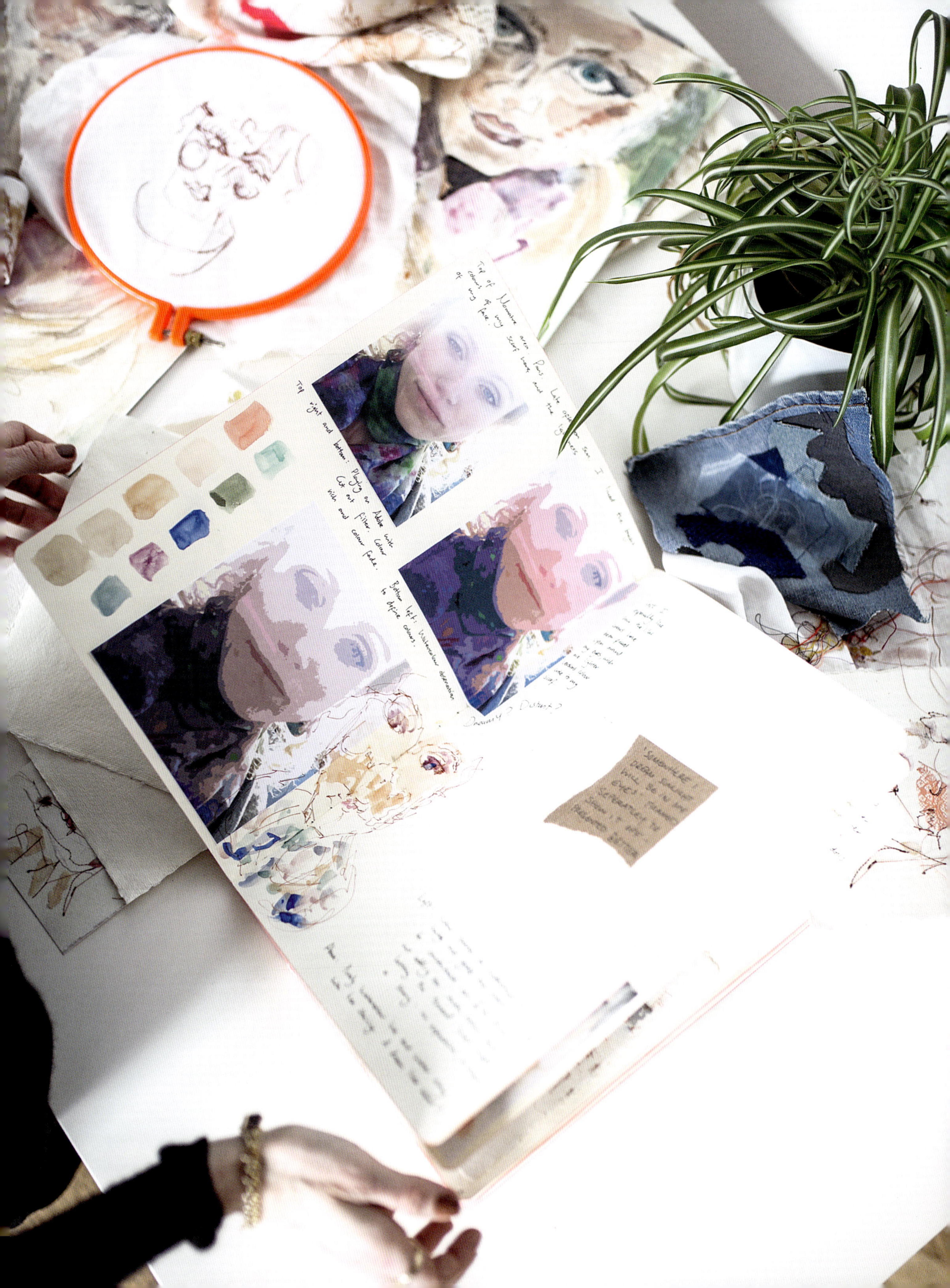

I want to focus on a few approaches that are less likely to be explored in other textile titles. I have listed below methods that are often regarded as being more complex to carry out within a home setting.

This section is divided into four subsections:

In print, where we will take an overview of many of the methods. Some of these are perfectly possible to do at home; for others you may wish to book a session at a professional studio that will have all the tools on hand.

Mash-up moments, mixed-media collage, for which I have become well known.

Stitching it out, where we will focus on the machine side of things, on using this tool to 'draw'.

Unusual sculptural. This can give a new dimension to our work, as well as a fresh excitement. Suddenly your vision may be more than wall-mounted. The key aim within this section is to ignite a zeal within you to be that explorer.

OPPOSITE: *Self-portrait outcomes in image, paint, stitch and print techniques, variety of exploratory works set in studio.*

In print

Often, print-making is viewed as a paper-based exercise, primarily carried out within a professional studio kitted out for the process. However, it can be a wonderful decorative method to weave into your material-based pieces.

In this section, I discuss experimenting with fabrics in a professional print-making studio, then suggest some print-making methods that can be used at home without access to any specialist materials or equipment. We also take an in-depth look at batik techniques to try at home, outlining the materials, process and possible applications.

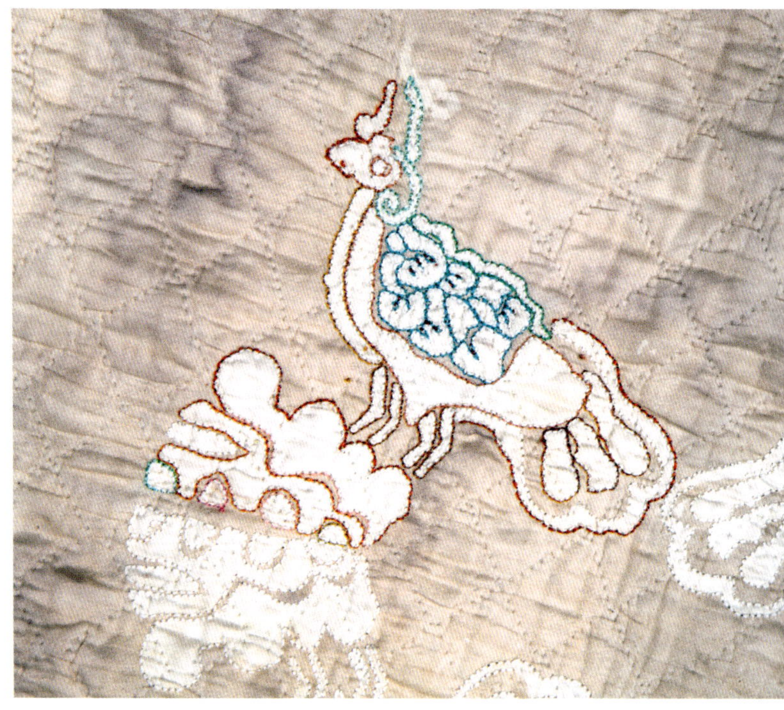

ABOVE: *Detail.*
OPPOSITE:
Remembering what is lost, creating the new from the gap of old (Ailish Henderson, 2024). Vintage cloth (various), decolourisation, silk thread, tea.

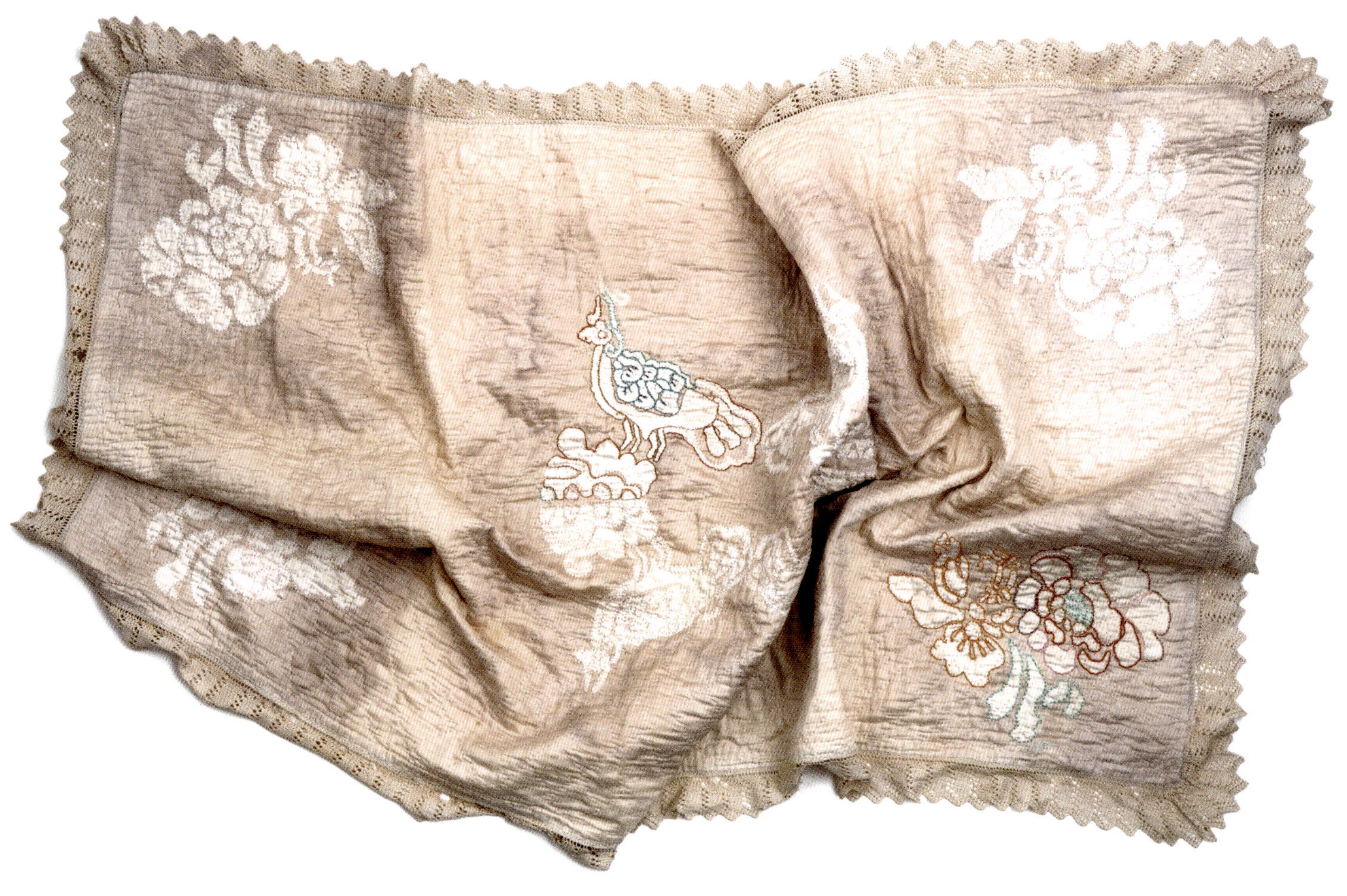

Professional print-making studio

I am lucky to have access to a print-making studio locally. In a print-making studio there lie many a perfect, sharp-edged wall-mounted offering. The sources are vast, the influences are large, yet all hold one thing in common: our views or expectations of them are paper-based. For the beholder, or the maker themselves, the excitement will derive from the excellence of the execution, or the weight of the paper used. There is variety, and one will pick up on this, depending on how experienced or observant you are in this method.

However, what if we approach this with textiles as our chosen media? Then we can simply use this method in conjunction with the skill set that we are already developing. When I wanted to try this, I approached the print studio first and explained that I wanted to work with fabrics and fabric-like papers, rather than the traditional ones they stocked. I prepared a few items to take in and had a few induction sessions to learn how to use the equipment. Then, I flew.

In the studio, I used the same copper plates and the same etching tools that are used for traditional paper printing, I simply used them with alternate materials. I chose thin natural fabrics, such as muslins, tight-weave cottons and handmade papers. I did not get anything 'perfect', nor was I trying to attain that. What I did get was a selection of samples that made me smile and which had character and depth.

Home-based suggestions

At times, such as during the COVID-19 lockdowns, it just wasn't possible to leave home. During our own personal 'stay at home' times, there are ways to develop prints without the need for extra support. There are too many methods to cover in depth; however, here is a short list of those I have had success with at home:

• Sun printing

• Decolourant

• Screen printing

• Batik (this method is explored in more depth on pages 46–49)

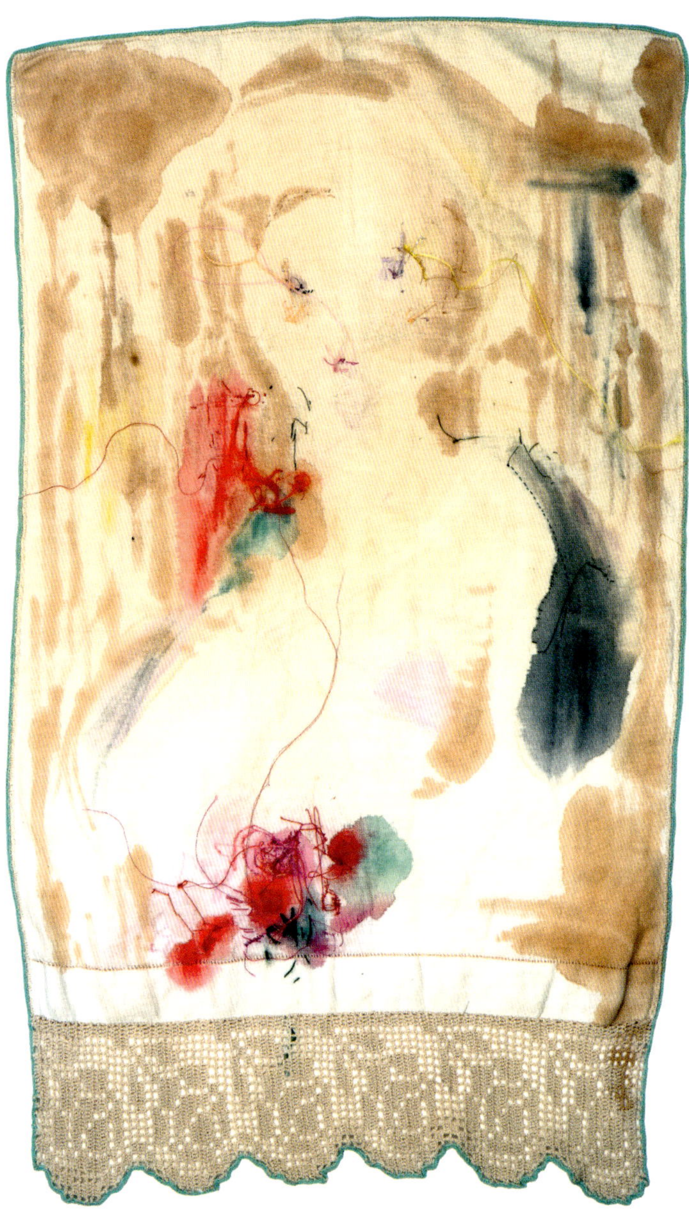

ABOVE: Washed-out, Hooded Parisian Jaunts *(Ailish Henderson, 2022). Vintage cloth, inks, oils, pastels, stitched findings.*

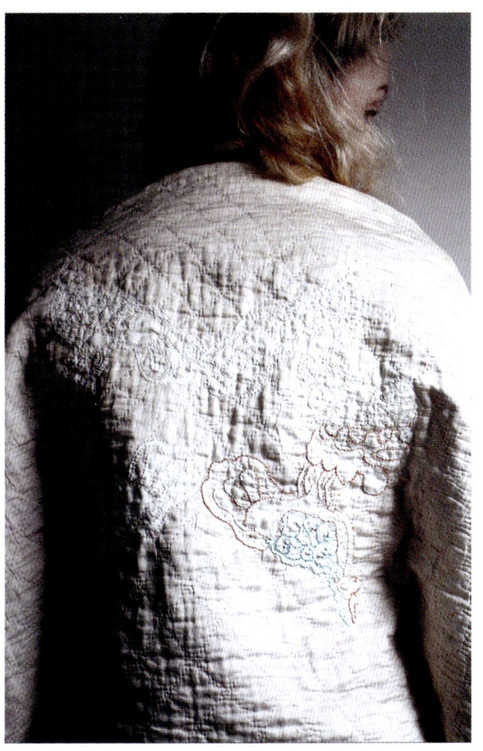

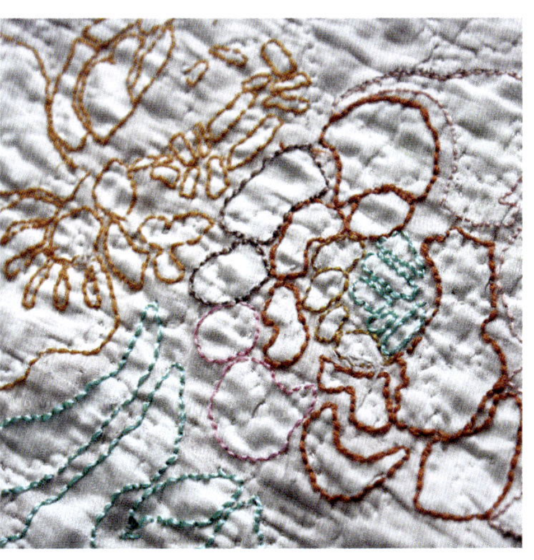

ABOVE: *New work inspired by the lost scarf (Ailish Henderson, 2019). Vintage textile, screen print with decolourant pastes and hand carved stencil.*

Narrative One:
The Lost Scarf

I will tell you a tale whereby two friends venture to Rome. The usual touristy spots covered, one final evening, aubergine parmigiana and red wine fuelled, I dragged her to the Trevi Fountain to have a photograph taken with ice cream faces next to this historical masterpiece. I wore my 'never get to wear' gown and my antique scarf, a piece passed down from my Parisian aunt. The captured visuals of this time tell the story of 'The drop' – the scarf teetering ever further away from my neck. Instead of leaving the magical coin at this landmark, I left a piece of me, my family and my story. Perhaps we should try not to become attached to transient items, but this scarf had seen me through many a fix on a wet day.

Maybe it was because it was therapeutic, but I decided to use this scarf as the inspirational launching pad for my artwork. I had only one problem: no tangible item to work from. Instead, I brought together all the images I had of me wearing the scarf.

Some simple ideas to create your own:

1. Locate any visuals of the piece that is going to become your inspirational resource, such as photographs or a diary entry that describes it.

2. Write or sketch some thoughts and methods you wish to explore.

3. Make a final design to use as a sun print (purchase an at-home kit for this method and follow its instructions).

4. For my piece, I drew and cut out a stencil to use. I then applied this to a vintage blanket that somewhat resembled the scarf and applied the sun printing techniques as I was instructed to.

5. You may wish to finish your piece with added detailing. Here, I explored stitching by hand around the printed shapes, using a subtle colour palette.

The narrative of 'Auntie Dom and the lost scarf' will now live on as a softer retelling of loss.

Batik workshop

Here, I will outline methods you can use at home, without a batik pot (a specialist pot to melt the wax in), as I see this as a skill you may enjoy and continue with, or one you are at least happy to try, but don't feel the need to further.

You need pots and pans and paintbrushes, and whatever primitive tool you do not mind compromising with wax.

During the lockdowns, I tried to find new ways of accessible working. I guess it was my version of the Second World War adage 'make do and mend'! I wanted to demonstrate to others how they could still achieve results and be arty, even if they were house-bound. So, much to my family's shuddering, my professional batik pot never left its studio cupboard, instead, the gas hob and a saucepan with water became my *bain Marie*.

Candles were melted down – no commercially bought wax pellets here. In terms of tools, I have had some success with spoons, forks, paintbrushes and the odd stick. If you want to get more recognisable results, a tjanting (the traditional pen-shaped tool specifically for batik) will not break the bank. For fabrics, use what you have; for paper, look at what you have in 'that drawer'. Blotting paper (even paper towels) along with an iron and an ironing board can be used to blot out all the excess wax after you have painted over the work in a colour, revealing the finished piece. Just remember to use your 'messy' iron, not one for pressing garments.

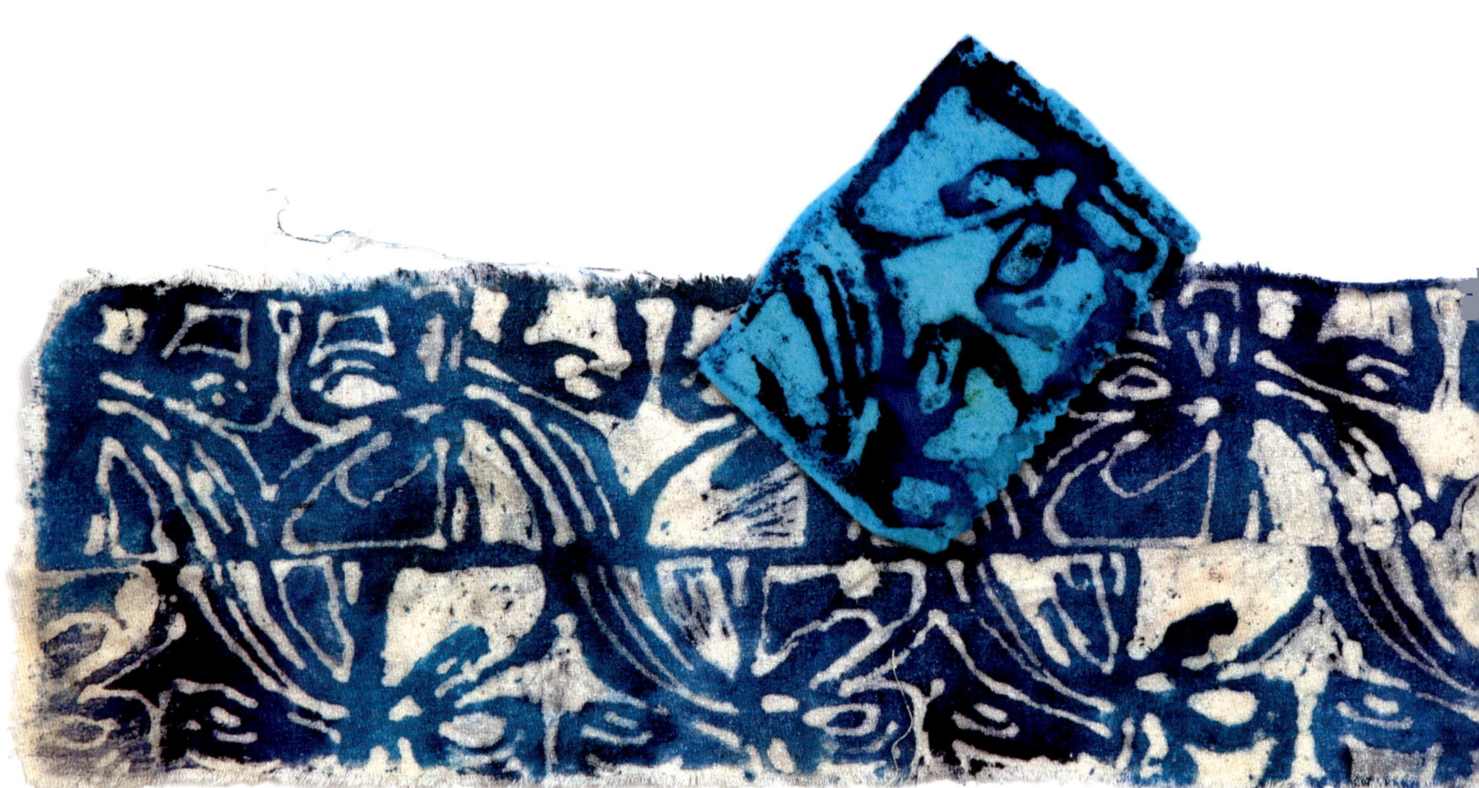

Suggested materials

- Kitchen hob and worktop

- A plastic sheet, tray or cardboard to protect your working area from wax splashes

- A selection of papers and natural fabrics, in white or pale colours

- Watercolour paints or Koh-I-Noor watercolours

- Fabric paints or dyes. Look for batik dyes or liquid fabric paints, such as Jacquard Dye-Na-Flow; use permanent colours if you want to wash the finished fabrics.

- An old metal pan to melt the wax in

- A household candle

- Marking tools. Try old paintbrushes, wooden spatulas, and spoons that you are happy to cover in wax, or you can use a traditional tjanting tool sourced online.

- Old newspapers to blot the wax out of your drawings

- A 'messy' iron

- Premade stencils, or cut your own design using a craft knife and thick card

- Basic hand-sewing kit

- Beads and buttons

The process

Set up a work area near to your kitchen hob or heat appliance. Cover your work area with protective material. Gather your papers and fabrics, marking tools, wax and melting pot/pan. Place any photographs or other inspirational resources nearby for reference.

1. Gently heat the wax in your pan. Use a very low setting as you do not want the wax to smoke.

2. Choose a brush, spatula or spoon. Dip it into the wax and use it to draw shapes and patterns onto the paper or fabric. As you work, you will begin to understand how fast the wax dries and how quickly you need to make your marks. Create several samples. If you have a particular subject in mind, try drawing it with wax. You might want to use a stencil or a traditional tjanting tool (this is optional). If you use a stencil, leave it in place until the wax is dry.

3. When the wax is completely dry, paint the paper/fabric. Use a clean paintbrush and a selection of paints and dyes. Add colour and make marks in a playful way.

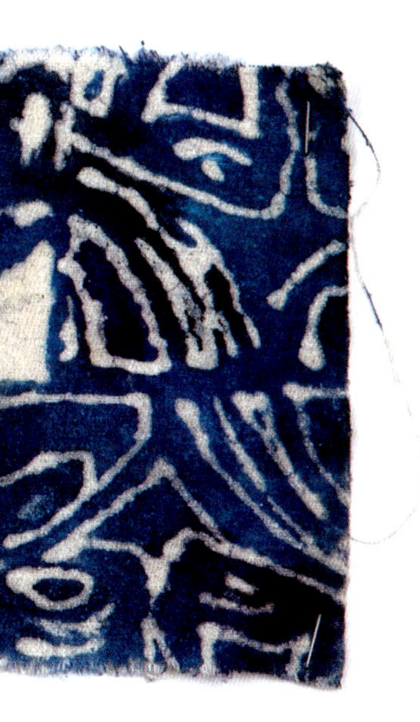

OPPOSITE PAGE:
Eyes Wide Yet Shut –
TKMaxx Tale
Untold *(Ailish
Henderson, 2021).
Taking the colour
out method trial.*

4. When the fabric/paper is
completely dry, iron out the wax.
Set the iron to a non-steam setting,
place one of your wax drawings
between some sheets of newspaper
and iron. Dark patches of wax will
come through the newspaper. Move
the fabric/paper to a fresh area
of the newspaper and iron again.
Repeat this until all the wax has
been removed. Iron the wax out
of the rest of your samples in the
same way.

5. You should now have a pile of
finished paper and fabric samples.
These can be used for further
development, stitch and collage.

Future possibilities

• Pick your best batik pieces to frame,
or scan and print the designs to use
as greetings cards.

• Hand- or free-machine-embroider
or embellish with beads. Or use the
batik fabric for a sewing project.

• Try painting one of your pieces
using colours you would not
normally use.

• Recreate your favourite piece on a
larger or smaller scale, or change
the subject matter. For example, you
could try making batik faces or a
self-portrait.

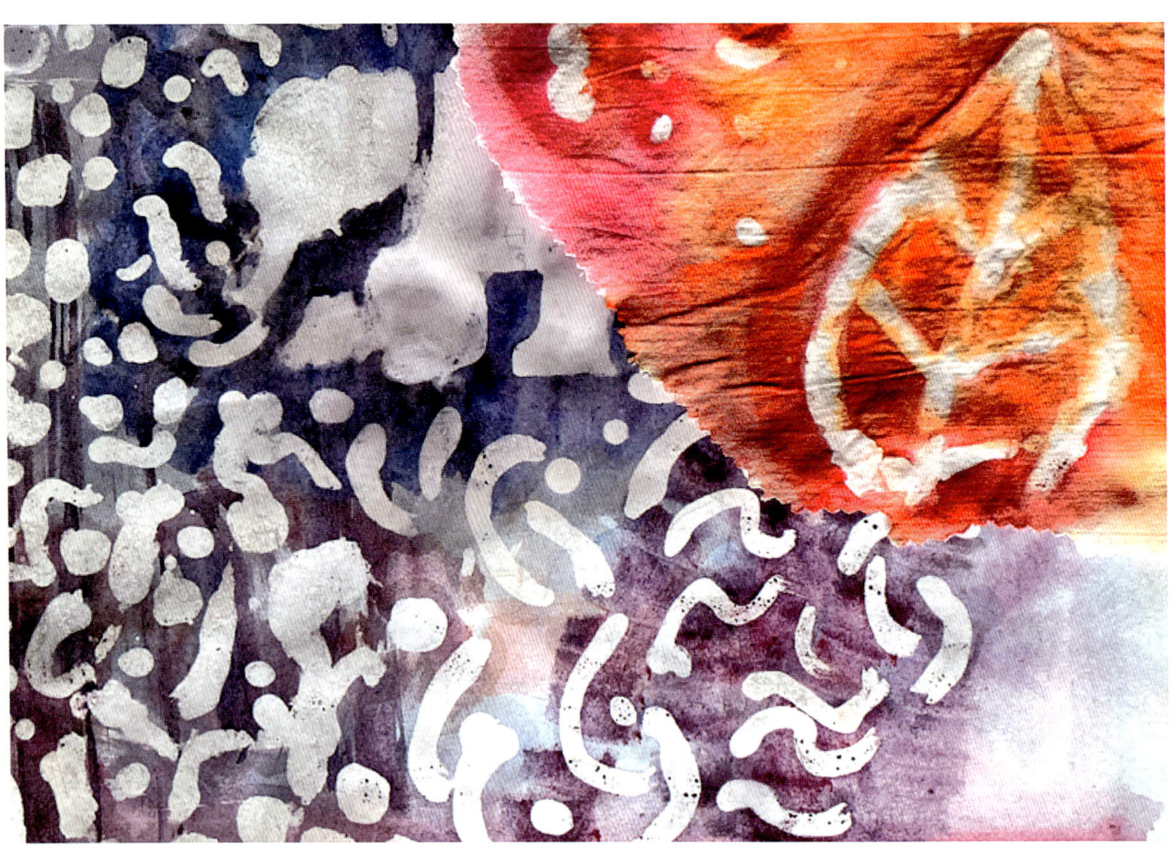

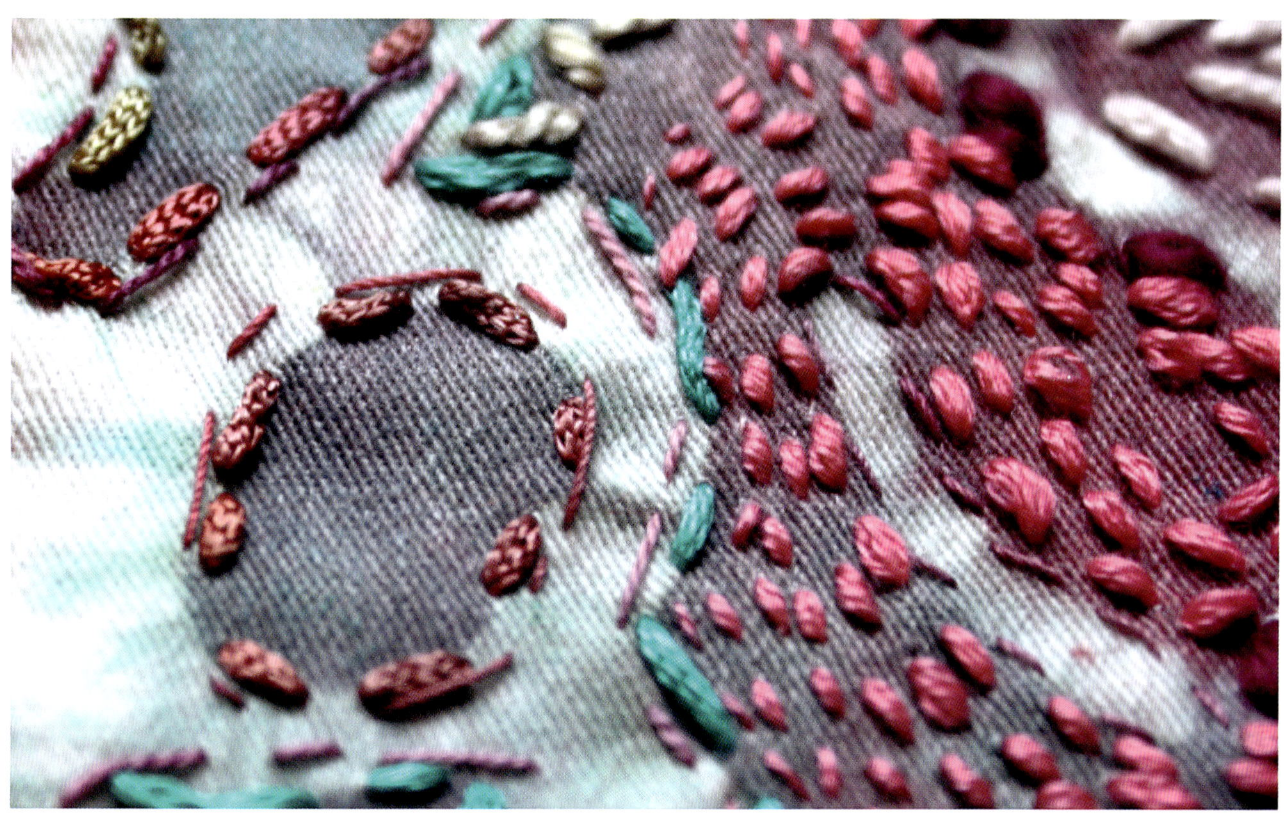

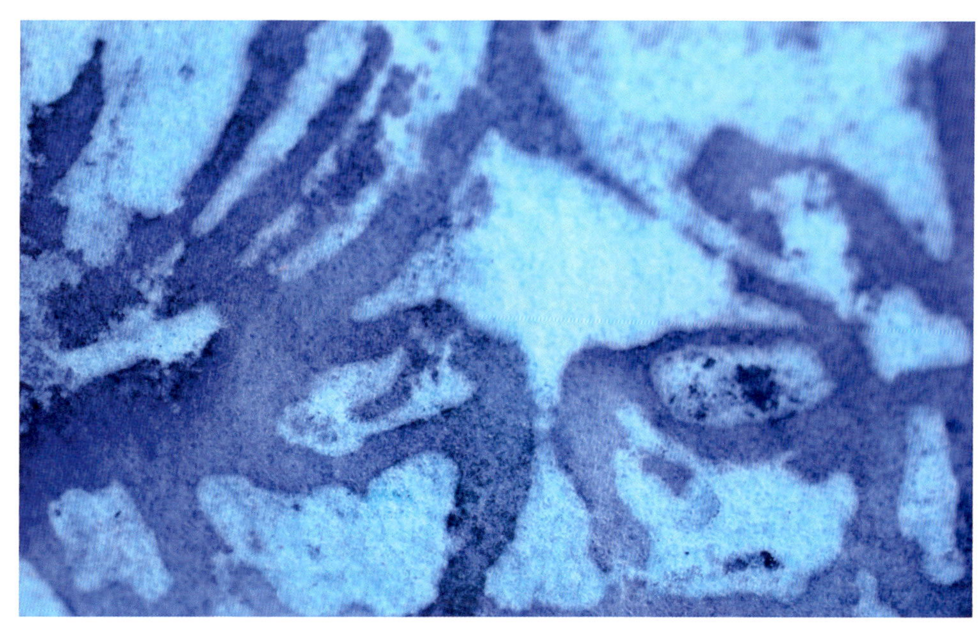

OPPOSITE PAGE: *The finished result! The blotted-out wax has left lovely patterns in white.*

ABOVE: *Why not try to hand stitch extra detail onto your Batik pieces? If you enjoy this method, purchase a tjanting tool. This will mean you can add small details.*

RIGHT: *Once you are confident, try out more planned pieces, such as facial details or hand-cut your own stencils from plastic or card.*

Mash-up moments

Cut and stick days – remember those as a child? The sticky residue of a glue stick was always a feature. As adults, sometimes we lose that joy; that moment of just being. Using our instincts, allowing ourselves to be an intrepid explorer, endeavouring to discover the unseen. Imagine being somewhere like Egypt in the early 1920s, just opening Tutankhamun's tomb – that thrill of discovery. It's ground-breaking; a moment in time never to be felt the same way again. Can you put that passionate feeling into your artistic practice?

This section includes a workshop on stitched collage.

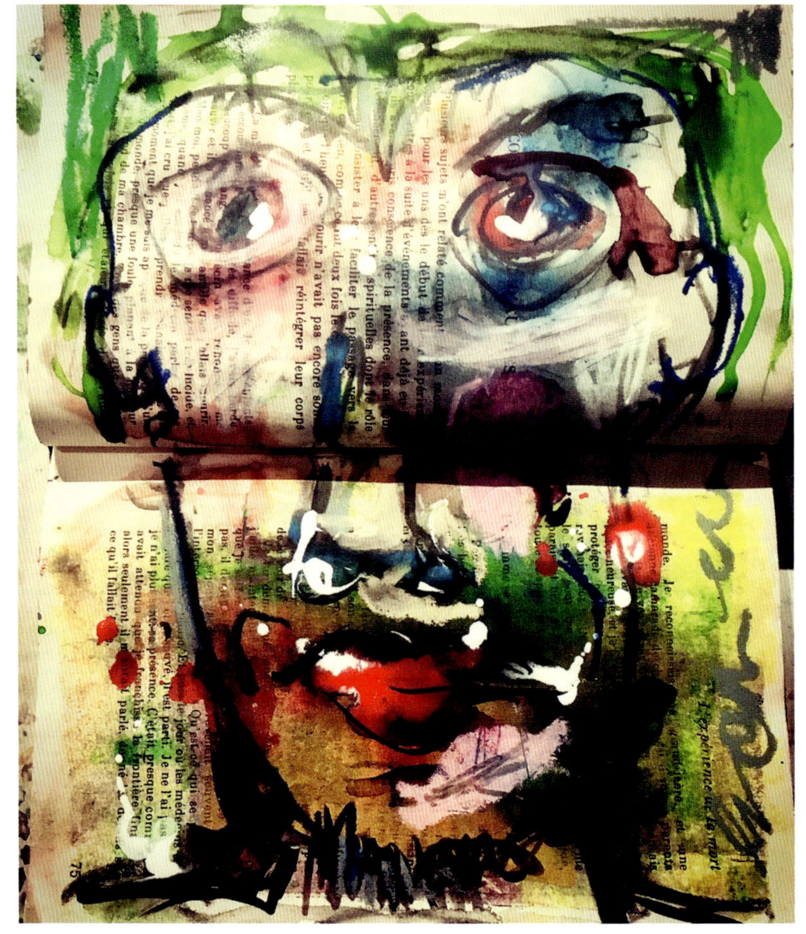

RIGHT: *Mixed media portrait with text base (Lise Howie, 2021).*

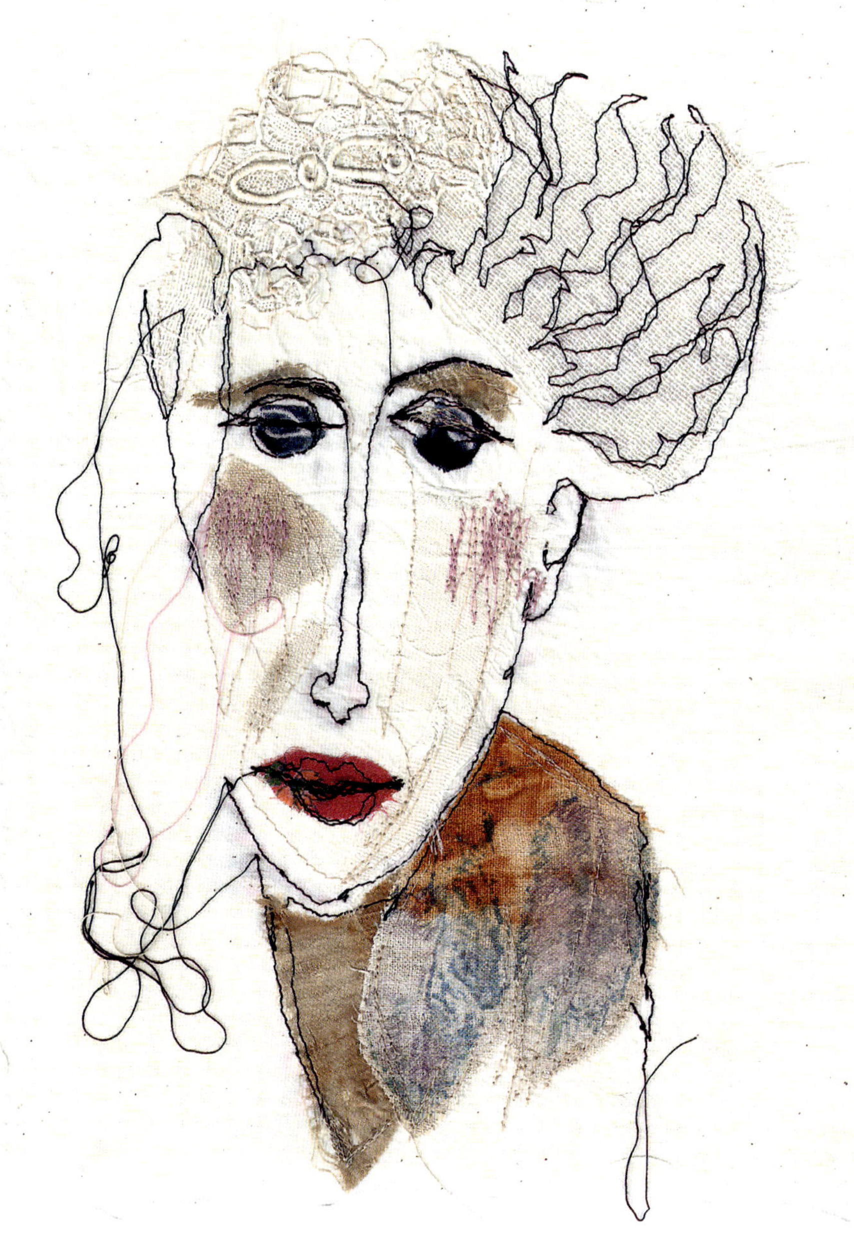

ABOVE: Portrait on Cloth (*Susan Forbes, 2020). Mixed media, thread (28 × 33cm).*

Narrative Two:
The case of the university coward (me)

Recently, I reflected upon my university days and a tutor who really helped me learn this lesson.

He told me: 'It's all about risk-taking, reflecting and remaking. I think you are working in the mindset of an accomplished designer rather than an explorer. I would like you to imagine yourself as an explorer of textiles looking for something that no one has seen or thought of before. How can you use stitch to create something totally fresh?'

We feel that now we are older and wiser, we must plan what we do, very much like our weekly food shop and life routines. What if we just began with a pile of photos, travel tickets and even clothing tags beside us and yes a tube of good old Mr Pritt?

Stitched collage workshop

It was thoughts like those in print above, which brought me to embark on my own stitch collage pieces, I am known to be a heart-sleeve wearer! I am a sentimental personal who strongly believes in art from head and heart, as it were. It was a time of self-reflection that ignited this type of work – questioning who I was and how I viewed myself. Using imagery taken at pivotal times in my life, I began to paint and draw what I saw.

I intuitively gathered collage material relating to the reference image – paper pages and receipts from a holiday where the photographs were taken. I then began to build up a self-portrait using these scraps, tearing them to my whim and fancy. I always use source material that has a direct meaning to me – my baby clothes and nappy changing bag have even made the odd appearance! Finally, I used a combination of machine- and hand-based embroidery to draw my own facial features and give the work the final finesse.

This is such a great technique because there is no right or wrong. You can tailor it to your own quirks and unique style. No two results will ever be the same, which I believe creates a wonderful sense of anticipation and excitement...the what if?

Suggested materials

- A table large enough to spread out your collage material and paints

- Reference photographs of your subject

- Handmade paper sheets (such as khadi rag paper)

- Paper and fabric scraps for the collage

- Personal source material, such as travel memorabilia, tickets, bags, as well as tissue paper, lace or old clothing

- Fine-liner pen

- Non-waterproof pen. I use Berol fine ink pens which are sold in blue and black

- A small container of water to use with your paints

- Small watercolour paintbrush

- Watercolour paints or dyes (such as Koh-i-Noor)

- Scissors

- Glue stick

- Sewing needle and a few embroidery threads in your choice of colours

Optional materials
- Gilding wax, such as Treasure Gold, for adding metallic highlights

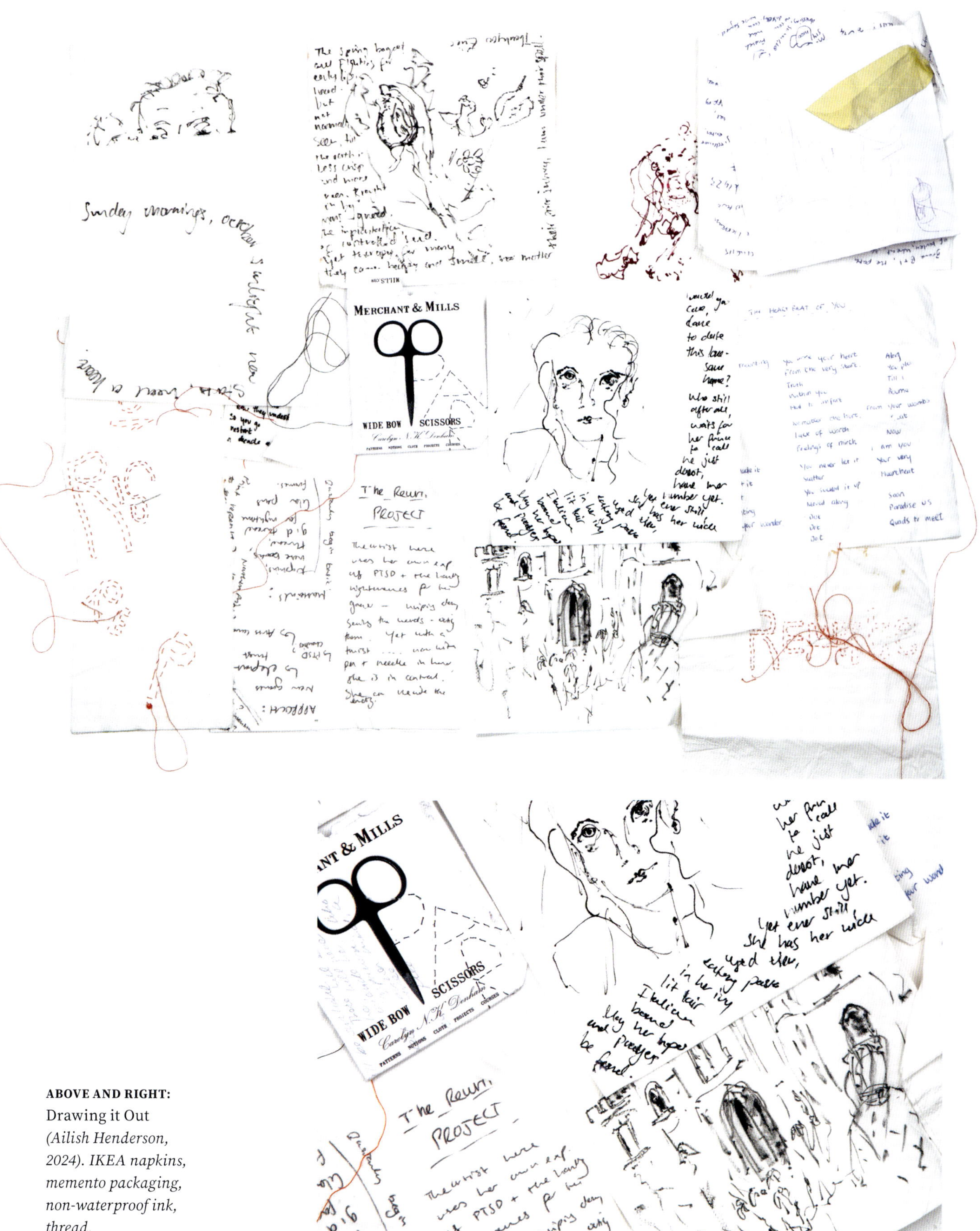

ABOVE AND RIGHT:
Drawing it Out
*(Ailish Henderson,
2024). IKEA napkins,
memento packaging,
non-waterproof ink,
thread.*

The process

Gather your inspirational imagery together and think about what aspects you would like to recreate. You might want to pin them on an inspiration board so you can refer to them as you work. You might also like to record your process and ideas in a sketchbook during this project.

1. Select a piece of handmade paper. Draw an outline of your image using a fine-liner pen.

2. Colour the image with watercolour paints or dyes, using a wet paintbrush to blend colours and blur the edges. Make a piece that is personal to you and expresses your style. It doesn't have to be perfect, as it will become the reference image for your collage.

3. Select another piece of handmade paper, then use your gathered collage material and the painted drawing to influence the colours and shapes you select for your work. Tear or cut fabric pieces from your stash and place them onto the handmade paper to build up the portrait.

4. Use a small dot of glue to tack the collage composition into place.

5. Select a thread colour. You could choose a thread that is darker than the collaged scraps, if you'd like the stitching to stand out, or something lighter and more subtle. Then start to stitch the features in your own style. Use a basic running stitch to emulate sketched lines. Be patient and go slowly on your first attempt.

6. Finish each thread by sewing a small stitch or tying a knot on the back of the work. Alternatively, you can knot the thread on the front and leave the tail hanging loose to add character.

Future possibilities

Using this approach, you can take any photograph and play with collage and hand or machine stitch to emulate what you see, in your own unique style. Have fun and explore a wide variety of materials and textures in your work.

OPPOSITE, ABOVE: *Duo of stitched portrait collages.* Stories My Grandmother Told Me, *collective works (Ailish Henderson, 2021). Thread, Irish linen, personal treasures.*
OPPOSITE, BELOW: Pistachio Smiles *(Ailish Henderson, 2016). Stitch collage self-portrait. Irish linen, intuitive curation of materials.*

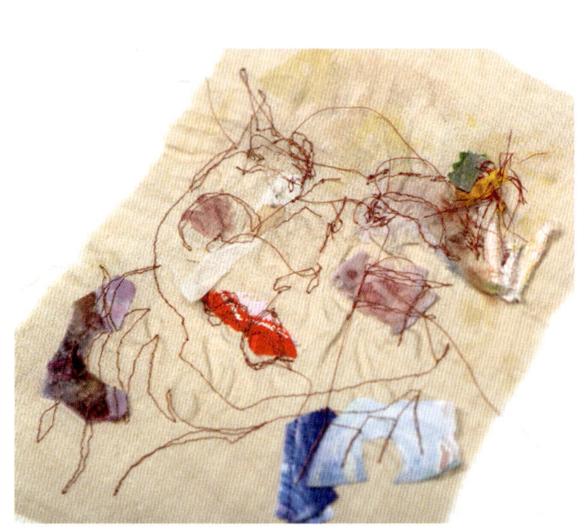

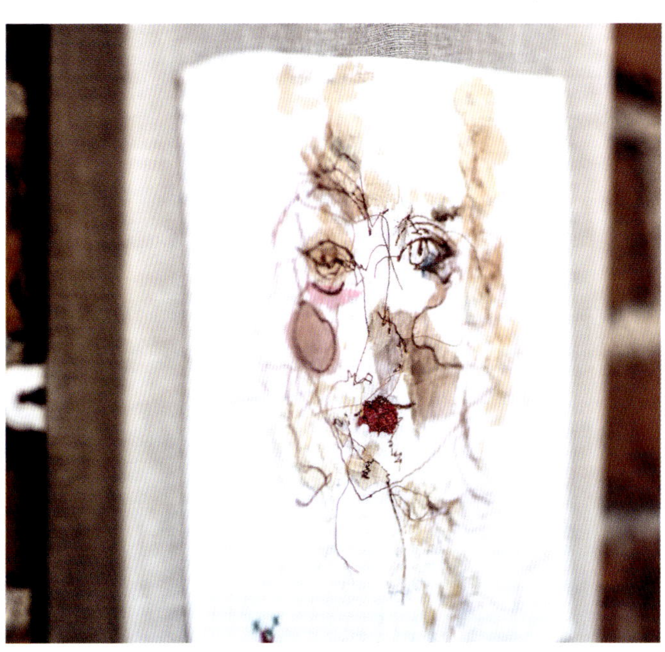

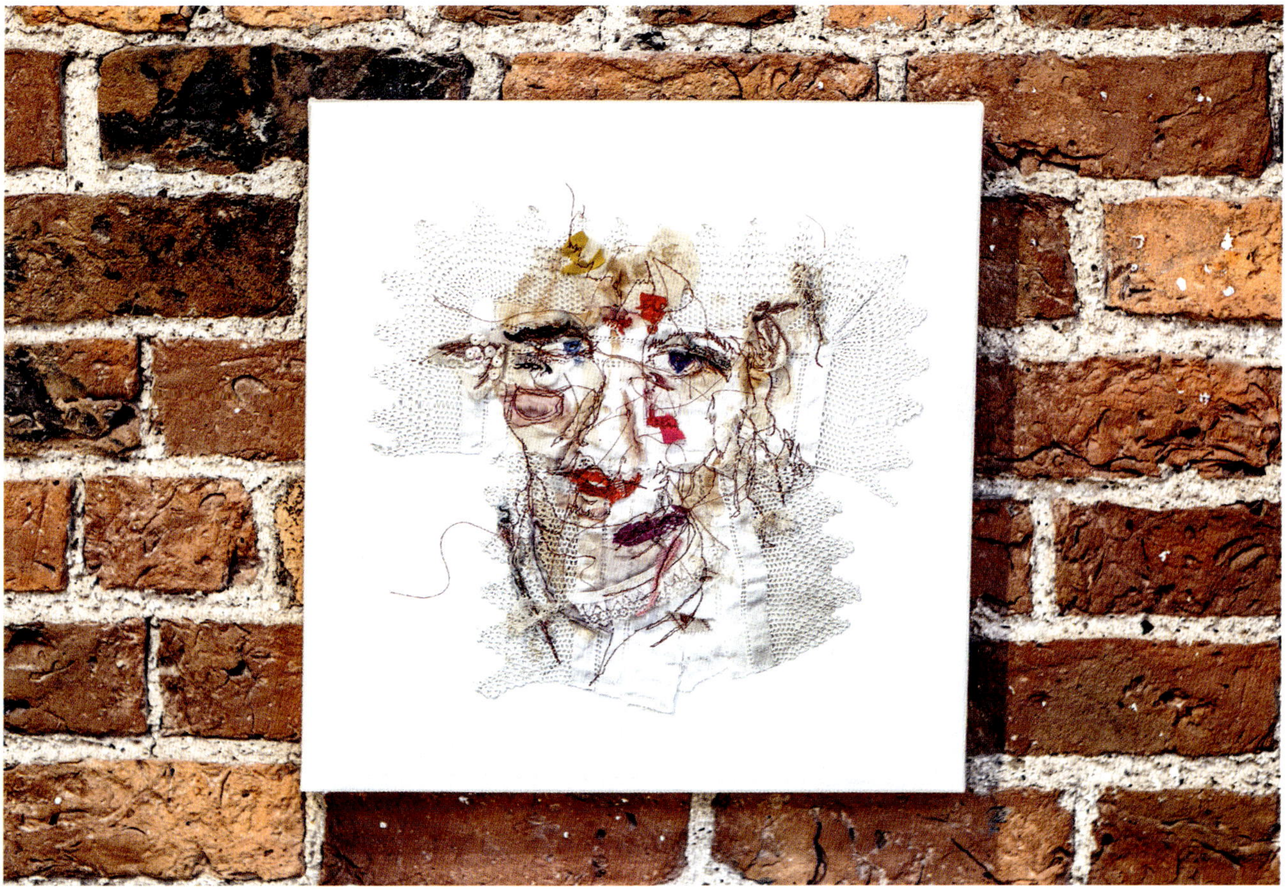

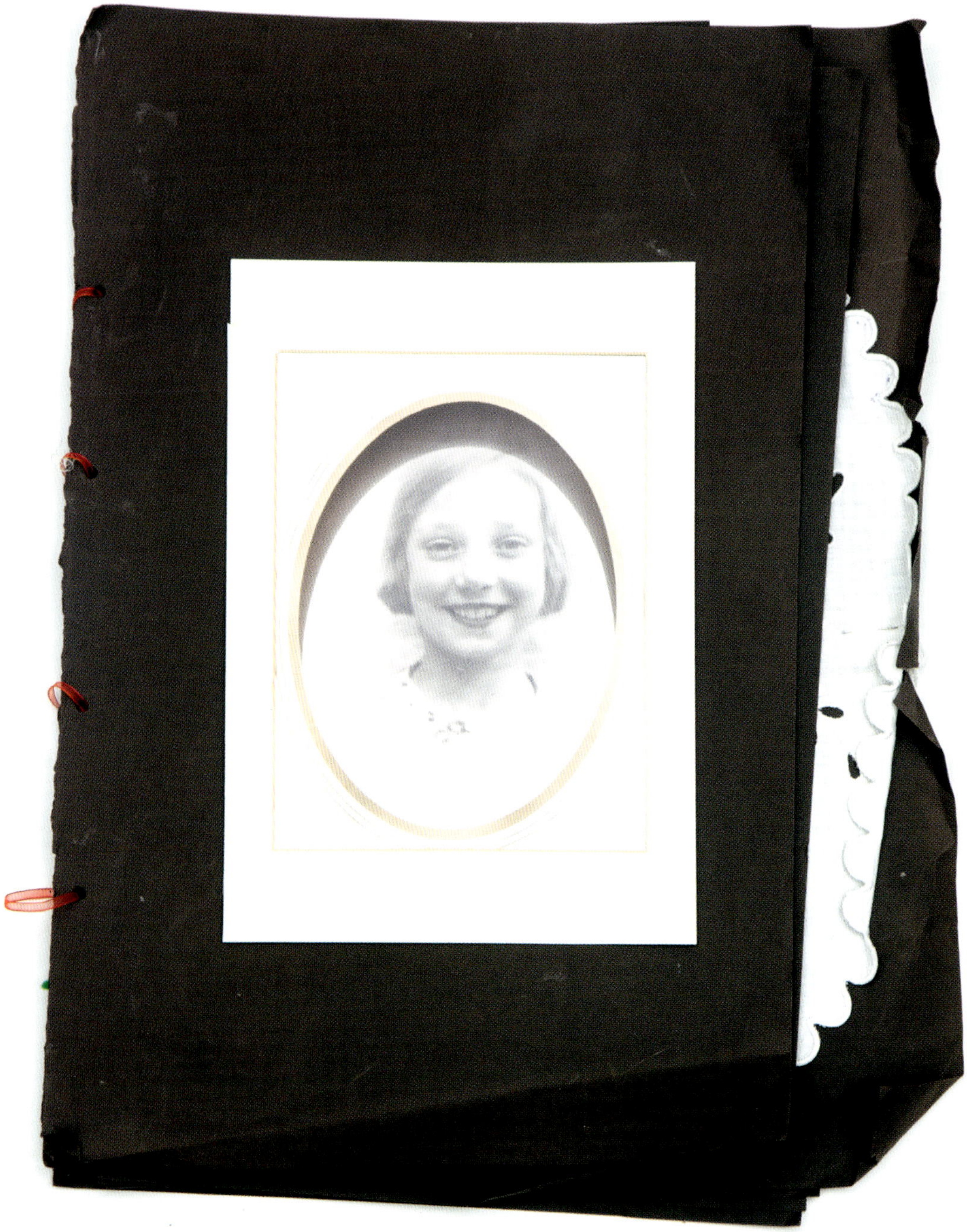

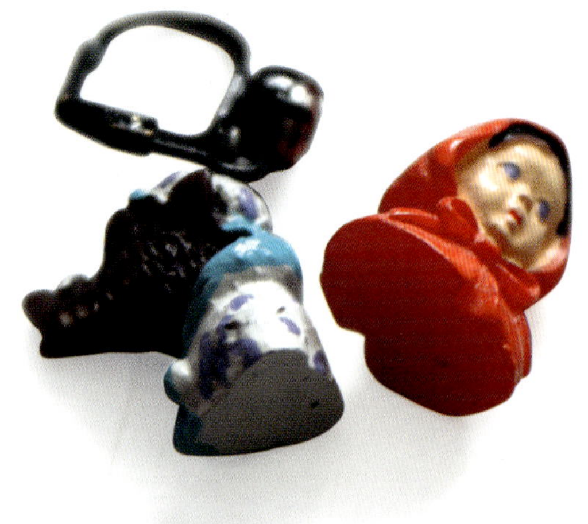

ABOVE: *Grandmother at 14. Print book of* Red Ties *narratives (2021).*
RIGHT: *The black hooks of Red and Wolf prove to be inspiration fuel (2011).*

Stories my grandmother told me

Stories my grandmother told me,
Never did she scold me,
When my mind wanted read again,
What she was never able to write,
By pen.

An ever changing,
Developing mind was I,
Never happy with her version,
Another change in her tale,
Pending.

Now I make my own paths,
Tales,
Travel abroad,
Tall structures seen,
Architecture stored,
Yet down these narrow streets,
It is not the buildings,
That my gaze meets,
But the tiny shop window,
With my grandmother's story,
Held on two black hooks.

In this place,
I remember her more,
All the words,
That were given verbally,
Stored,
Passed from her mouth,
To my grasp.

And now I want her,
To sit and tell me her story,
That ever changed,
Yet the ending always remained the same.

Peace and a happily ever...,
Was all I ever after.

She crafted words,
That have become such strong memories,
That even in this foreign place
I am at peace.

I now carry them,
In a visual form,
On those black hooks,
That adorn my ears.

I shed a tear,
For the girl I once was,
For the little girl,
In the red coat,
Yes,
I once was.

For the wolf that is now locked up,
Dormant in my bed of childhood.

I must make my own story,
Yet her words remain,
Just outside my listening parts,
They have left their hole of glory.

Grandmother,
What a big mouth you have.

Thank you for telling me your story.

AH 2012

Stitching it out

In this section we will look at the two main types of stitching: hand stitching and machine stitching. Both methods can produce beautiful results.

FEATURED ARTIST:
Sharon Peoples

I came across the work of Sharon Peoples quite by accident via Instagram. I loved the diversity of her hand- and machine-embroidered pieces, but it was those which were quite miniature and figurative in form that struck my interest. She has been a part of many exhibitions and often leads classes, where she generously imparts her knowledge to audiences. She co-curated and co-authored the book titled *Exuberance an Embroiderer's Perspective* which was created during the COVID-19 lockdowns and focuses predominantly on hand stitching. She has depth of knowledge which flourishes visually in her outcomes. She has a PhD in art History and is based in Canberra, Australia.

'Although not obviously apparent, the touchstone for my work has always been the Bayeux Tapestry, an embroidery that has a strong narrative. It is also an explicit

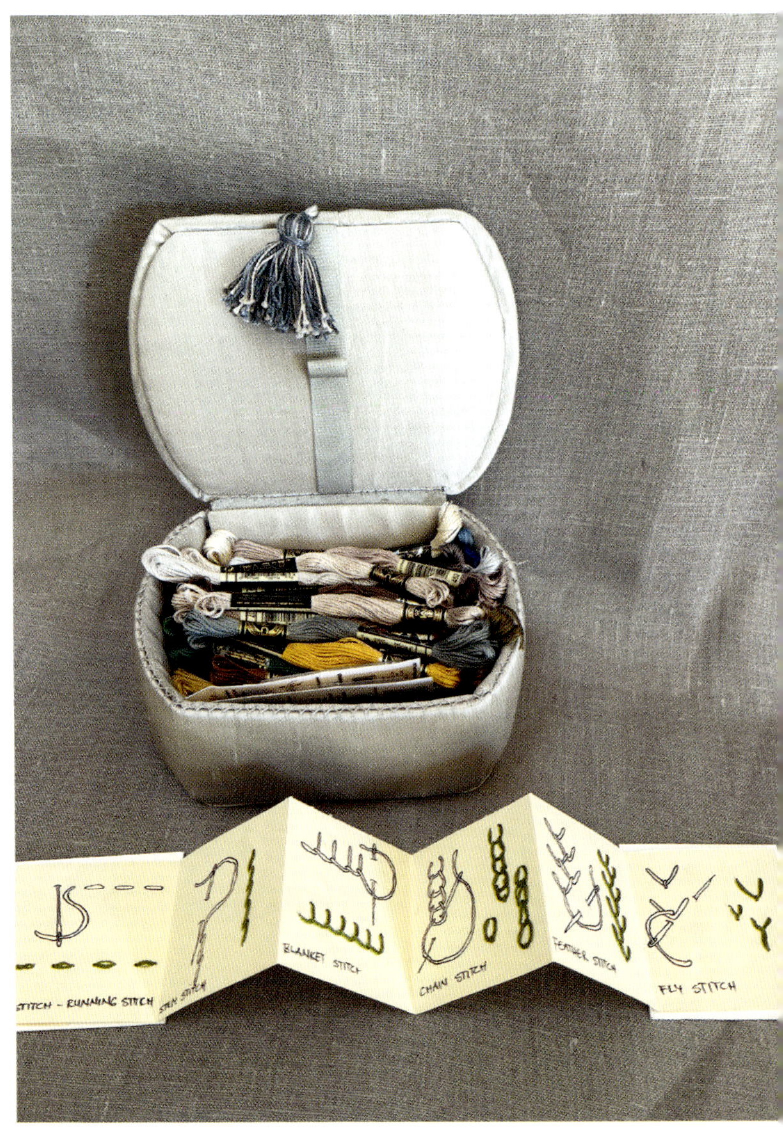

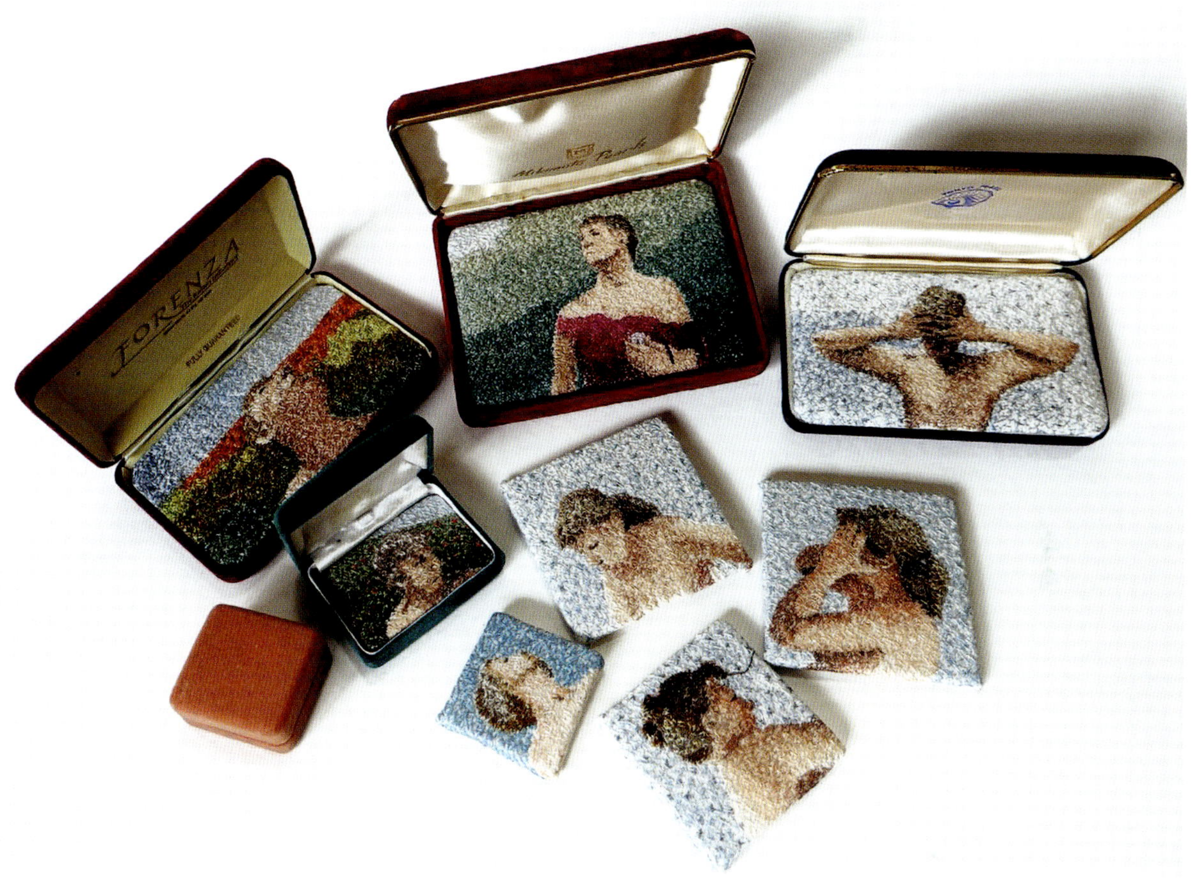

example of embroidery as a metaphor: embellishing, exaggerating, decorating and often covering up and darning over existing stories. The embroidered cloth also shows the marks of repairing, mending and restoring. I take this as a springboard to repairing the fragility of both the environment and of the human condition in my own stitched works.

'I have been involved in several very long narrative embroideries, commissioned for cultural institutions, either as a stitcher or as the designer. Yet, it is the small works I stitch that tell other, more intimate, chronicles. These works may not necessarily begin as a narrative. The portrait of my husband working while sitting in the morning sunlight during the pandemic lockdowns of 2020 shows him still in his dressing gown and pyjamas. The stripes and the play of light were the motivation of the piece, but now, in perspective, it tells of a worldwide event within a personal story.

'Textiles are created at a specific moment; they are given the imprint of a precise instant in time. Embroideries also have their own memories of the maker. They are projections of the expectations of the maker: the maker's energy, thoughts, and life flow through the threads. Textiles

OPPOSITE PAGE: *Mending Box illustrating supplies for hand stitch (Sharon Peoples, 2021).* **ABOVE:** *Group of boxed embroideries (Sharon Peoples, 2019).*

remember moments of happiness and tragedy; they are recorded on the surface and embedded into the structure of the cloth. Staining, dyeing, piercing, stitching and printing are ways that document moments, both personal and social.

'Our bodies also react to constant stitching. I build up calluses on my fingers when I am embroidering heavily. Initially my fingers are pricked, but it doesn't take long – maybe a couple of days – before thick skin develops. I am not deterred by the anticipation of soreness, as experience tells me that subsequently the speed of my embroidering picks up.

'These are small works made in recent years that began while I was on a residency at a local arts centre here in Canberra. I wanted to make small pieces that could tell a story. Matching the narrative to the housing was time-consuming but nonetheless added depth. Sometimes, the container in which the textile is housed leads the direction of the work. I spend time collecting interesting boxes from secondhand shops and garage sales.

'Capturing a story in any form opens us up to reflection. Reflecting can take us to surprising places, and perhaps opens a path to creativity, if we allow it. Creativity is about capturing those moments that make life worth living.'

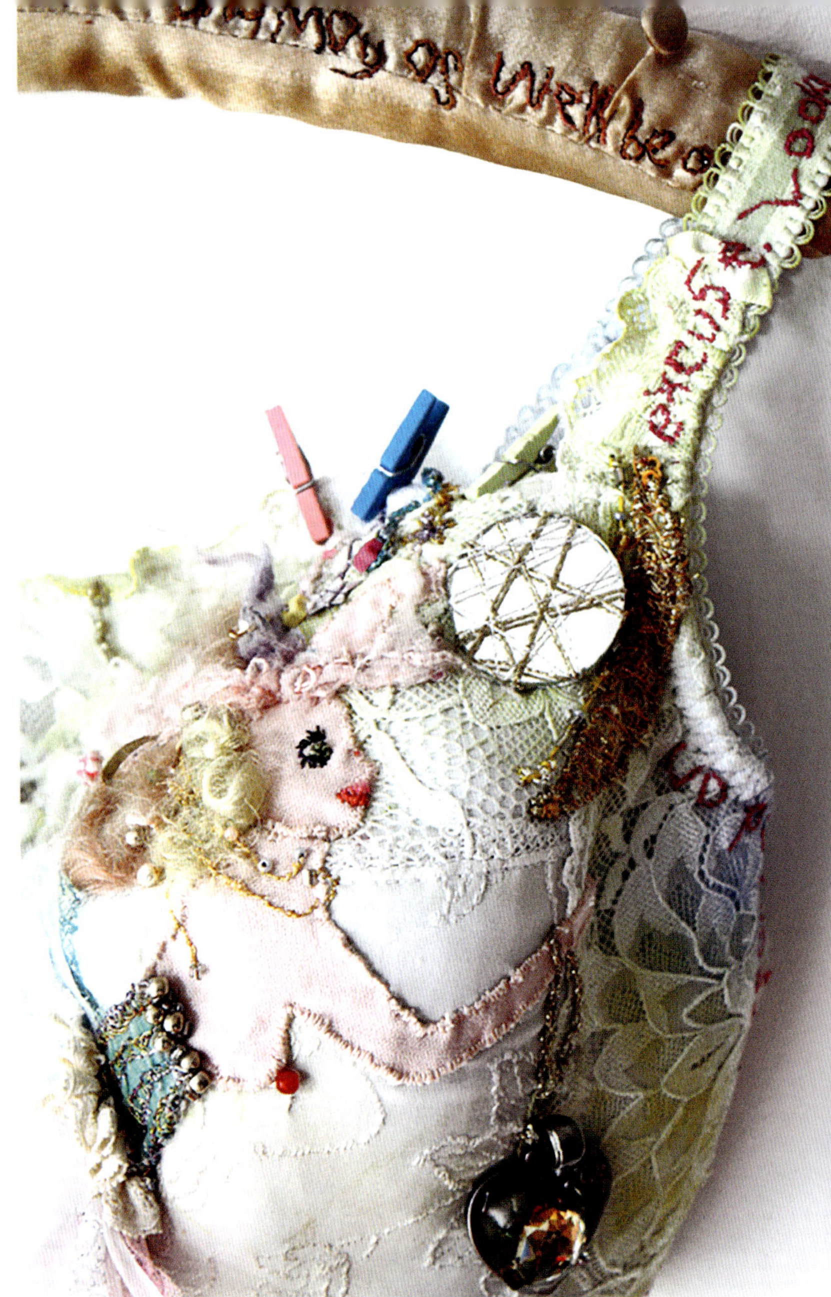

ABOVE: The Star Catcher *(Ailish Henderson, 2016). Inspired by mother's twice survival of breast cancer and our shared bond. Post-surgery brasserie, dye, embroidery, embellishments.*

Machine stitching

A free machine embroidery foot can open up exciting possibilities; it is like having a new style of pen to draw with. This concept takes the heat out of any prior trepidation: simply view the machine as another drawing tool, one that you will gradually feel more control of through experience. Just be careful to watch where your fingers are – it is easy to get one's digits too near the eye of that enthusiastic needle!

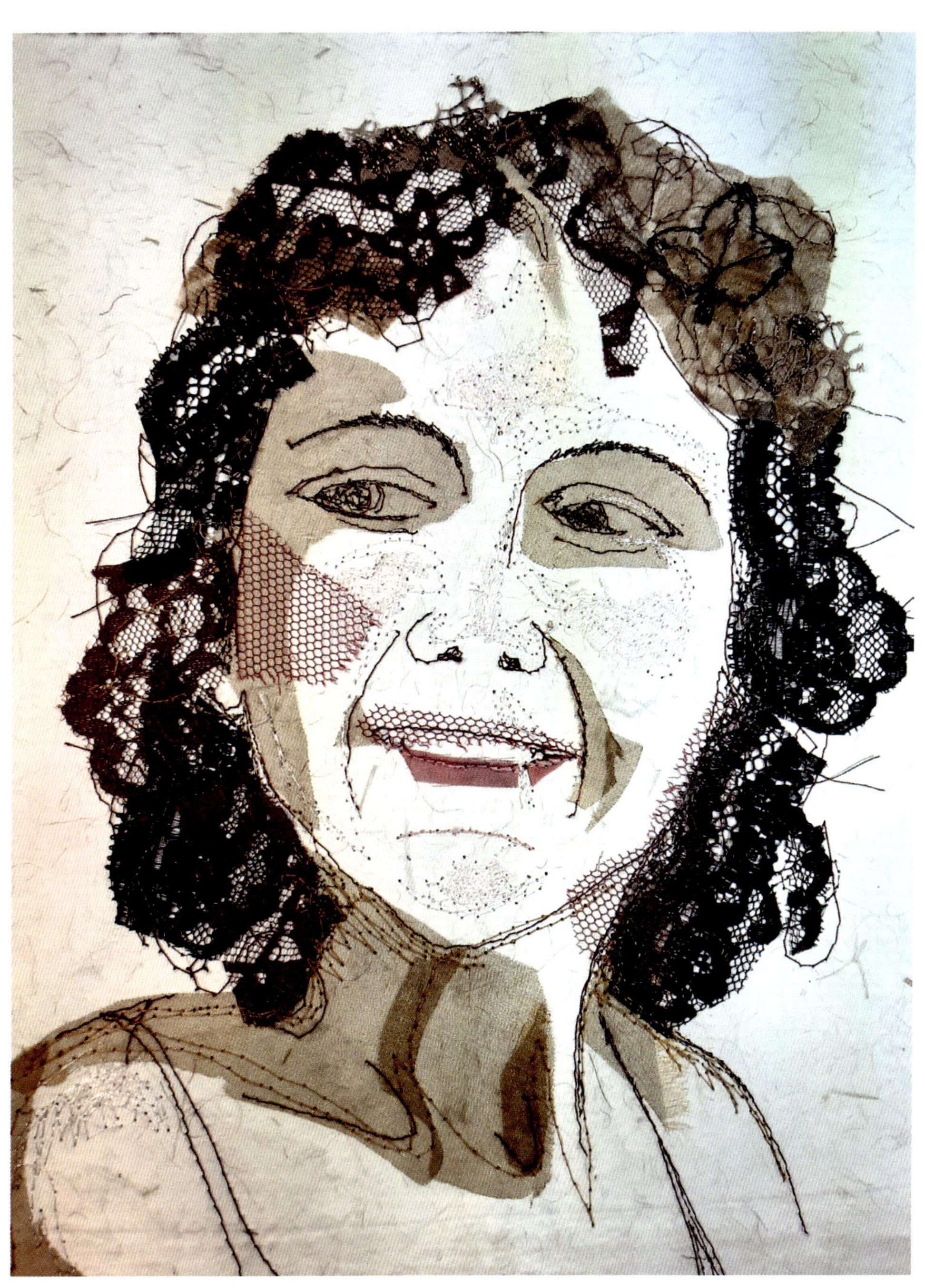

BELOW: *Portrait in free machine embroidery (Linda Carswell, 2020). Applied lace, net and sheer materials on handmade paper (24 × 30 cm).*

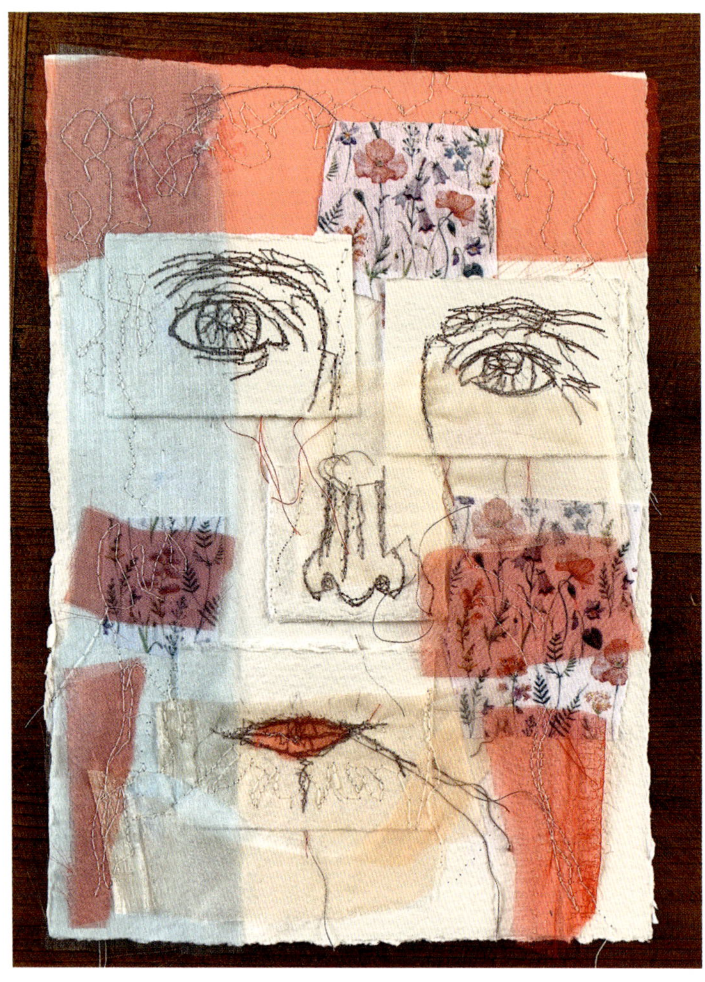

FEATURED ARTIST:

Gill Tyson

I first met Gill Tyson through a portrait workshop I was teaching back in 2020. I was drawn to her samples and outcomes because of their beautiful, pieced-together nature, for example the square blocks in this piece, which become a part of the portrait itself.

Gill explains: 'I was inexperienced with free-motion stitching at the time and the prospect of doing a full portrait was daunting. So, I practised on the separate parts of the face and this piece just came together. It was a serendipitous process in the end and the expression rather appropriately conveys me in a moment of contemplation. I am interested in the process of making and constantly reflect on how inspiration and the creative art of making comes about.'

Gill likes the slow, hands-on approach and to allow a piece of work to evolve. She enjoys the meditative process of the making where ideas swirl around until the final outcome becomes clear. This can be through sketchbook notation and experimentation with design, or by auditioning different materials and techniques until something feels right. She is drawn to the natural world, and in particular, the intricacies of surface patterns, shapes and textures. Gill uses natural fibres and recycled fabrics, print and mark making, collage and stitch to explore her ideas. She likes the serendipity of the process, the intrigue of inspiration, and the feel of the materials in her hands, all of which contribute to the creative art of making.

Unusual sculptural

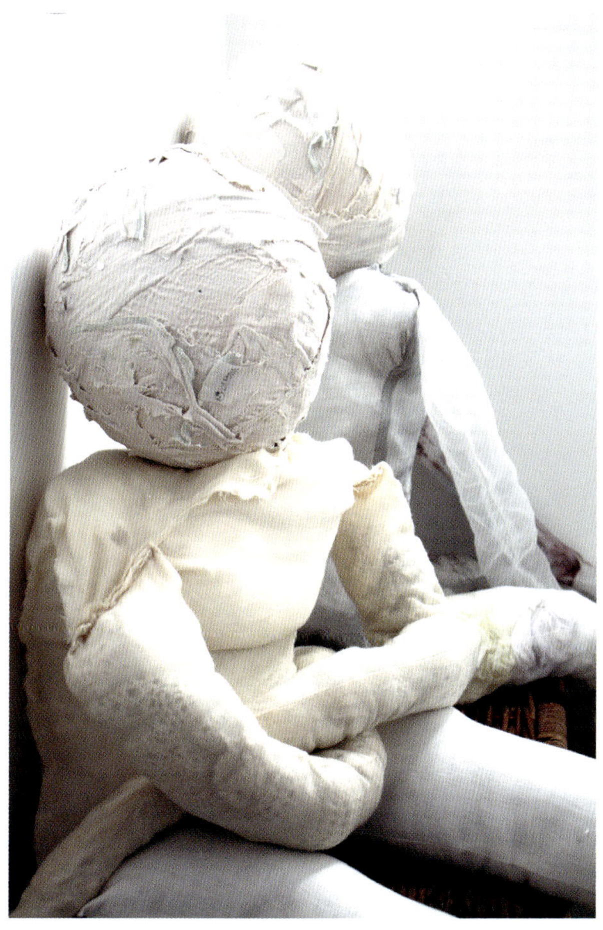

ABOVE: *Two selected sculptures made from personal items and Irish linen (Ailish Henderson, 2020). Jesmonite, mixed cloth.*

Telling our stories through textiles doesn't have to take a flat, well-trailed embroidery form. In fact, it does not have to be literal. If we know the backstory, as it were, then we can choose how much to reveal or conceal.

What can we show with as little as possible? I set myself a deliberately bland palette for this project, to show what emotion and character I could convey with much thought and little detail. So, I began a body of work, which is not yet ended.

What I found interesting about the development of this project was:

1. Keeping a neutral colour palette.

2. Using little detail, and instead planning and thinking out the work much more.

3. The feeling of excitement about using materials I was not familiar with; in a way this took the weight out of how the work looked in the end. I had no prior expectation or vision, I only had my imagination.

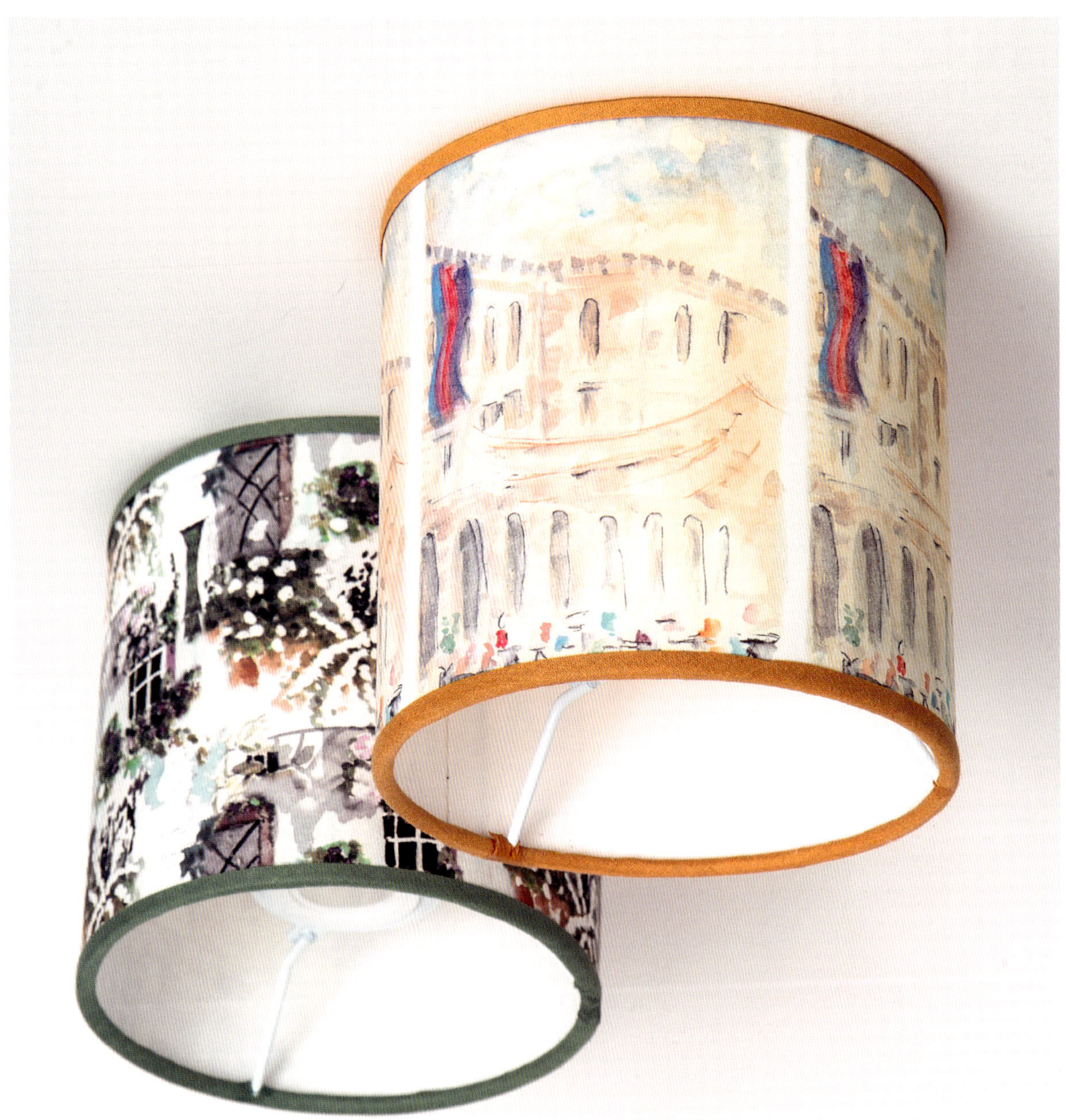

ABOVE: *Duo of shades, derived from original watercolours of* The Royal Academy *and* Gigi's Garden *(Ailish Henderson, 2023).*

OPPOSITE PAGE: *Pottery gets personal. On site of the story.*

Narrative Three:
Pottery gets personal

As we were having a meal at a local pottery studio, repurposed as a restaurant at night, my friend and I were offered a free pottery lesson. How could we say no? My last experience had been at the Early Learning Centre, with a plastic turning wheel and many safety-checked 'tools' when I was around seven.

We are ushered in, with a quiet, respectful bow, by an unusual character. We sit down on wooden benches with a table to work on. I catch my companion's eye. We are smiling, yet transfixed, distracted by the grey mound of matter in front of us.

As I shape it, mine turns into a planned bust, a woman's form. I find myself trying to make it exactly how I want it, only as we near the end, a sadness descends over me. It dawns on me that I have forgotten how to make this woman's form feminine. What does this say about me? I am perplexed. Is this a mirror for how I feel about myself? Am I overthinking this? Going too deep? It feels like this earthen grey mound matters more to me than I could ever have realised.

I have carelessly taken something for granted: that we will all fire our pieces (or rather let them be fired), then pick them up on a future date. Maybe this is a ploy to bring us back to play and – let's face it, as nothing is free – maybe to pay this time. I ask our master, but he simply smiles. He describes why he has created these free spaces: they are simply for us to play, to become children. This is his gift, his joy to share.

Once armed with this knowledge, dare I admit, the light goes out. No longer driven, I feel rather lethargic and spend the remaining minutes playing without care or direction.

As we are about to leave, he gives us one command. 'Now, get the weight of your hands and smash'. WHAT? Yet we all obey without argument, all under his gaze, in a trance – there is something hypnotic about this wise-eyed person.

Relief flushes over me. I no longer have to achieve the perfect, I don't have to walk my own tightrope of 'how it should be' rules. This command has crossed my 'known'. I leave with a gap, but I had arrived with a nothing. I only lost what I had come to know.

What is the point to this narrative? How does it relate to your own personal creativity? Personally, I found introducing a creative activity that I was less familiar with an exciting opportunity for growth as an artist. We all have our preferences, but it can be rewarding to 'dabble' outside our comfort zones. It also caused me to reflect on my own identity and where I saw my creative life going. Periods of self-reflection can have positive results for all of us, as they may provide a foundation of ideas to build upon. For example, from this experience, I have since found myself making textile art that is more three-dimensional in form. Have a think about this within your own circumstances – what creative activity could you experiment with? Remember, it doesn't have to be a forever journey! Try something new and if it is not for you – move on. Oh, and finally, remember that you can learn to play without purpose – I am still trying to learn this fact myself.

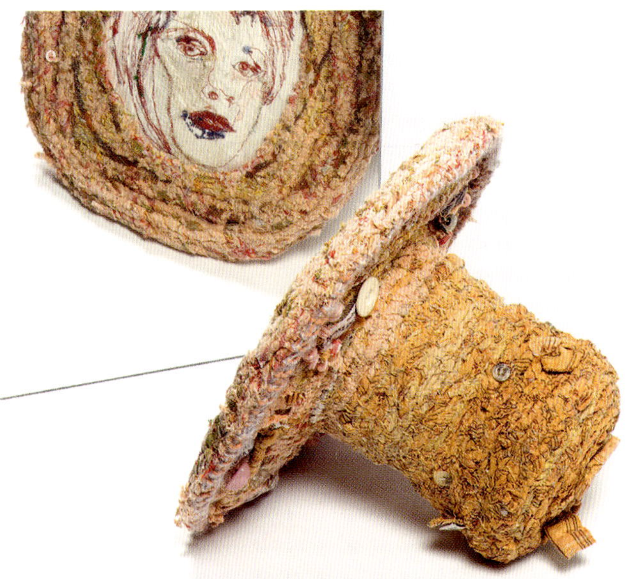

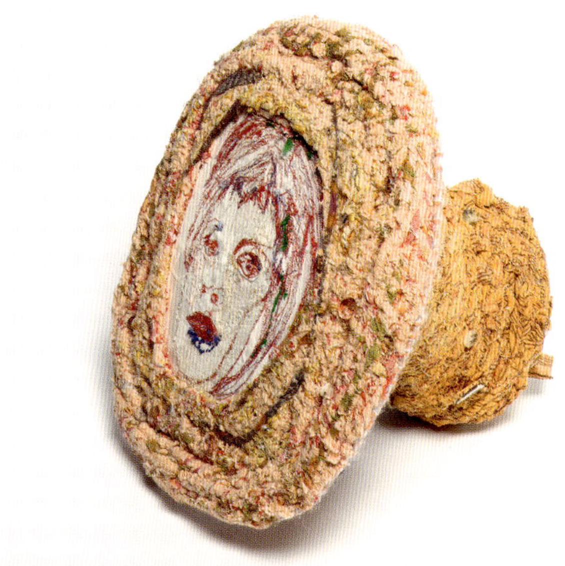

FEATURED ARTIST:
Rosalind Byass

I would like to introduce you to Rosalind Byass, a textile artist who intuitively incorporates personal themes into her work.

Rosalind's work reflects her love of pattern, colour and texture. She enjoys using materials that others discard, and her three-dimensional works explore the properties of recycled mesh, which she uses to construct colourful vessels and objects. Unique, whimsical forms are expressed in a distinctly individual style, exploring the interplay between man-made fibres and the natural properties of wool. Rosalind's textile sculptures challenge the perception of everyday objects, taking them to a new dimension.

Rosalind has this to say about one of her textile sculptures, titled *Fossicker*:

'*Fossicker* pays homage to the childhood fun of hunting and gathering. It takes me back to another time when the magic of life was to be explored and enjoyed. As a child, fossicking often rewarded me with treasures that not only caught my eye but also fed my imagination and enlivened my spirit.

'The repurposed labels and buttons accompanying this self-styled portrait are there for the viewer to quietly discover. They not only represent treasured finds, but also create a metaphor that exemplifies my style of creative endeavour, fully supporting my love of reinvention in artistic expression and storytelling.'

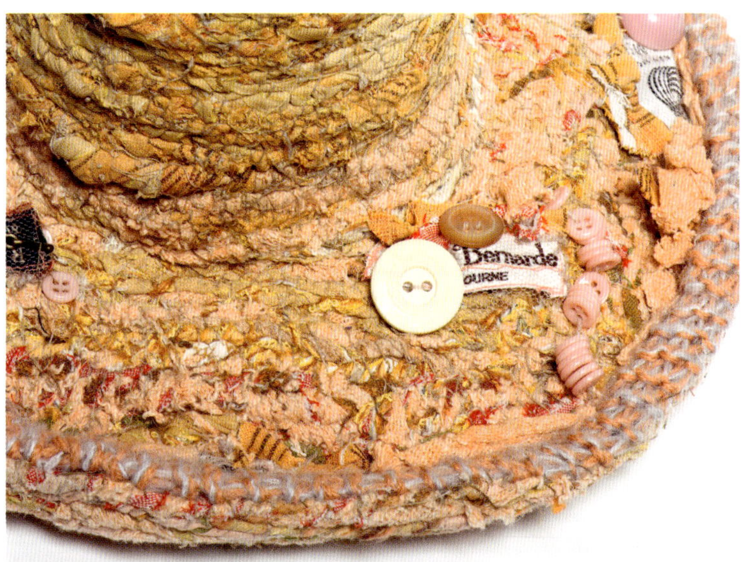

ABOVE: Fossicker (*Rosalind Byass, 2012*). *Recycled clothing, wool, cotton, buckles/ buttons, canvas, wool wadding (H31 × W32 × D23cm).*

Daisy May Collingridge

The works of the British artist Daisy May Collingridge lie in opposition visually to my own body of humanised sculptural works. I find myself smiling every time I come across one of these beautiful celebrations of our human existence.

She confides a little about her works and core practice:

'The core of my practice is an exploration and celebration of the human form. Working across sculpture, photography and performance, I study anatomical properties with exaggerated flesh and limbs. I harness the tactile and haptic quality of fabric. Fabric makes sense as a medium to explore the organic fleshiness of the biological body. It is a material that everyone is familiar with, since we physically encounter it every day. It can evoke deeper connections because of that daily sensory experience. The form and structure of fabric offers skin-like qualities. In looking at bodies and the relationships we have with our own bodies, it makes sense to use an emotive medium like fabric. There is something fragile and impermanent about it, yet it is resilient, stretchy and forgiving.

'Growing up with a medical and scientific family influences the way I look at things. It is a pragmatic and logical view of the body. This was compounded by a formative experience that awoke my curiosity further: the exhibition 'Body Worlds' by Dr. Gunther

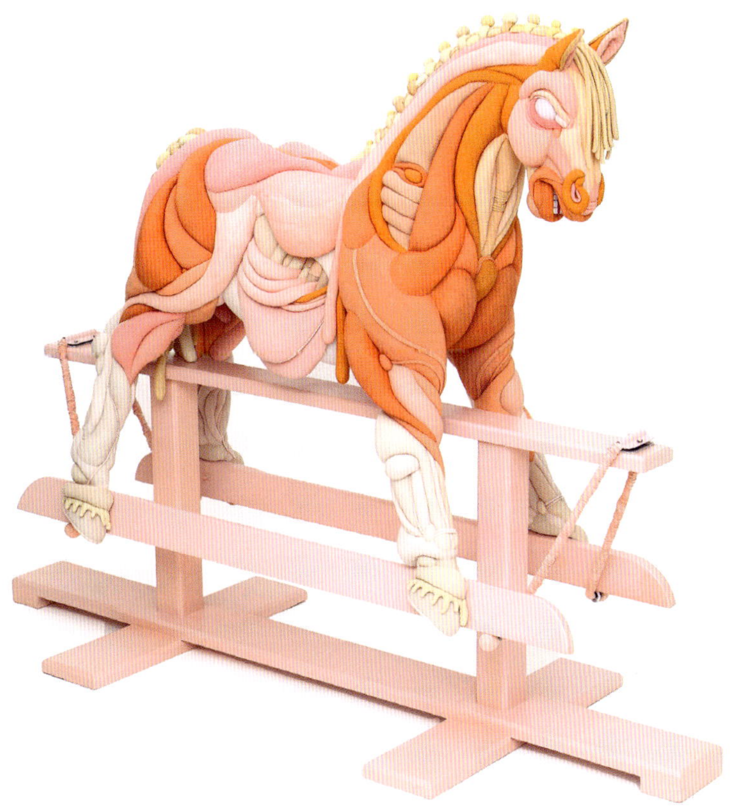

RIGHT: Pippa *(Daisy May Collingridge, 2022). Reclaimed rocking horse, fabric, wadding, thread, sand (120 × 60 × 160cm).*

von Hagens, of real anatomical bodies, which I saw as a child in London in 2002. The idea that we are all composed internally of things of which we have only a very basic understanding or concept of intrigues me. The work is a physical rendering of those things invisible and internal, making them external and tangible.'

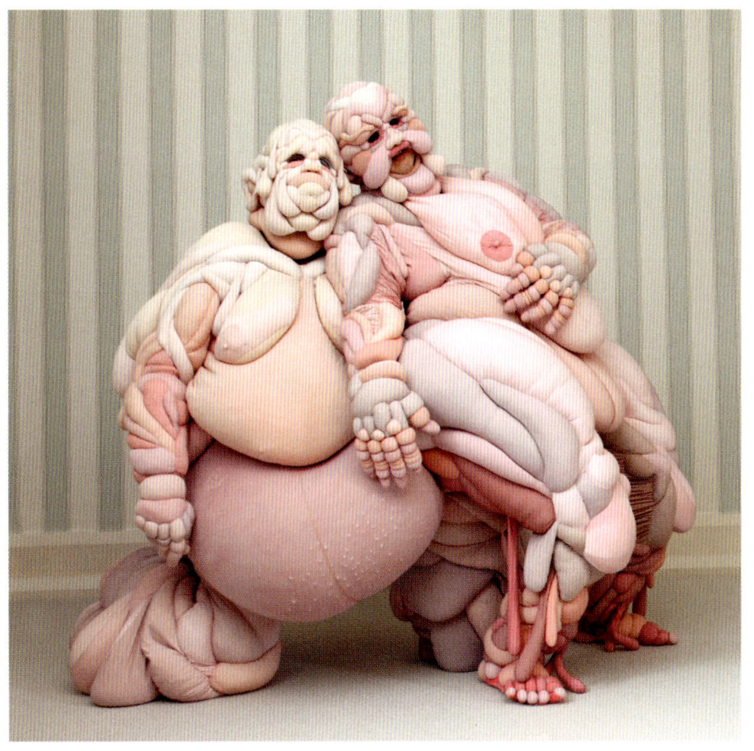

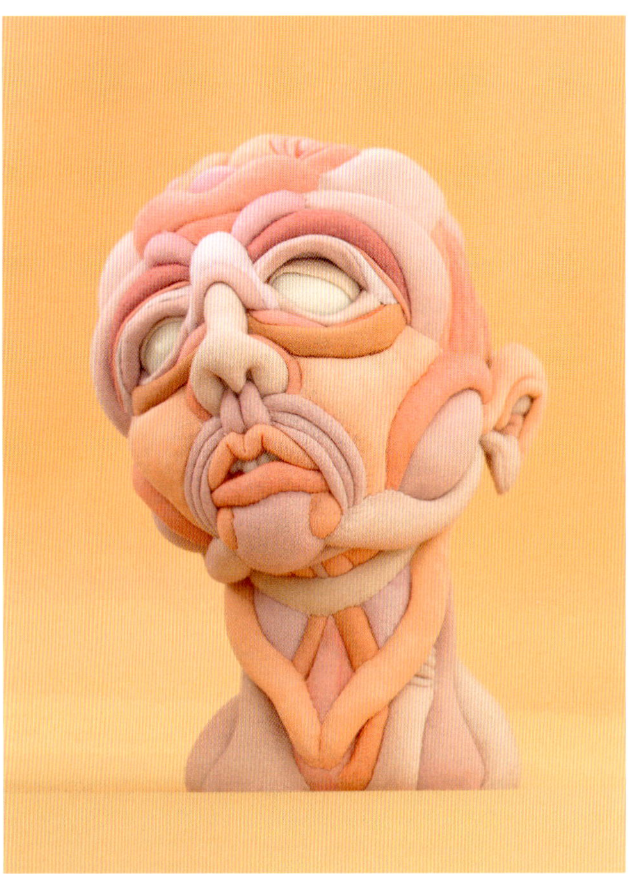

RIGHT, ABOVE: Lean on me *(Daisy May Collingridge, 2021). Archival pigment print of photograph, various dimensions.*
RIGHT, BELOW: Annie *(Daisy May Collingridge, 2021). Fabric, wadding, thread, wood (29 × 18 × 18 cm).*

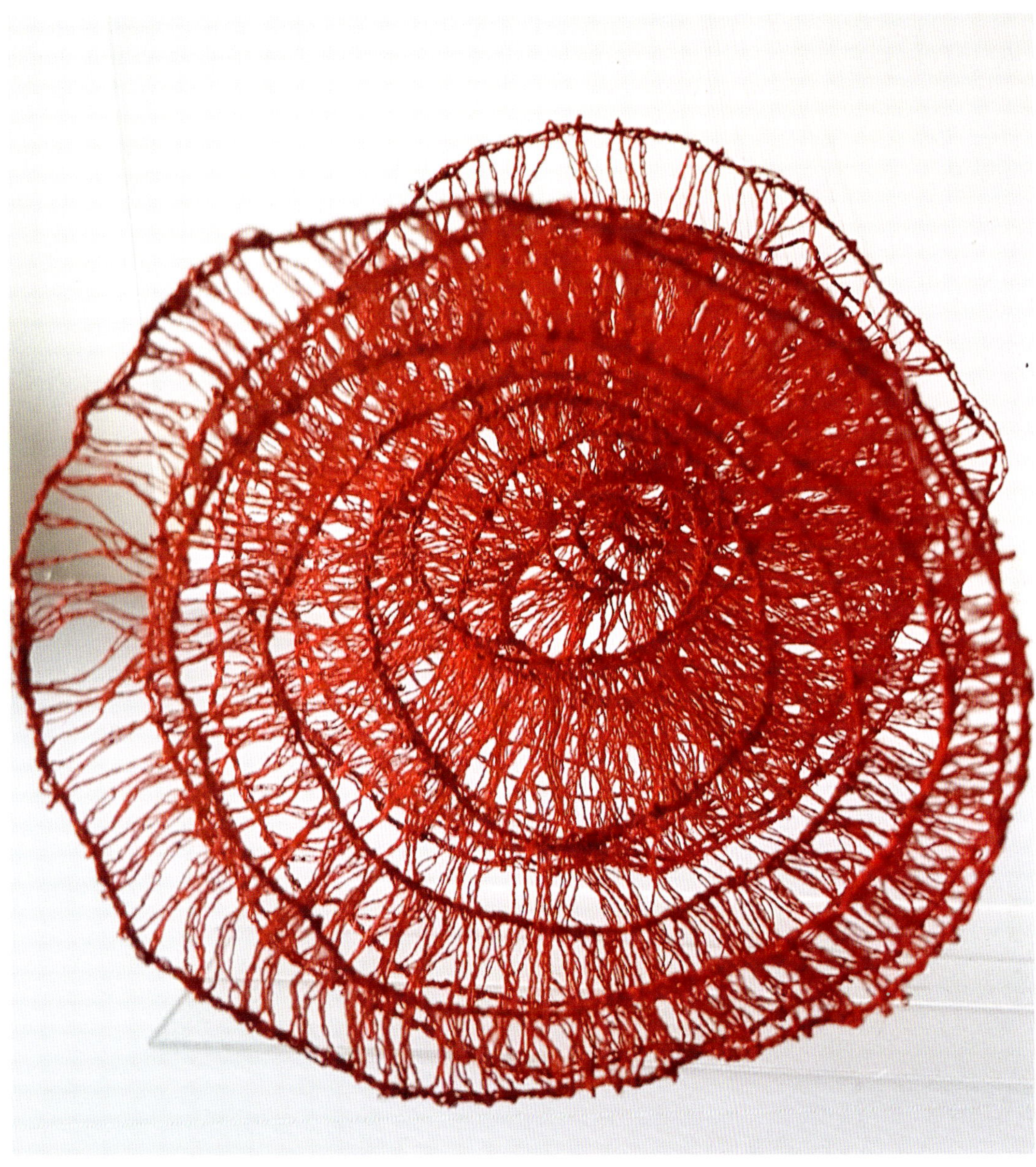

FEATURED ARTIST:
Wendy Ward

I first met Wendy Ward within a formal learning setting. I value her key core practice values and how as an artist she has made the positive through the outworking of her hands.

'I've used my work for a narrative when words don't come easily. This work was made using thread machine-stitched onto water-soluble fabric, which was washed away once complete. The work is hung by invisible thread onto an acrylic stand.

The work is of gradually diminishing stitched circles, portraying the feeling of being lost in a tunnel and not knowing the way out.'

What is your method of visual narration?

RIGHT: *Sketchbook page of stitched portrait collages.*

Walking the narrative line

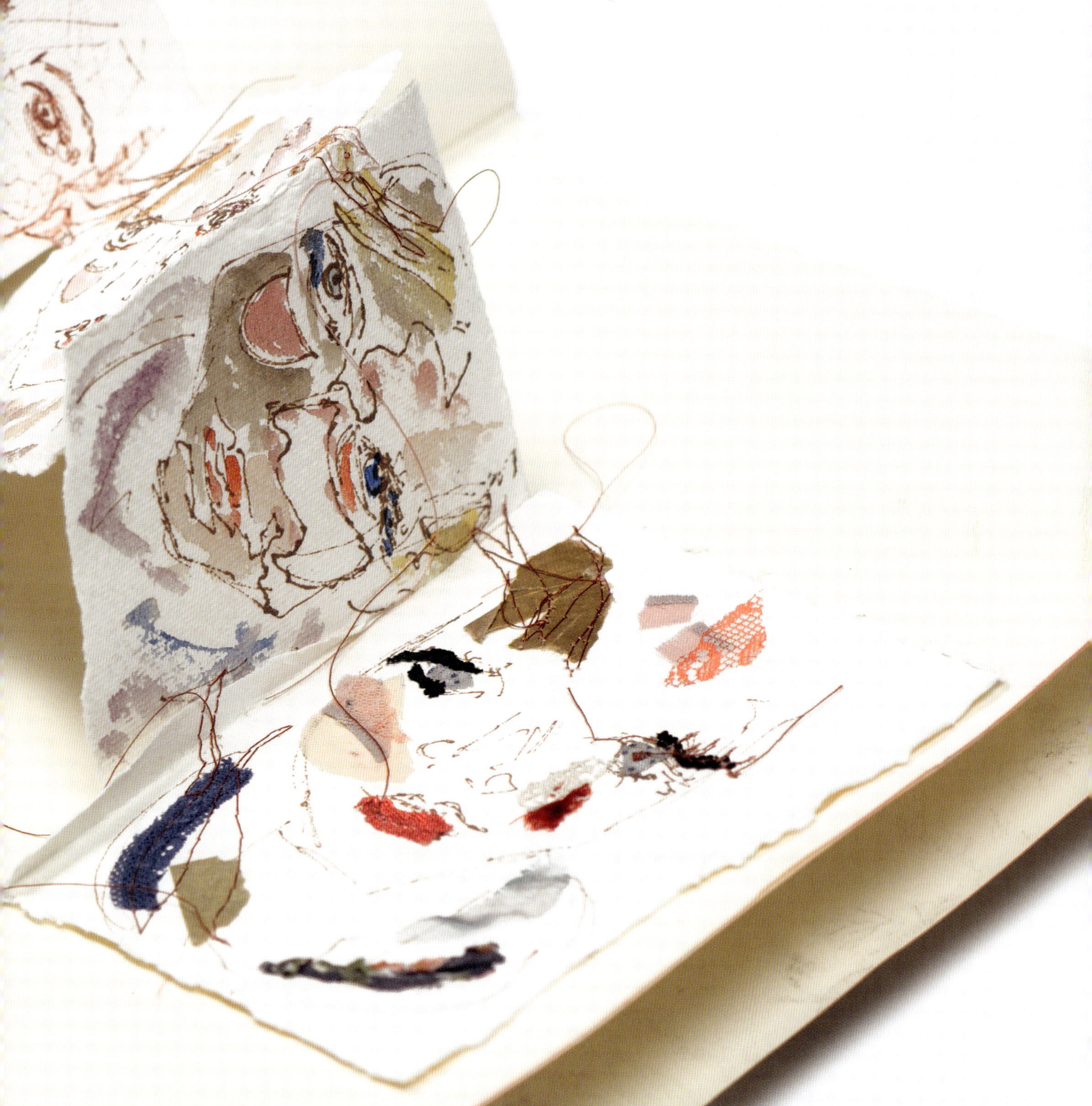

The meet cute
The happy happenstance
The moments matter
The moment in time
The who knew? It must have been serendipity.

The moments that make your heart start.
The reminder that life has worth.
It matters.
Don't let the memories scatter.
The taking for granted.
The times it all turned out okay.

I want to remind you of the narrative; the real story of you.

The narrative line. What can it be? How can it be translated
into textiles?

We all have a story to tell, we might just not have previously
named it a story, or a tale, a narrative line, a pathway, a life
journey, a life lesson.

We may have designated ourselves as ordinary, but we are all
unique. We must just tap into that definition and not pass it by.

How? One way is by discovering your textile-based narrative.

Remember what a narrative can be:

'a spoken or written account of connected events; a story'
– Oxford Languages

It is simple, so do not overcomplicate it or feel you need a better
story to start with. It is yours, so bend it to your will.

Throughout this section I will give you my own narrative
examples, stories I have been told, which I have somehow
connected with. They are a glorious mix of the fabricated, the
frivolous and the true. In other words, all the wonderful features
that make our lives meaningful.

OPPOSITE PAGE:
*Unfolding the
narrative of stories
my grandmother told
me (Ailish Henderson,
2022). Sketchbook page
within sketchbook
(concertina mixed
media).*

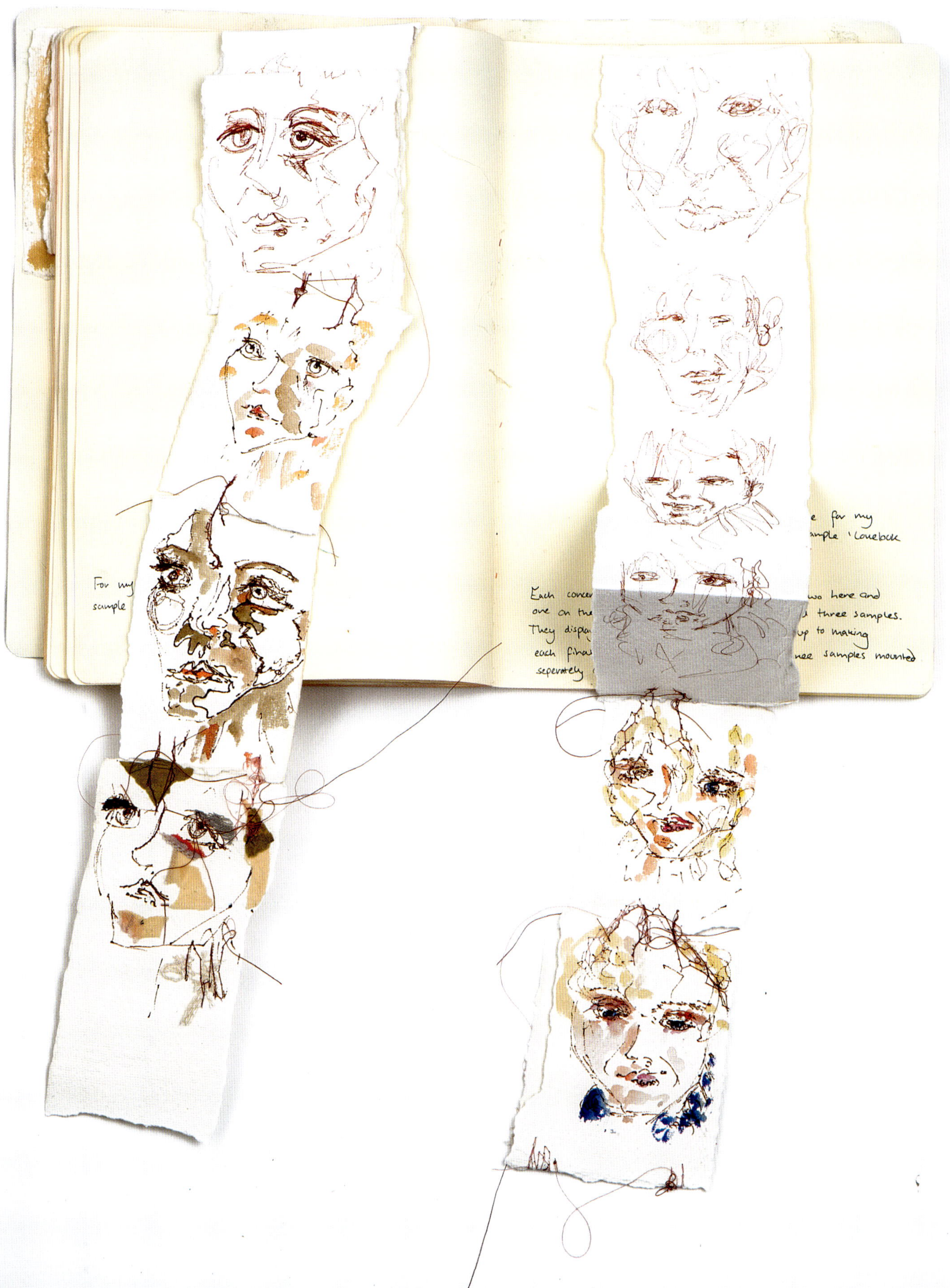

For my
sample

Each concer… …wo here and
one on the … three samples.
They displa… …up to making
each fina… …ee samples mounted
seperately …

… for my
…mple 'Lovebook

Yourself

*'My shadow's the only one
that walks beside me
My shallow heart's the only
thing that's beating
Sometimes, I wish someone
out there will find me'*

'Boulevard of Broken Dreams' – Green Day

You now need to lose the identity you connect with yourself and view yourself as a character called the 'shadow', not as you. We all have our flaws and the things we do not like about ourselves – do you echo the lyrics above, feeling the need for someone to 'find me'? Maybe we must work out our own identity – art is a wonderful method to use to do this.

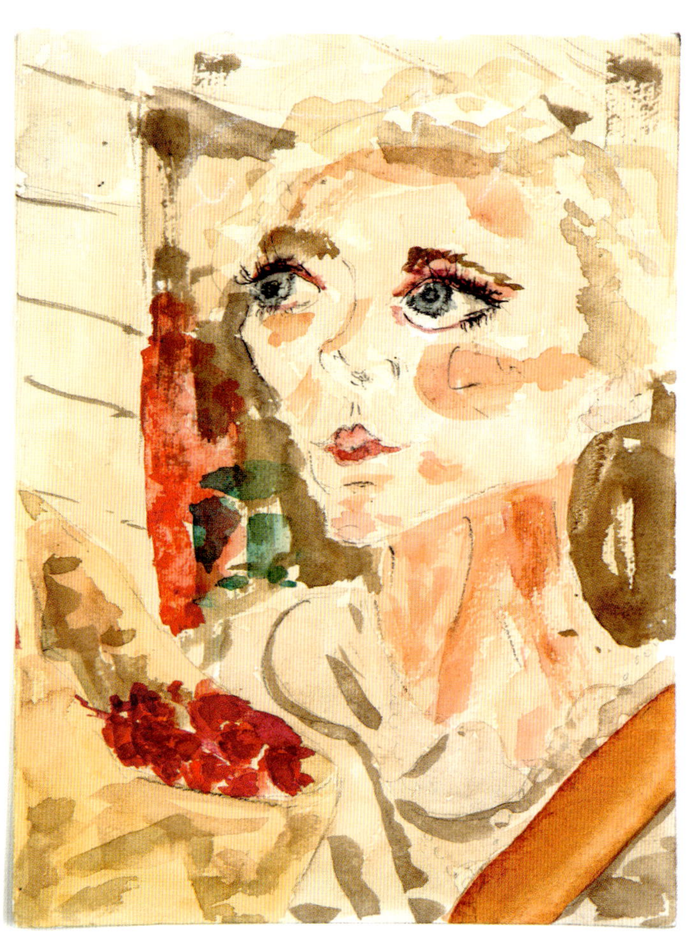

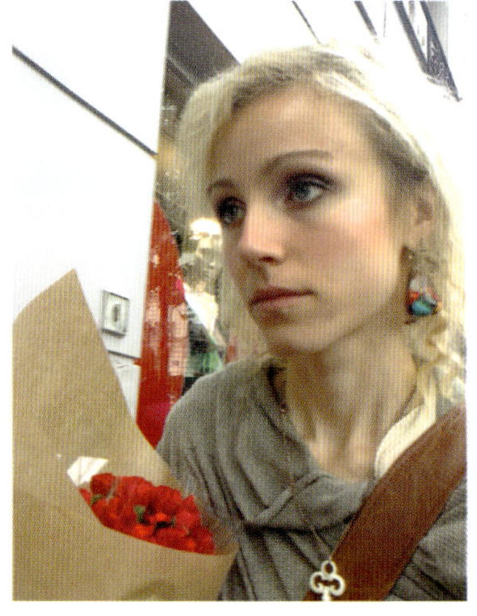

ABOVE: Sunday morning flowers, will she like them? *(Ailish Henderson, 2021). Original watercolour on canvas alongside the photograph which captured the ambience.*

Narrative Four:
The working-class hero school roundtable

As the bearer of an Arts Council grant, back in 2015, one of my visions, and in fact provisos, was that within the period of the allocated grant I would work with a group of school-age children. This came to fruition within the walls of my first solo exhibition.

I introduced myself to this wide-eyed group; eight girls and boys from a year five class. A rare escape from a tired classroom, this was part of a bid to widen the education values of the ones who might get left behind. The children were given tools and encouraged to draw impressions of themselves on a canvas bag. This was a practical blank canvas that could not only serve as art for art's sake, but as something to carry their books between lessons.

I noticed that they were not drawing exact representations; no fine art portraits here. This involved the feelings and faults that characterised them. One girl drew a Mr-Blobby-style character. Recognising this figure as female by the hair length only, I asked the girl if this was her. 'Yes. I am fat,' she replied. Surprised by this straight statement, I was reticent to push the matter. I was not their teacher or their social worker. I was not permitted to intervene, only be the once-met quiet noticer, who left with a smile, forgetting anything, because I could not heal these children.

I still have the photographs of their masterpieces. There was the boy with his impressionist cloth, revealing too many dads (stepdad, boyfriend on the side, no DNA here). The northern child brandishing himself on the bag in full football gear, along with his beloved football, of course. No pets were illustrated. Most were, I guess, not in a stable enough place to provide the care or finance for this unneeded item. A bunch of characters, all at such a fragile time; ready to fly given the circumstances.

Reflecting on this time, I realise what is important. It isn't so much what they have drawn, how good it is, or any perceived lack of talent or milestone achieving. Rather, are they happy? Do they like their own skin? Are there any worrying traits forming that are revealed through this creative play in a relaxed environment?

What can we learn from this story? This is not only a narrative of the observation, but also about the individual: how one – in this case, these children – views oneself. How do you view yourself?

I think these questions can promote reflection in all of us.

FEATURED ARTIST:

Julia Triston

Self-identity can be a wonderful feature point of contemplation for inspiring artwork. Julia Triston is an internationally renowned textile artist, educator, mentor and published author. Her work focuses on the themes of sustainability, identity and gender. I first met Julia by happenstance when I was a young student and she walked into my life as a stand-in tutor. I owe her for the final push to begin my own tale within the textile art genre. In her own words, she divulges the thematic underbed of her practice:

'There are many aspects of our lives that shape our personalities and perspectives. From day-to-day routines to once-in-a-lifetime travel opportunities, or from happy occasions to tragedies and loss, we experience events and adventures that, as artists, motivate and inspire us. In turn, sometimes after many years of absorbing these experiences, they build and connect to inform our practice.

'For some time, my practice has been concerned with the interpretation of the theme of identity. Through this broad topic, I have explored aspects of historical costume and its constraints; how the media portray women (as opposed to how we, as women, view ourselves); issues and campaigns about consent; location and environment; and personal relationships and circumstances.

'In consideration of the theme of identity, I have investigated how our relationships to textiles change when our raw materials have a history or personal association; they command more authenticity. This is never more the case than in my work with women about their own identities and life stories through my Underwear Projects.

'The memories that materials hold are important to me. I have collected old textiles

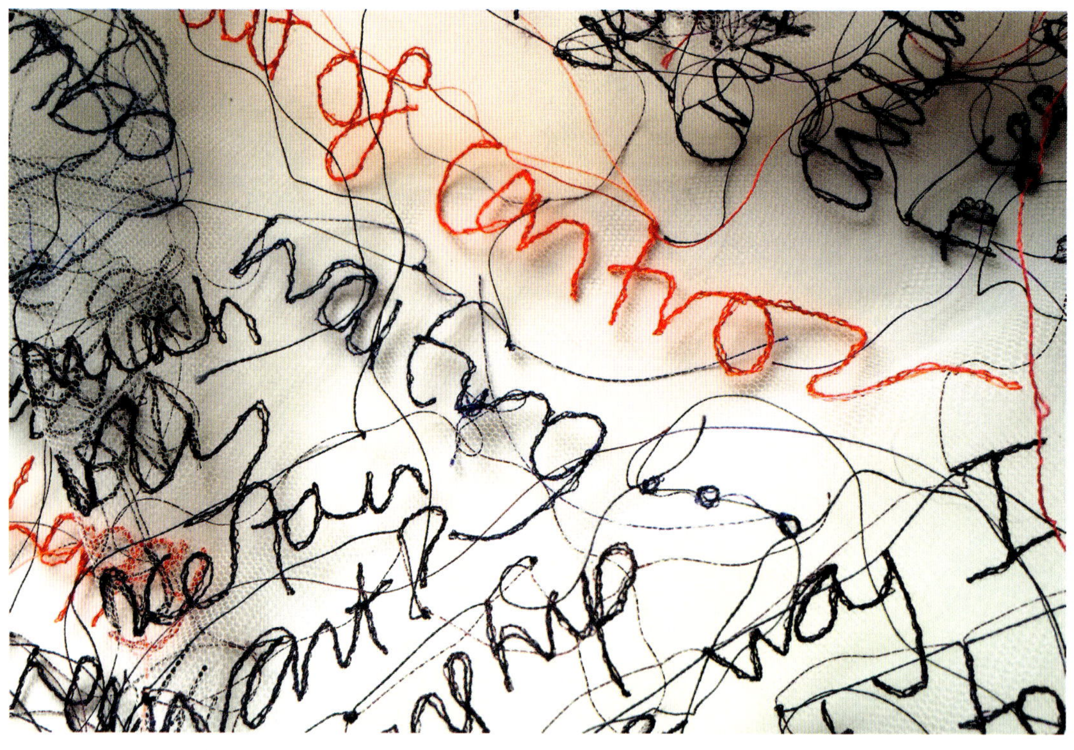

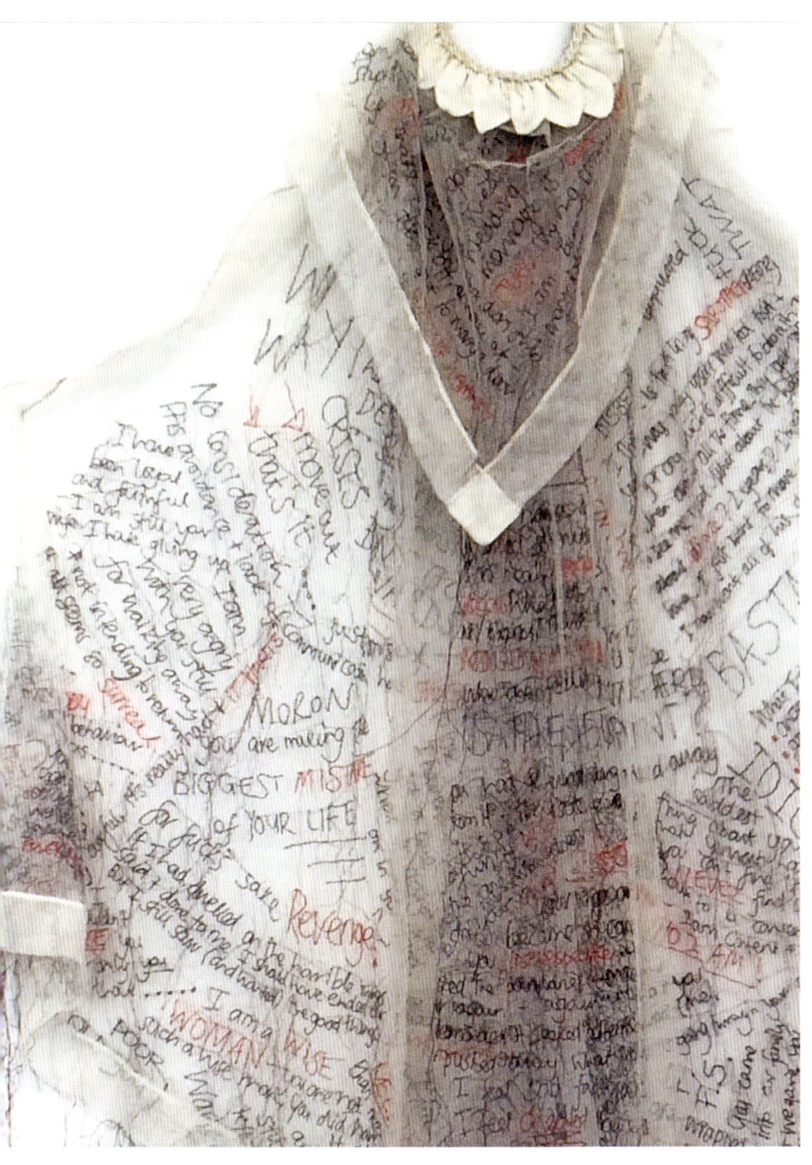

from my travels in India, Peru, Mexico, Tunisia, Morocco, New Zealand and Europe. By examining these treasures, I have not only learned about technique and traditions, but also about upcycling, sustainability, construction, and the economical use of cloth, thread and stitch. As a consequence, the majority of my raw materials are repurposed and upcycled. They include secondhand textiles, old household linen, discarded clothing, cast-off school uniforms, and previously worn underwear.

'I often start a piece of work by deconstructing my chosen textiles into elements and "landmarks", such as plackets and hems, or buttonholes and embroidered motifs. Then I reassemble them in new ways, thus giving the original materials a new identity, a new meaning and a new narrative. The stains and marks of wear and tear are included, as they are a fundamental connection to the identity of the previous life of the textile, the wearer or the user.

'Other bodies of work might be inspired by a title, or action, such as The Textile Study Group's DIS/rupt exhibition, for which I made *To Know A Veil*, my most autobiographical artwork to date. The content documents the upset, anger, resentment, conflict – and finally the "resolution and repair" – that I went through during a traumatic divorce.

'The text is taken directly from my journals over a turbulent four-year period. Sometimes my sentences did not make sense, and my language was very explicit, but every word was transcribed as it was written, including the bullet points, underlinings and capital letters. In the making process, I transformed a vintage wedding veil from 1938 into a piece about relationships that had a different narrative and a new identity, which was extremely cathartic and therapeutic.'

FEATURED ARTIST:
Caren Garfen

Caren Garfen is a London-based artist specialising in textiles and meticulous hand stitching, creating carefully considered pieces with profound messages. She is an award-winning practitioner who has established an international reputation for her accessible yet challenging issue-based art. I admire Caren's work due to its honesty and raw embodiment of previously shied-away-from themes.

Here, Caren reveals a little of how the narrative, and a particular aspect of wellbeing, has captured her soul and subsequent research-based textiles practice:

'Narrative has always been intricately entwined within my art practice. My research has led me through a range of subjects, such as women's roles in the domestic sphere, dieting trends, eating disorders, and, more recently, the Holocaust and contemporary antisemitism. Initially, I employed hand-drawn silkscreen-printed imagery onto cloth, combined with meticulous hand stitching. However, this approach has transformed over time. While textiles and sewing techniques remain, I have introduced carefully chosen objects as vehicles to construct narratives.

'Having dedicated four years of focused exploration to the relationship between women and dieting, which culminated in a room-sized kitchen art installation called *She Was Cooking Something Up* at The Knitting and Stitching Show in 2014, I subsequently began researching the devastating subject of eating disorders. This thematic shift was not initially intended but was inspired by a message from a courageous schoolgirl who had been struggling with anorexia nervosa from the tender age of eleven. Her message imparted how viewing my installation had sparked a wish to recover.

'Visitors' reactions were profound and moving. Tears flowed, and many shared personal experiences relating to eating disorders, whether suffered by themselves or by family members. For some, witnessing the installation marked their first steps towards healing, while others found a fresh means of communication with their child and their illness. One teacher even mentioned adopting ideas from the room to assist students in finding their own voice through their stories.

'This experience was emotionally charged, physically demanding, yet undeniably inspirational. It underscored the pervasive reach of issues relating to dieting and eating disorders in our society, but also provided viewers with a space for contemplation, dialogue, and action.'

What has been a part of your own life that you wish to use as inspirational power to create?

'The things that make me different, are the things that make me ME'
Winnie The Pooh by A.A. Milne

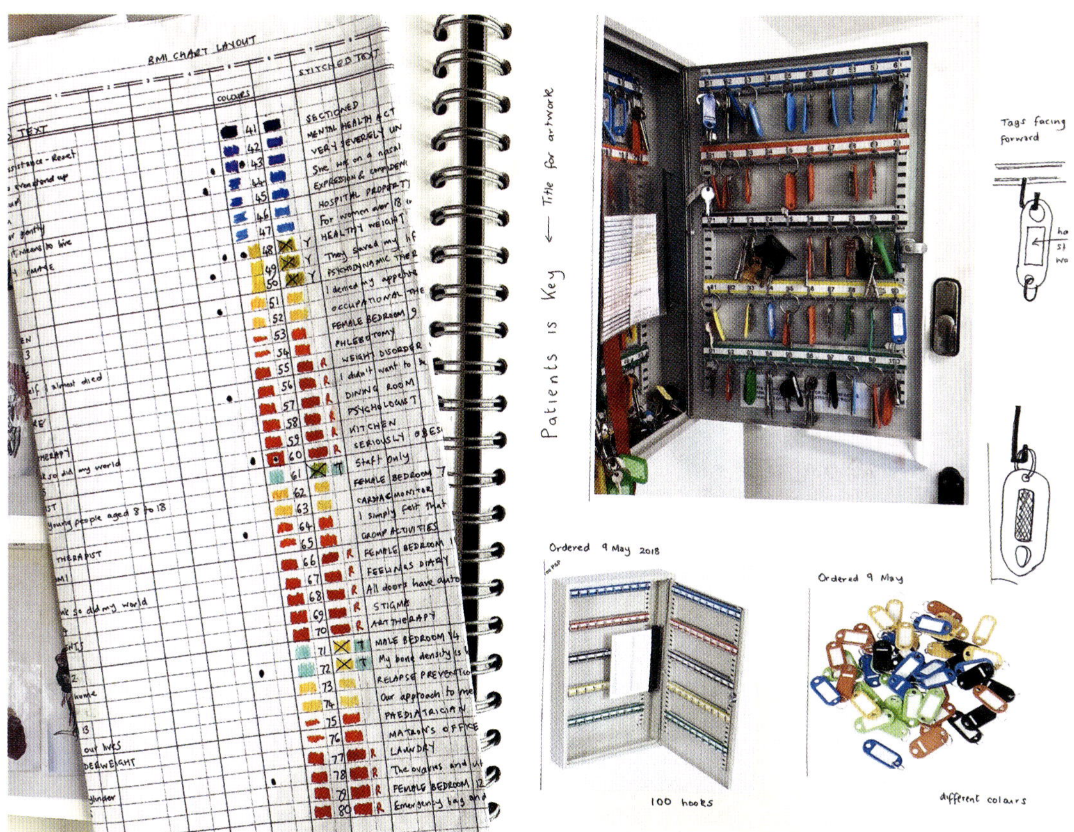

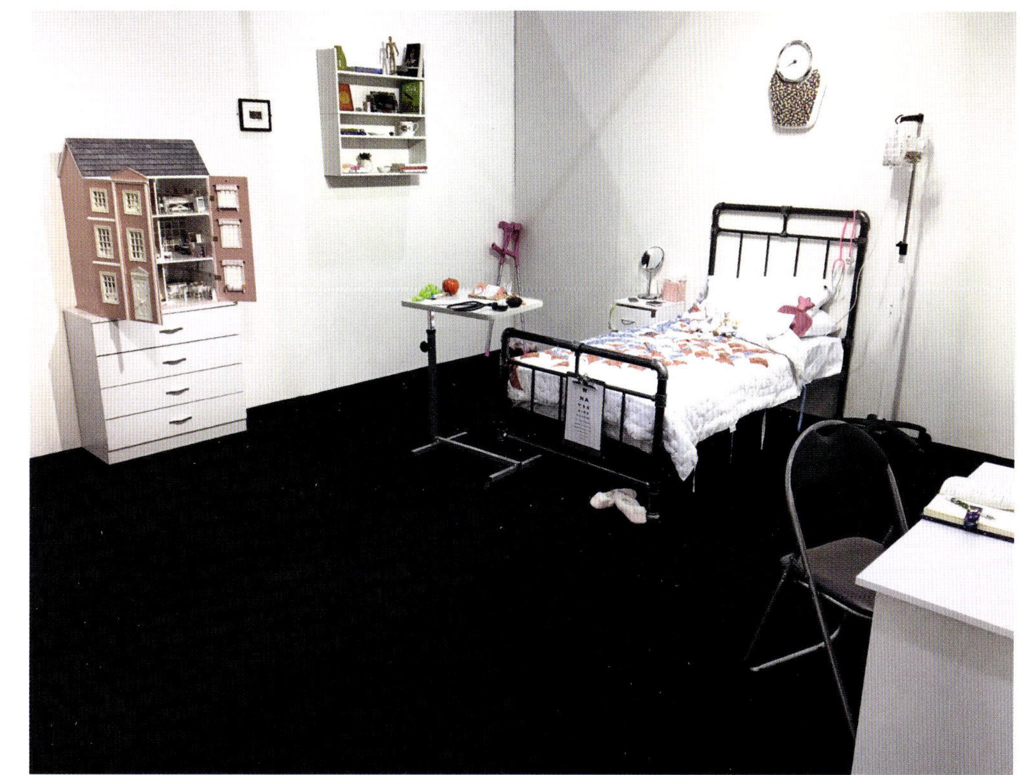

ABOVE: *Sketchbook – documents working process of* Patients is Key *(Caren Garfen, 2018). Textile, silk threads, key tags, keys, key-safe. Hand stitch (35 × 55 × 9cm).*

RIGHT: What's Going On Upstairs *(Caren Garfen, 2018). Textile, silk threads, bedroom furniture, medical equipment, dolls house, accessories. Hand stitch, digital printing (6.5 × 6m).*

Family ties

From parents to children, uncles and aunts, brothers and sisters… most of us will have some form of anecdote database, derived from the moments of matter, the cherished memories of times spent with those whom we loved, even if lost to us now. I wager a smile may grace your face, when remembering an experience involving those close to us. How can we use our familial links to inspire the creative side of us? Let's look at two initial tales.

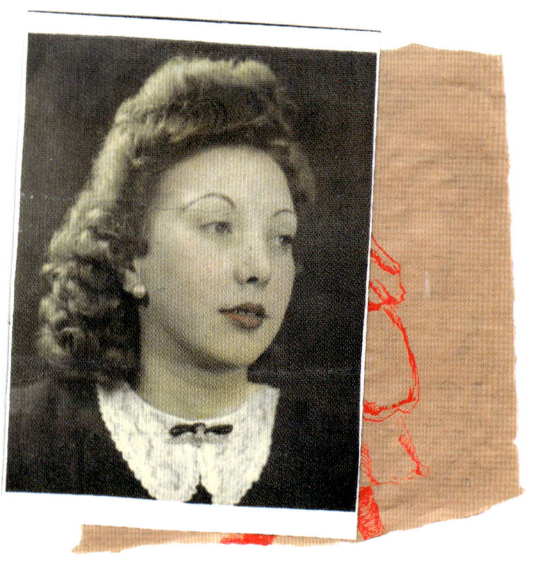

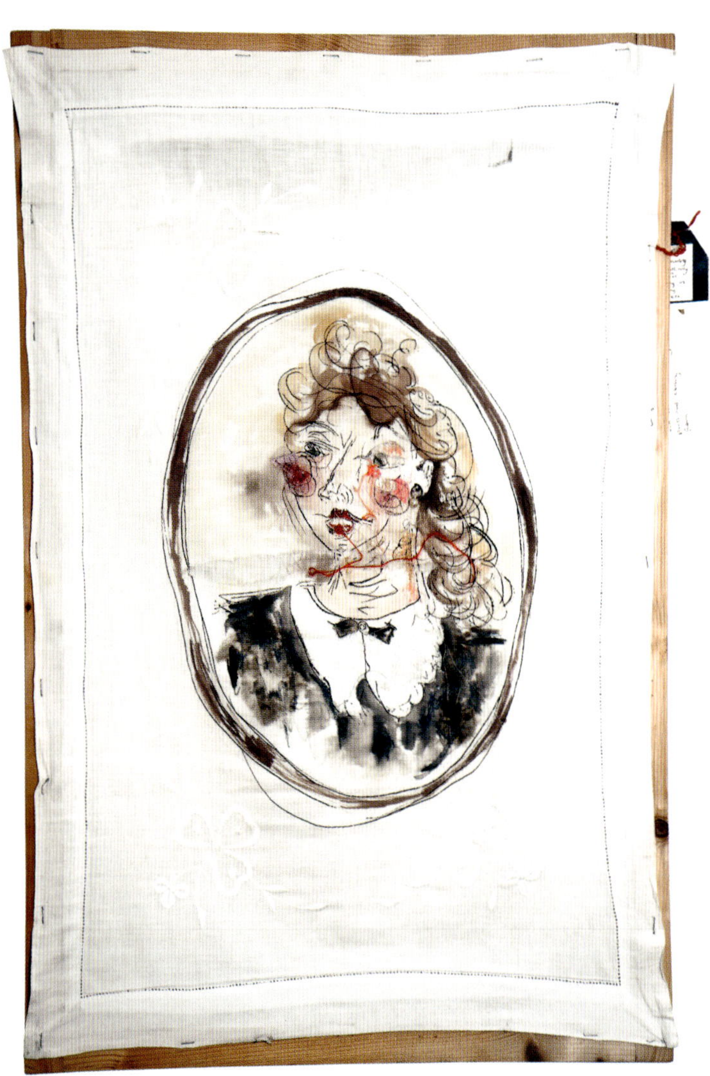

LEFT: *Narg, now I believe your war badge story. Original war-based photograph in sepia (1939).*

ABOVE: Red Ties *(Ailish Henderson, 2021). Antique pillowcase with printing press etching in sepia.*

Narrative Five:
The lost Narg

I lost my dear grandmother, my Narg, within the time of writing this book. At 99, some would consider her age an achievement, yet I knew how much she still had inside of her to live. I have found that grieving was an unexpected process. It wasn't the photos, so often popping up on my phone, reminding me, 'you were here with her last year at this time', or the ones of her and me on my shelves at home making my heart spark with pain. No, it was the discovery of her character. Finding the sweetie wrappers when we stripped her bed, from all the: 'can't sleep so I will suck sweets' nights. The lipsticks, half used in her bag, and the lack of jewellery; the main rings coupled with a load of nothingness, weighing up to so little, yet saying so much about her. She didn't give any value to material things; her family was her life. Selfless bread-and-butter nights to

prioritise feeding the kids, that was her premise in life – first look after others, second, look after yourself.

The qualities of a person, their little quirks and lovelinesses, can form the premise for a sort of 'therapeutic art' for the grief-holders, namely ourselves. The ones who are bearing the loss, the left-behinders. Take this as an example: could the sweetie wrappers become part of a stitch collage, a montage of memorabilia centred around the person? Not the usual materials, perhaps, to build a characterful piece based on the person you love, you might think. So, are there items like vintage cloths that we could use for our own creation?

As visual fuel, I have illustrated one of my own examples, inspired by the relationship I had with my dear grandmother. As I feel the loss, I also celebrate the connections we had.

ABOVE: *'That's my lilac lace', she said. 'Solo' Exhibition opening party (2016).*

Narrative Six:
The Liberty print dress

This is the story of my mother, and the dress that fashion and mind forgot. Made by hand, on a 'stop the world I need some quiet' day.

From a young age, my mother loved two things: making her own clothes and Liberty print fabric. This flooded through my own life-course. There is a very faded photograph of her wearing this particular dress, but the issue is, I have never been able to work out what the exact fabric was, as an old print in sepia does not offer many clues.

It itched at my brain for a very long time, and it was only when I was halfway through my own degree in the arts that I had any success finding out the history. I wanted to do a project on my mother, focused on this dress. In my interview with her, I found out where and when she had bought the fabric. This led to me interviewing members of staff within Fenwicks and John Lewis, the two firms she mentioned. I later travelled to London to visit Liberty and look at their own historical resources. It certainly crossed the degree brief; was I now more interested in history or art? Anyway, finally, after blowing up the images I had, despite their aged tones, I had something to work on.

All the above came to fruition in fine-art pieces, portraits and characters of my mother. Working from the print, or at least my drawn-up slice of it, I played with stitching, collage and finally even brought it into print design and repeat patterns. It has become one of my success stories: a wallpaper, a lampshade, a cushion, a scarf are all available in this design. 'She gave me Liberty' – eventually.

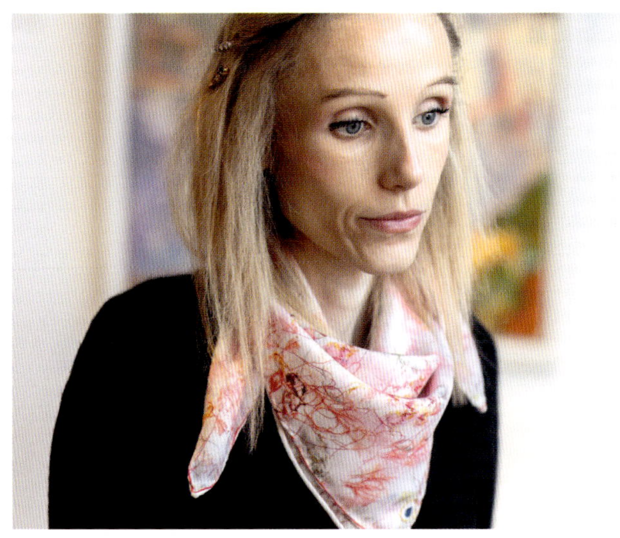

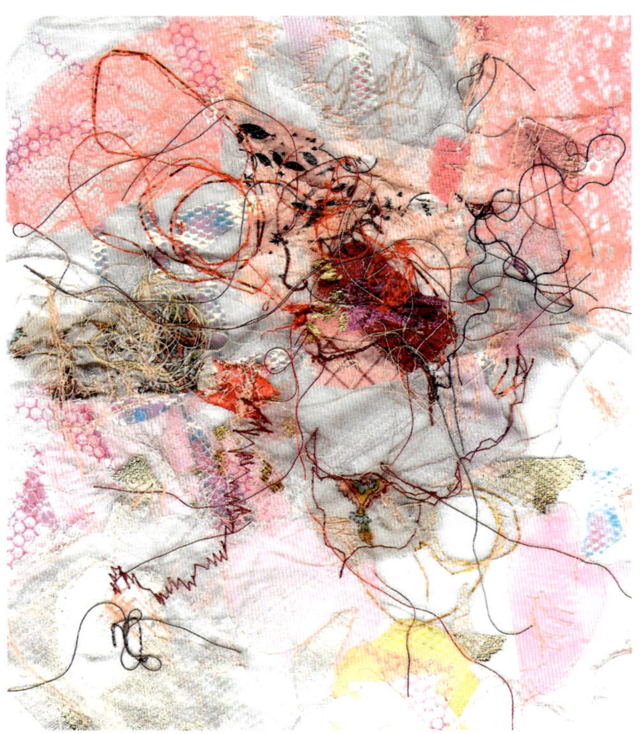

ABOVE, TOP: You gave me Liberty *(Ailish Henderson, 2022). Silk square model view.*
ABOVE, BOTTOM: *Original connected cloth template for all subsequent works.*

You gave me Liberty

My mother and I
I knew we were tied,
Yes it took years,
For me to reach the hem,
Her,
Your,
Starting stem.

Two paths,
Liberty Print proof.
Worn by you,
Made by your hand,
The very one I turned away.

Years apart,
It took time,
For your inspiration to start,
Thrown off by my youthful stance,
Never a needle's glance.

Now I stare at the florals before me,
Now I know the name,
Of the fabric you worked so hard to gain,
Yet gave up,
While I became your work in progress.

Your dress,
Fabric,
Liberty Print proof,

I know my path,
Trapped in layers,
Stitches through,
Made by me,
Instigated by you.

You,
You gave me Liberty,
In more ways than cloth.

AH 2018

It is all very well me telling you my personal tales, but how can you use your own?

A first step could be delving into your family history. I bet there are a few characters. What can you find out about them? Could you create a small family archive book, perhaps with collage material, mementos and photographs? From this you may discover a few images you wish to use as reference material for a stitched piece. I certainly didn't plan my finished work, it came about naturally, based upon simple family tales – so do not feel that you have to create something remarkable… play at first.

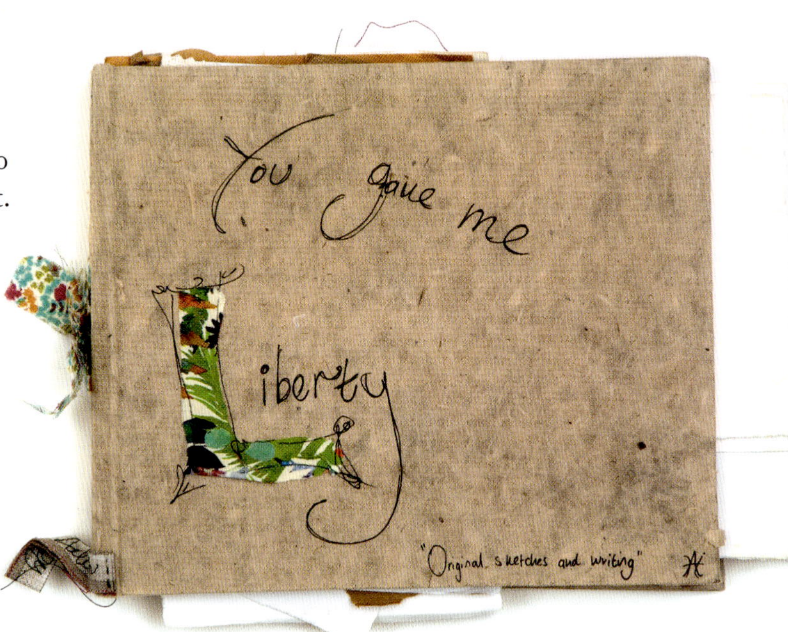

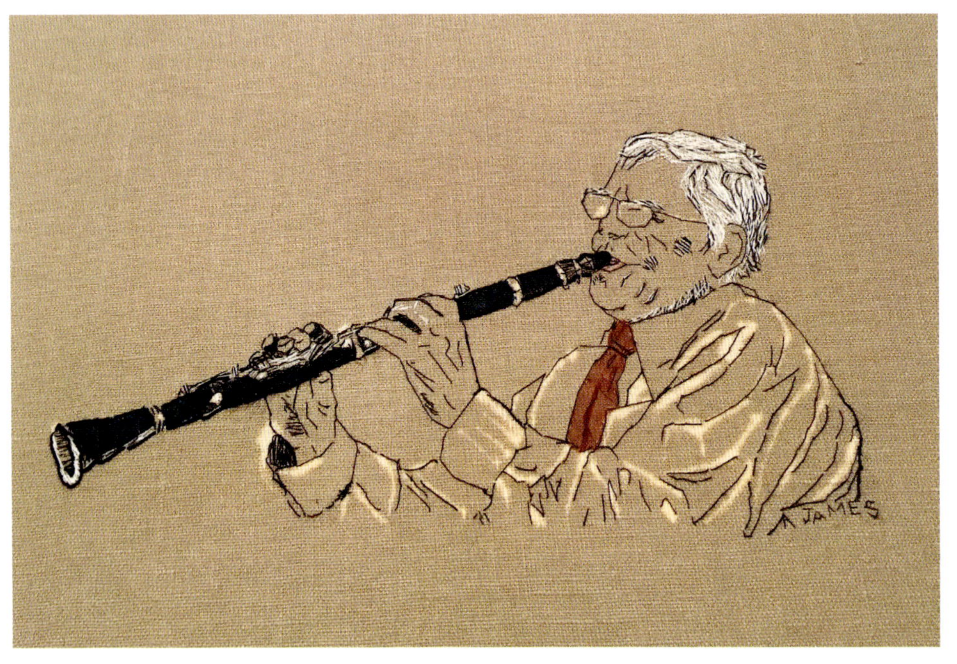

ABOVE: You gave me Liberty *sketchbook (Ailish Henderson, 2018).* **LEFT:** Eric Newton – Jazz Musician *(Angela James, 2020). Mixed media, stitch.*

FEATURED ARTIST:

Jenni Dutton

Jenni Dutton is a multimedia artist based in the UK. Her work explores time, memory, identity and loss. Jenni is an artist I admire strongly; she fits beautifully within this section. Her 'fragalistic' tenderness speaks through her heart-hurting and sublime works. In her own voice:

'The title *Dementia Darnings* implies repair. The physical building of the image slowly over time helped me to deal with my mum's increasing frailty and ultimately her death. Using her as the focus for my practice helped me not to feel resentful about having to take care of her. She and I were collaborating. The intensity of each portrait reflects the nature of our relationship, the practical and emotional aspect of intimacy. I was trying to convey the realities of dementia, of ageing, not to avoid what might be deemed to be uncomfortable images, as well as honouring my mum.

'The sixteen portraits were made over ten years. I found there was a therapeutic effect, a mesmeric quality, as I slowly built her likeness. The slowness was healing. It gave me a purpose. I've been moved to realise that viewers of the series are profoundly affected by it. They say things like, "They could have been my mum's expressions. I recognise her in them. It was very, very emotional, and very, very moving for me. Thank you so much."

'During the ten years of making this series, I have been in touch with threads that bind and unravel. The work makes tangible the emotional, as well as biological, ties between mother and daughter. It's about love.'

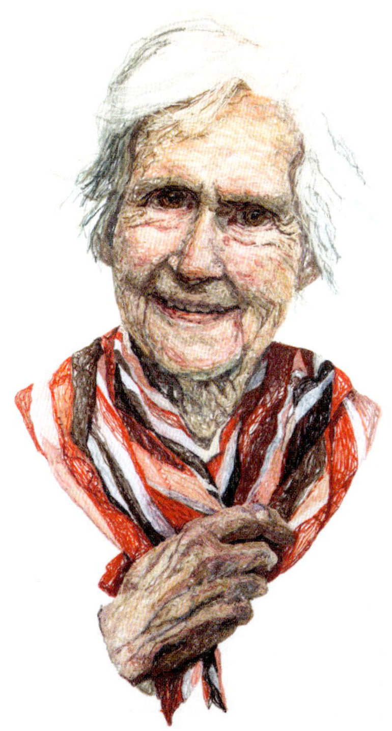

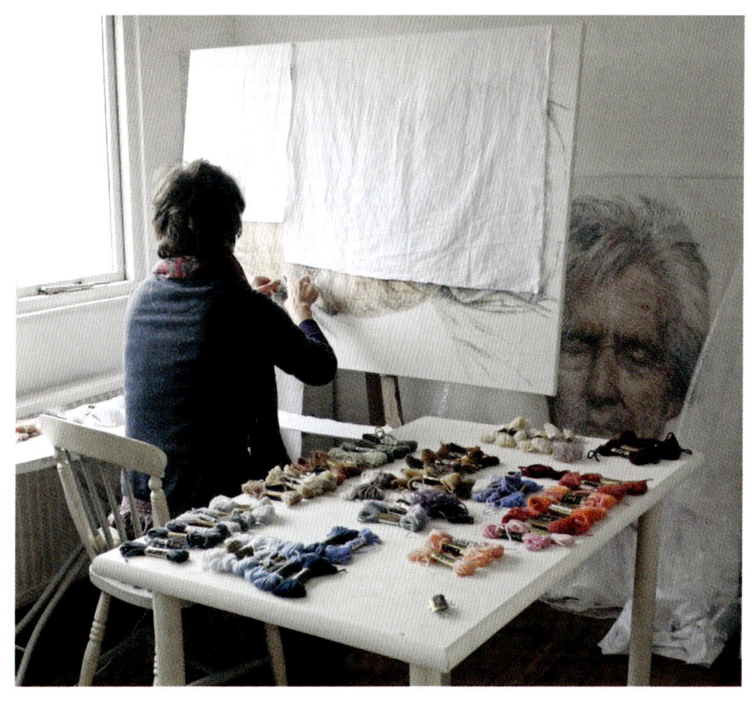

ABOVE: Mum wearing a red scarf *(Jenni Dutton, 2012). Woollen thread sewn through fine netting stretched over canvas (130 × 90cm).* **RIGHT:** *Work in progress (Jenni Dutton, 2017).*

Narrative Seven:
'He Slept Through it'

The boy who slept through it all. This is just one tale that my dear Nargdad recounted to me, before his age caught up with his mind. I don't think any of us understood the damage of war, and the trauma that came after it. After all, he was just a boy, a boy who thought he was on his way to be a part of the greater good, defending his country on waters unknown. (Sadly, he did not pass on his iron seafaring stomach to me; I take after my father's landlubber line.)

He was an officer in the Navy, and the threat of a fatality was ever-present. One night, a bomb went off literally outside his cabin porthole, and yet, somehow, he slept through it all. This time, shipwreck was avoided, but during the war years he found himself in the lifeboats on at least three occasions! After the Second World War he emerged unscathed except for a finger half missing, the claw of a nail protruding.

I didn't have my Nargdad for long, but here are the things he taught me:

1. Always use 'the bairn' as an excuse to buy an ice cream!

2. Choo-choo trains are great distractions when trying to convince baby Ailish to open her mouth and consume her limited trio of acceptable foods: boiled eggs, bananas, and Heinz spag-bol.

3. Braces, when on the body (not on the teeth) can define a character.

4. Sleep is a healer.

5. 'Jack and the glory...' I am still waiting for it to happen.

I did not have enough mature time when I would have 'understood' my grandfather, so much of what I remember is more of a visualisation.

How can you be inspired yourself? It may be that you use something literal as a starting point. Most of us will have a sentimental garment in our care, be it our own baby clothes or, as we will see with the next featured artist, a grandparent's jumper. It is precious to us, we will be reticent to touch it, as it's a unique item, one which we cannot remake or buy – it's priceless. But could it be taken out of that drawer, its protective resting place and at least be used as a reference point?

You may wish to use the garment itself, stitching it, darning it... sometimes the object will make its future use known to you – such as a hole you observe, do you want to celebrate it with some added embellishment? Or maybe you wish to cover it, soothe it and elongate its life?

If the garment is too sentimental to use, why not stick it in front of you and draw it? Or use a medium you feel comfortable with to remember it by.

Now let's look at an artist who has literally used their grandfather's jumper as artwork itself, bringing it to life within their trademark art style...

FEATURED ARTIST:
Jordan Cunliffe

Jordan Cunliffe is an embroidery artist with a specialism in data visualisation and storytelling. Using data collection, methodical planning and meticulous hand stitch, Jordan creates encoded pieces which celebrate the everyday moments of our lives. Here, Jordan describes the inspiration behind their piece *Grandad's Sweater*.

'After my grandad passed away in 2019, I asked if I could keep one of his sweaters. Whenever I picture him, it is in one of these M&S knitted pullovers that he would wear and wear until they were falling apart.

'I reflected for a long time about how I wanted to create this tribute, and what it was about our relationship that I wanted to commemorate. As I thought about it, I considered our lives and how they had intertwined. My grandad knew me from the beginning, but it struck me what a small proportion of his life I was privy to. I decided to use this idea as the basis for my embroidery. The piece is almost a cross stitch, but each stitch is separated into its two opposing diagonal lines. In one direction is a red stitch for every day of my grandad's life, and the opposite direction is a pink stitch for every day of my life, and where they overlap it creates the cross. There are so many singular red stitches, every day he lived before I was born. As I stitched them, I thought about what that day must have been like for him: What had he done? Who had he been with? Some days must have been momentous, like getting married, the births of his daughters or moving overseas for work, and then some days would have been the general day-to-day monotony. All these different types of days are given equal importance in the same repetitive red stitch, because I believe that every day does carry equal importance; these small, ordinary moments that make up each of our lives.

'Towards the end of the embroidery, there are a few singular pink stitches, where my life now carries on without him, and this section will grow with time, creating a living document that will constantly evolve, a testament to the closing of one chapter and the continuation of the next.'

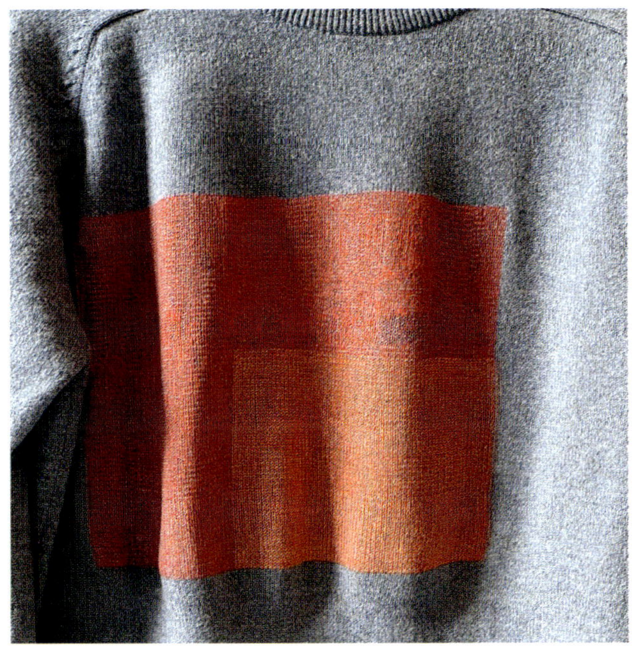

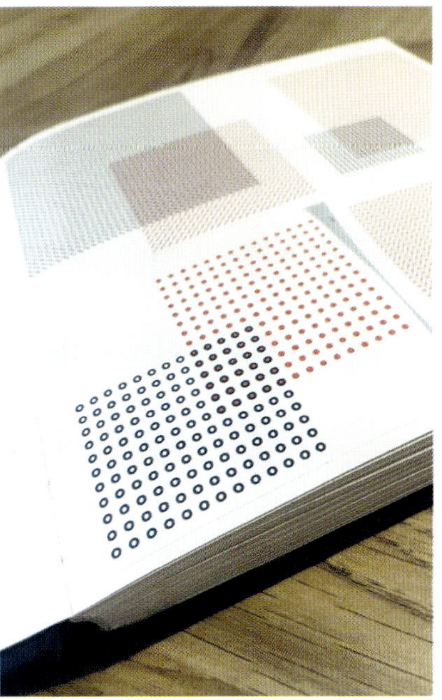

FAR LEFT: Grandad's Sweater *(Jordan Cunliffe, 2020). Embroidery thread on M&S knitted sweater (61 × 63cm).* **LEFT:** *Jordan Cunliffe, Sketchbook (2020).*

Nosy notions

I am a nosy human – or should I say 'curious'? I love to people-watch. Maybe you relate to this trait. Many of my days are spent, generally with a coffee on the side, just letting the theatre of life outside float by. As emotional beings, we thrive on being relatable; soothing ourselves that we are as ordinary as other people are, just as normal.

No special destination is required; it could be a local IKEA or the Royal Academy of Arts. I have done it all, and drawn it all. I guess it is my way of making sense of the world.

We do not have to own a story to feel the emotion surrounding it. It does not have to be our story; we can be captured by another's. We may know them personally or they may be on TV, a soap opera character, or even our nextdoor neighbour.

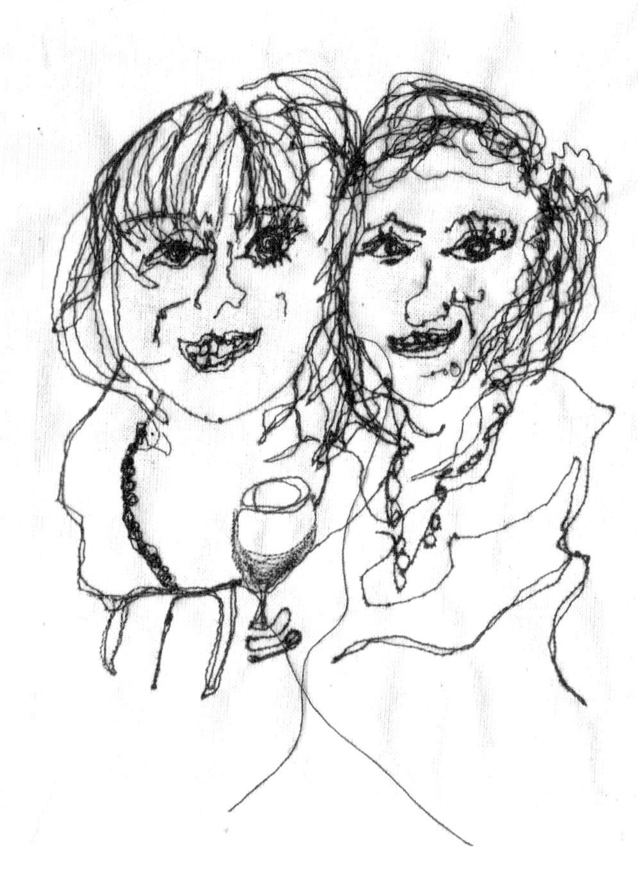

RIGHT: Mum and I at Jamie's *(Ailish Henderson, 2016). Black needle drawing on muslin cloth.*

OPPOSITE, TOP: *Blue and white RA courtyard collection (Ailish Henderson, 2019). Watercolour.*

OPPOSITE, BOTTOM LEFT: I got to the RA despite... *(Ailish Henderson, 2021). Watercolour.*

OPPOSITE, BOTTOM RIGHT: *RA lampshade (Ailish Henderson, 2023). Digitally printed onto handmade paper.*

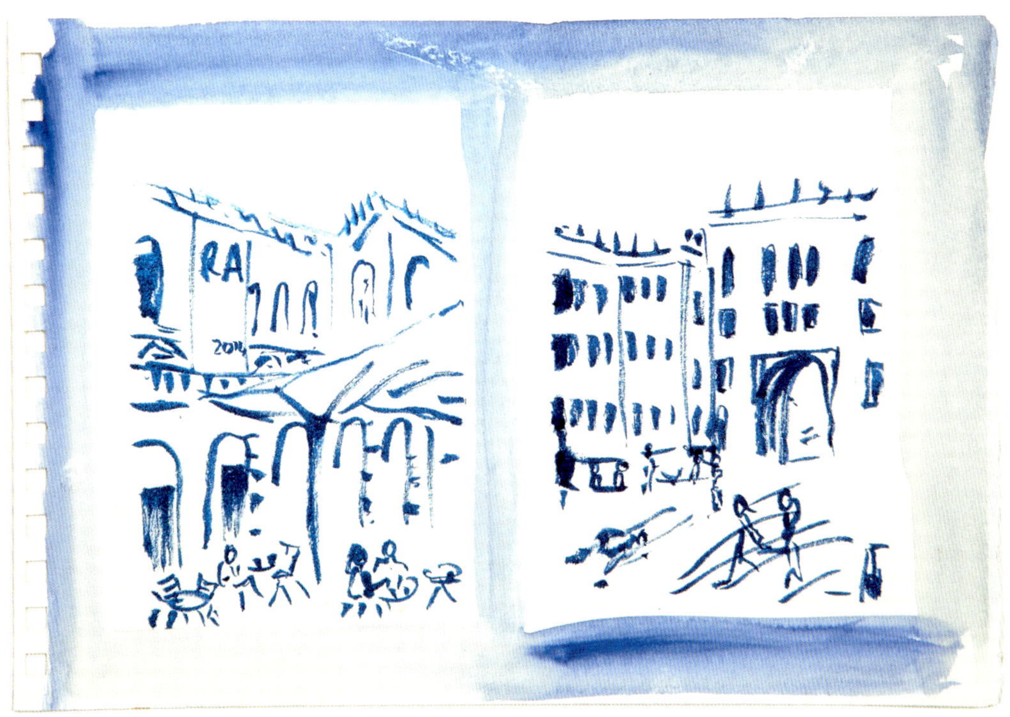

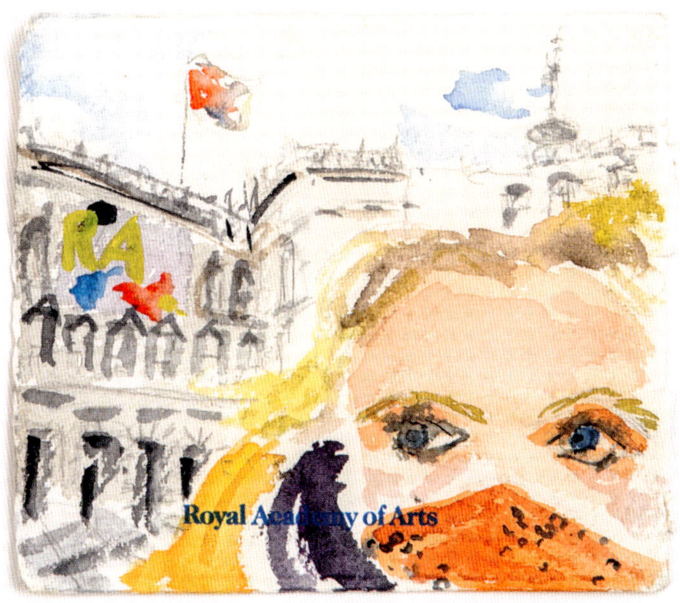
Royal Academy of Arts

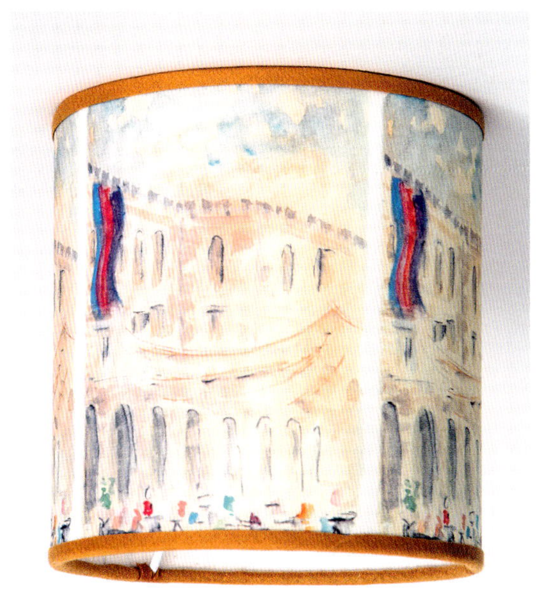

Narrative Eight:
The meet cute

I want to tell you to story of Eunice and Tommy, my dearest non-family. We met by moving into the house nextdoor to them. Then they were a couple in their seventies. They give their hearts, they care, we phone each other most days, we knock, we are there. They know my eating habits better than my own DNA, and will offer the greenest granny smiths, cheese scones and quiches to dry my tears when the day has gone awry. I associate them with white lilies, which, in my third decade, made me love this floral perfection for the very first time; with 'leather' soap to soothe my panic and travelled Canadian maple syrup to end my days.

This is just a sample of their kindnesses. They watch, yet do not nose. They observe, but never say. They are the people I cry to; go to when fear has snapped me, and their shower is the one that heats my bones when mine is no longer useable. They were neighbours, who became so much more than great friends.

This kindness has its downsides. I worry every time I hear a siren, praying for it not to be for them.

On coming out of their shower one bungalow-bound morning, I came across their desk of photographs in the hallway; many normal family photographs, the usual proud grandparent array of Carrie's graduation pictures. At the very back was a black and white print. A simple pose, two children, a boy and a girl, holding hands as they walk down a country path, far into the distance. I comment, of course thinking that

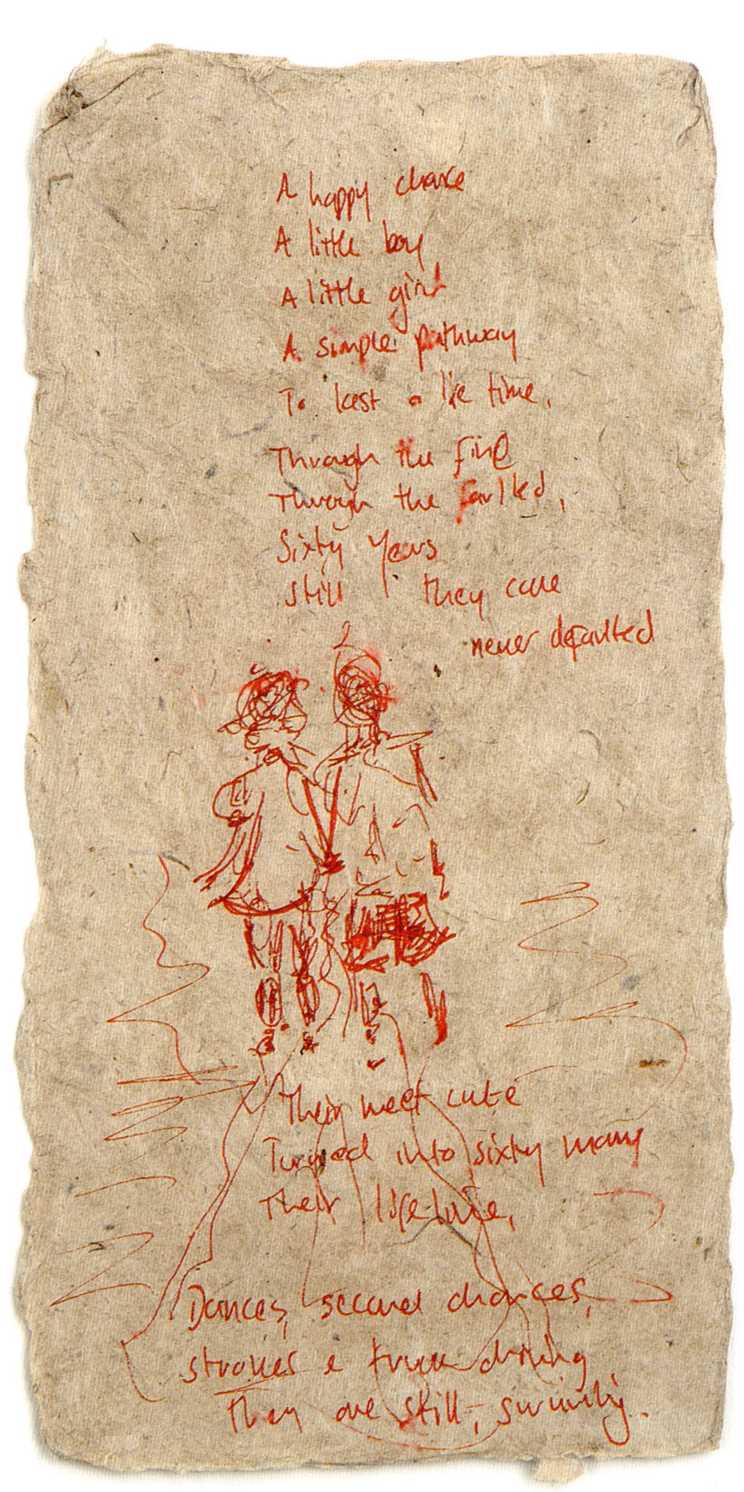

this is just a beautiful print of a common scene. Eunice surprises me with her words: 'Oh yes, we were about seven then.'

'What?' I say. This CANNOT be them. Surely?

But it is just that! A 'meet cute'!

War years, battles, illnesses, kidney problems; they have had it all, yet their path continues. Together. One of my greatest (nosy) delights was being in my own garden, earwigging on their conversations, their knowing back and forth bickering. No matter what they say, this couple is there to stay.

Who is your Eunice? Who is your Tom?

In case you are unsure what this is, a meet cute is a chance meeting of two people in a cute way. More than that, it is the push, the pull, the discomfort, the whole world of a love story. Really, though, as this couple pass their sixtieth anniversary, their platinum year, they have no idea how much they would inspire a neighbour to retell their story. It has taught me once again, 'moments matter, don't let them scatter'.

A meet cute is generally said to be set in a romantic context. It is that look across a room, the bumping into each other on a road that develops into a marriage made in heaven and a 'happily ever after'. It's serendipity. Let's face it, no matter how bitter in love or life we may be, don't tell me that you started your own 'Once upon a time' and didn't want a 'Happily ever after' before 'The end'?

So, who will be a part of your textile-art-related script?

Narrative Nine:
She caught him with her hooked-out foot

I am cheating a little here, as this is about two close family members, but due to the fact I was not born when it happened, I feel a sense of isolation from the retold narrative.

There was once a Scottish boy and an English girl, who happened to be living separate lives in Ireland, doing voluntary work. By some serendipitous manoeuvrings, they happened to be at the same large convention hall. The English girl, by the way, was my mum. She had a nervous habit of shifting from foot to foot when standing, and as luck would have it, having given up on finding her own tall, dark whatever, managed to floor the Scottish boy as he passed by.

So of course the relationship developed, there was a subsequent marriage and I arrived not long after. The Scottish boy? My daddy. This narrative left me with a glazed look in my eye as a child, yet now I view it as evidence of hope. All is never lost, and I am the artist I am because of my dual familial heritage.

What will be your own serendipitous 'hook'?

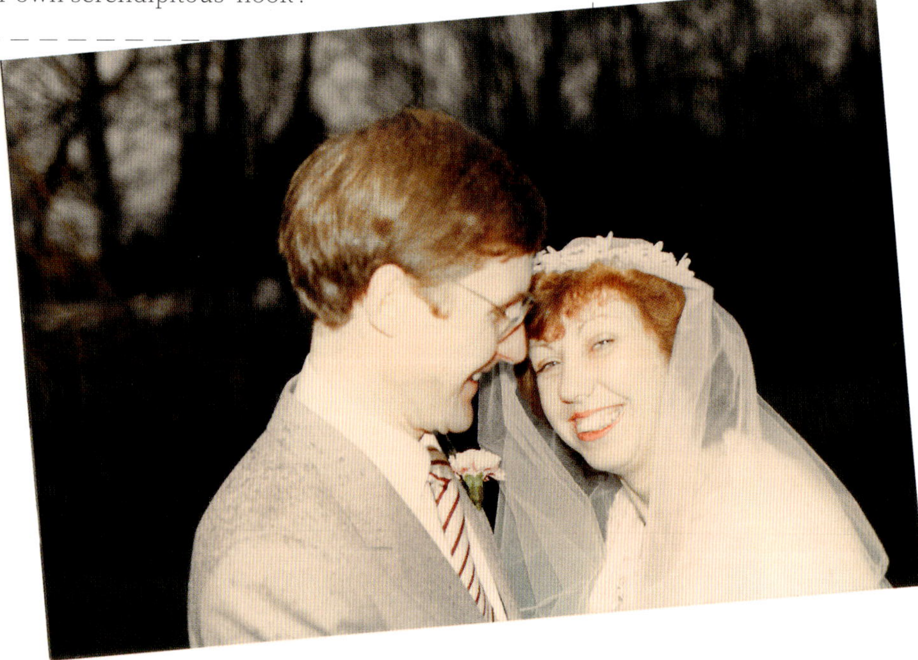

ABOVE: *She caught him – proof (1984).*

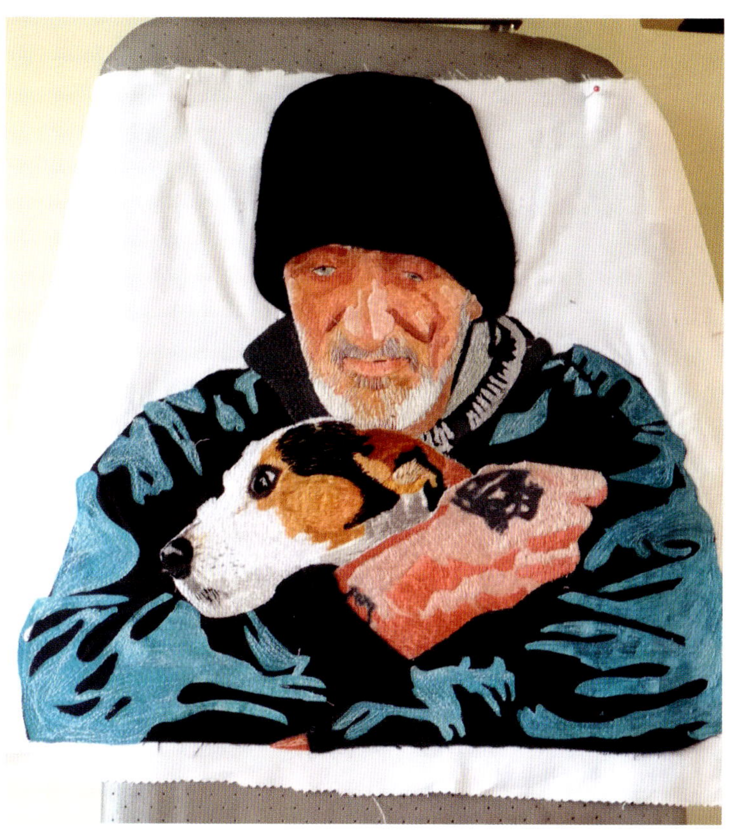

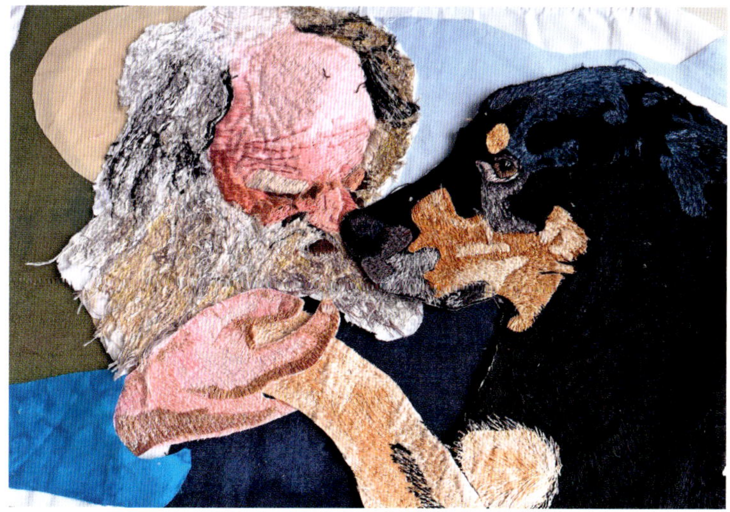

ABOVE, TOP: The Man and his Best Friend *(Aran Illingworth, 2021). Recycled fabric, appliqué, hand and machine stitch.*

ABOVE, BOTTOM: The Man and his Best Friend *(Aran Illingworth, 2022). Recycled fabric, appliqué, hand and machine stitch.*

FEATURED ARTIST:
Aran Illingworth

Here, Aran Illingworth discusses her work *Pareidolia.*

'Perspective and perception are two separate but intrinsically linked concepts. This piece, *Pareidolia,* an ambiguous, colourful quilted pattern, allows the viewer to remind themselves that our perception of an object or an event is in part dependent on our own previous experience and how we feel. However, this piece should also remind the viewer that we have the power to see other points of view through reframing our perspective. When we look at a cloud and see a horse, we should remember that we can also see a zebra.

Before my career in art, I trained as a psychiatric nurse. After I had my son, I left nursing and went into part-time studies, culminating in a degree in Applied Arts at the University of Hertfordshire, specialising in Textiles. On leaving university, my work has focused on feminist issues and on poverty and its relation to women and children. I have always been fascinated both with textiles and with creating realistic images. My art sets out to combine these two sources of inspiration by using fabric instead of paint to create an accurate portrait. It has taken me several years to establish myself as a textile artist, and during those years I have tried to perfect my work and the techniques that I use. I currently exhibit my work both in the UK and internationally.'

Fabricated

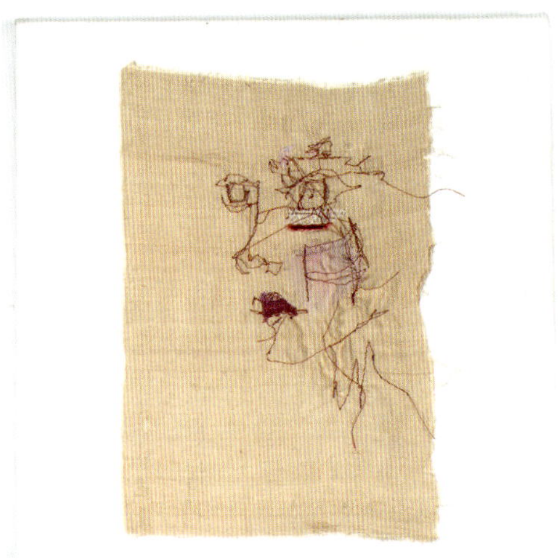

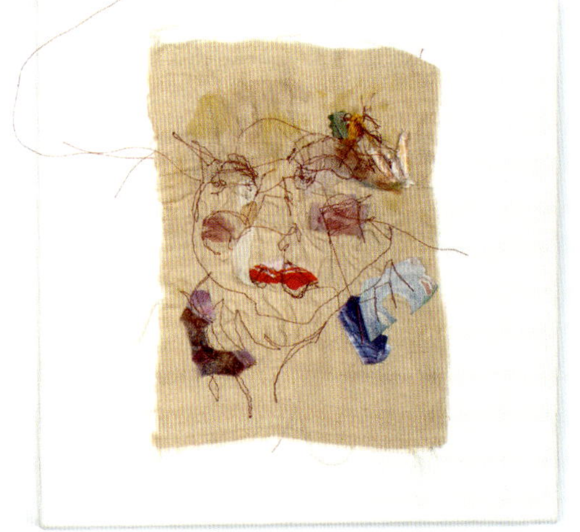

As children, we yearn for stories. They soothe us, unite us, connect us, and help us to learn life lessons within comparatively safe contexts. As adults, let's just put it out there, we would still love to be read to, and we still yearn for Prince Charming and the oh-so-magical moments. Isn't that why audiobooks were created, or why we guide ourselves through life's path with audio meditation apps?

Can this impulse be entwined with our creativity? Of course it can. I have spent a lifetime strolling down the narratives once told to me by my grandmother. Red Riding Hood was the main starting point. Because of my grandmother's inability to read, caused by the cruel condition of macular degeneration, the story always changed, which helped make it so addictive.

I didn't ask her to continually retell this story as I matured; I think in those early, youthful years, we profess to be over the stories stage. We want life: real life, boyfriends, husbands, partners and children. But it only takes a small life change, a broken heart, a loss, to bring us back to stories and wishing for a happy ending.

The fabricated is sometimes the only thing we can control. If we write something that is purely fictional, we can be in control of its happy (or not-so-happy) ending. *This is text-based, not visual*, you may protest. However, the narrative does not have to remain unused. The characters you have written about are real and three-dimensional in your mind. So how do we draw them out?

I find that the best way is through a few simple pieces of prose or poetry on paper. Nothing that would win any awards, just words that might create pictures in our minds. Then we can extend this to imagine what the people or situation or landscape looks like and draw sketches, even if they're rough. Continue this until you have a more polished view. Then think about how this could be shown in a textile art context.

ABOVE, LEFT:
'Looking forwards back' (Ailish Henderson, 2019). Stitch portrait collage. Drawn stitch, intuitive cloth.

ABOVE, RIGHT:
'Somewhere, someday there will be sunlight behind her eyes, enough to see' (Ailish Henderson, 2019). Stitch collage portrait. Intuitive cloth, drawn thread.

Red Ties

Lines that bind us,
The colour of blood,
A story that's stood,
The test of memory,
What was once yours,
Is now mine.

We have had so much time,
I promise it's all kept,
In my mind,
The story told,
Sold,
To me,
In so many ways,
That pathway,
Your pathway,
Defines me,
Underlines me,
Who I am.

I trudge on,
I've met my grandmother,
I've dealt with the wolves,
A father there to guide me.

When you were once,
What I am now,
You walked the red line,
To become mine,
Time was all it took,
For your vocal prose,
To collide with my hearing.

We have walked the woods,
Held our baskets close,
Scares have come,
Yes in different guises,
We make our own bed.

Thank you,
For giving me your voice,
Yet it is my choice,
Paths collided,
Journeys the same,
Now it is my turn,
To tell the red stain.

Red Ties,
They mind us,
Align us,
Your memory,
Tucked in,
Embedded as a duvet

AH 2018

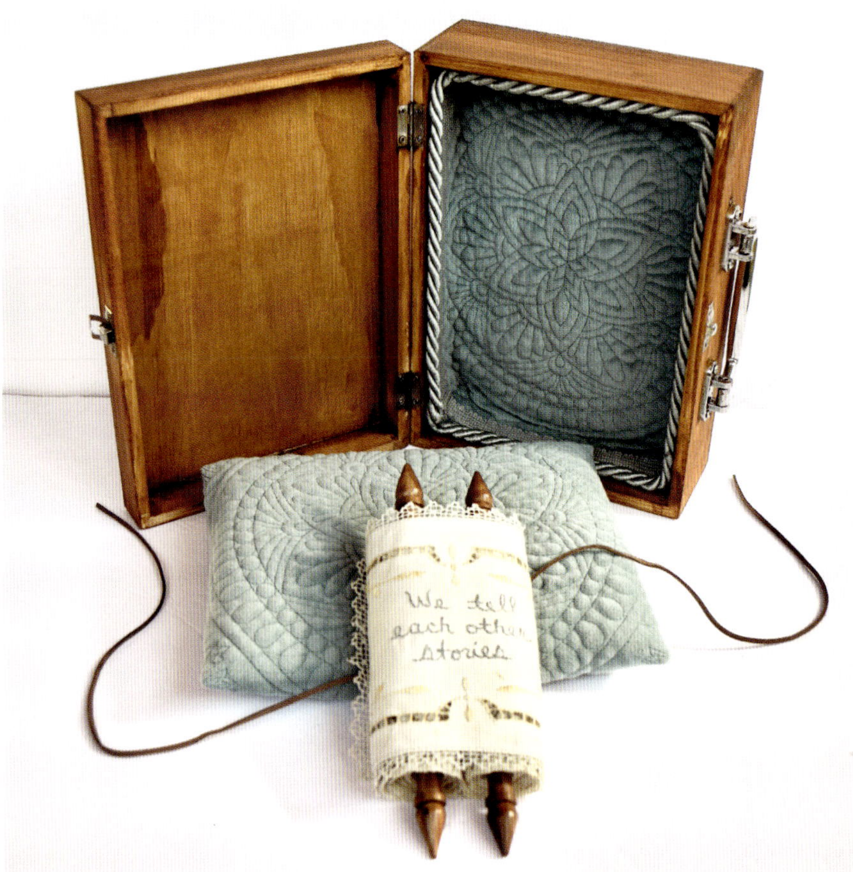

LEFT: We tell eachother stories *(Michelle Kingdom, 2023). Wood box lined with velvet, velvet pillow, embroidered lace cover and the scroll itself.*
OPPOSITE PAGE: We tell eachother stories, *scroll (Michelle Kingdom, 2023). Long vintage lace, vintage silk blue edging and wooden dowels.*

FEATURED ARTIST:

Michelle Kingdom

I asked Michelle Kingdom to tell me a little about one collection of her work that I felt fitted my narrative theme:

'*We Tell Each Other Stories* was made in March 2023. It was the very last piece for my fourth solo show, *A Thousand Past Days*. The piece wasn't planned and fell into place organically. It was also not typical of my work. Nevertheless, it seemed to be a fitting way to complete what felt like a transformational point of my life and work.

'The artwork for *A Thousand Past Days* began with inspiration from the enduring work of ancient textiles, with many of my narratives stitched on vintage textile grounds. But four months in, my beloved mother passed away from cancer. There are no words to adequately describe her

loss. We were incredibly close, and it was very traumatic. But at least I was able to be there and take care of her during this time. I was with her to the end. And I am forever changed; forever heartbroken.

'Eventually, I managed to resume working. Much of the rest of the art created for the show attempted to make present, honest and vulnerable work that reflected my state of mind, while grappling with the momentous complexity of life. After finishing what I thought were all the pieces needed for the show, I looked through some old family fabrics on a whim. There I rediscovered the vintage lace trim I would use for *We Tell Each Other Stories*.

'I'm sure it was my mother's, probably from when she used to sew my childhood clothes. I think I had it boxed away since I left home thirty years ago. I had never stitched on open lace before, but something made me want to tackle it. I was thinking specifically of two perennial influences for me: the horizontal, linear, graphic storytelling of the Bayeux Tapestry, and a humble ancient Egyptian textile fragment with a sparse row of people connected by a line. Somehow, I felt connected to the people in that line. It was my turn to make marks of connection.

'The piece would tell stories, though the specifics of the narrative would be less important than our need to try continually and collectively to make meaning in this world. Using a collage of vignettes, a vague story began to emerge. There would be spinners on either end to open and close the narrative, never letting us forget that this is a tale and that people, flawed and wandering and imperfect, are always the tellers. The figures represent stages of life, growth, and retraction, all amidst societal eyes and claws. The figures are executed with an even hand, using simple lines, the same weight and colour, the same gestural drawing quality.

'There is no judgement, just life unrolling and unfolding. Pared down to the essential line, the piece acts as a blueprint, revealing a skeletal core usually hidden under fancifully embroidered lives. The reverse would be just as important, exposing the vulnerable, messy, incomplete side we try so hard to conceal.

'To house the piece, I stained and lined a simple wood box with a rich, matching quilted velvet lining and pillow. An unrelated vintage textile would serve as a protective cover with one last detail that I never do – a title in stitch.

'Now objet d'art, the scroll lives in a sheltered, protected box. We tell each other stories, whether truth or precious fictions.'

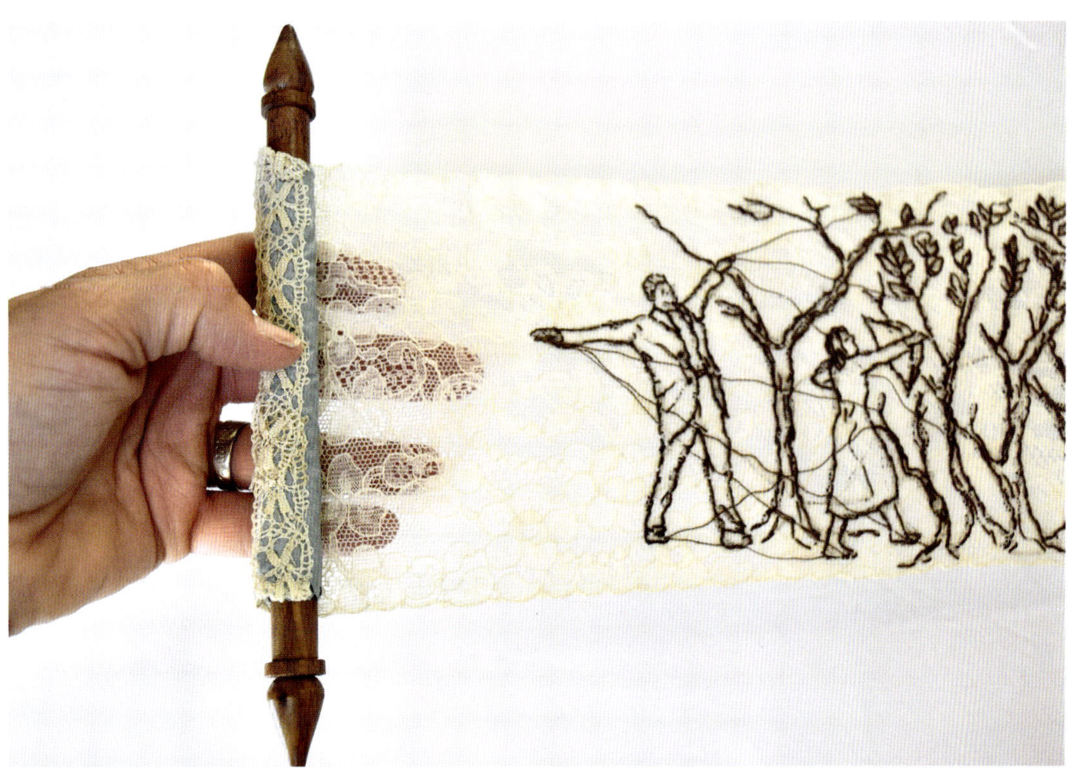

FEATURED ARTIST:

Gaynor Devaney

I would now like to introduce you to Gaynor Devaney, a dear friend of mine who has a studio to die for. Gaynor Devaney is an experienced multimedia artist and educator. Creative play is the strand of joy running through her work. She grew up in the tradition of 'make do and mend', learning to knit, playing with buttons, constructing models and collages from whatever was to hand. She is inspired by folktales and folk art, by her family and friends, by moments and memories.

'Sometimes, entering my studio, I have a sense of returning to times long past – to people and places and selves. The room is filled with mementos and with the evidence of lifelong creative activities. I first became aware of this when I spent more time in my

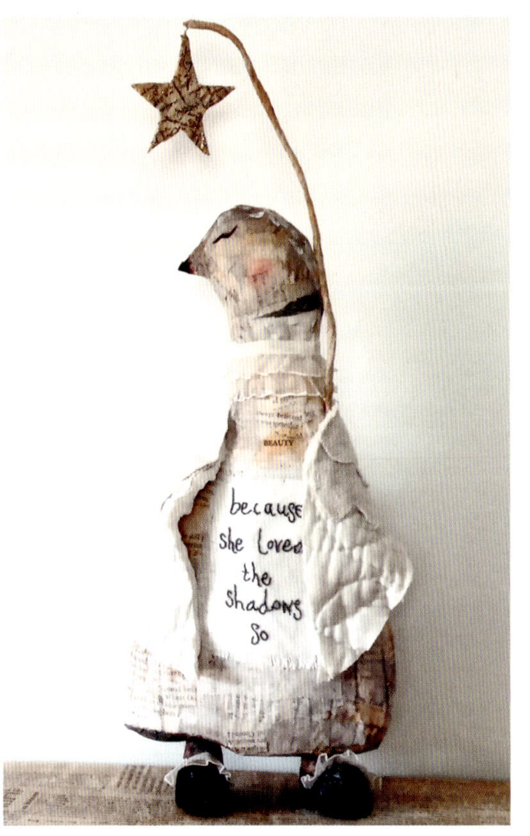

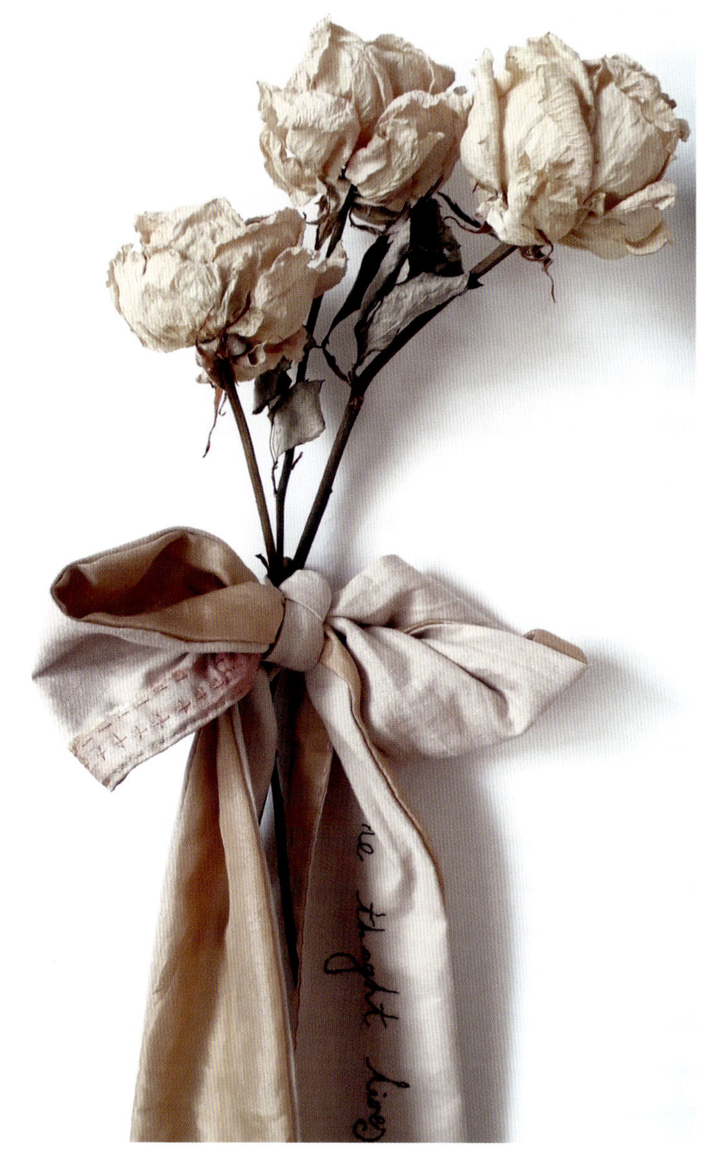

studio during the Coronavirus pandemic. I focused on making personal art, after years of working in museums, galleries, and schools.

'Through my making, I began to explore the idea that positive memories can help sustain us throughout our lives, even through the most difficult of times. I began to practise what I thought of as pre-emptive repair, culminating in *The Theatre of The Happy Ghosts*.

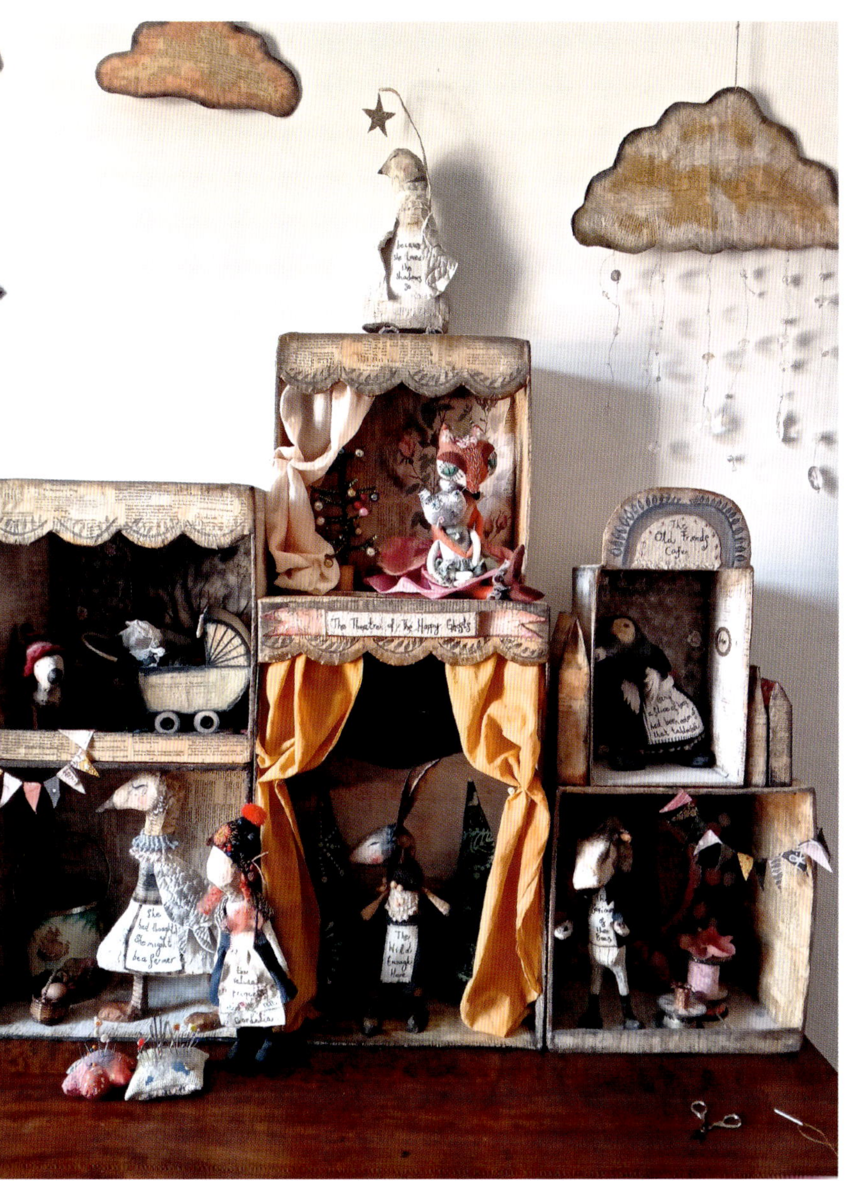

OPPOSITE PAGE, LEFT:
Pigeon *(Gaynor Devaney, 2021). Papier maché sculpture, hand painted, embroidery. 37cm tall.*
OPPOSITE PAGE, RIGHT:
Mother's Day Roses *(Gaynor Devaney, 2022).*

ABOVE: *Studio view (Gaynor Devaney, 2023). Worktable with the* Theatre of the Happy Ghosts *assemblage.*

'The Theatre is compiled of boxes strengthened and decorated with hand-stitched textiles. Each of these boxes contains an assemblage of found and made objects. The principal occupants are creatures either modelled in papier-mâché or stitched from fabrics imbued with memories, such as children's clothes, a pair of old overalls, a grandmother's tablecloth. The Theatre is also a repository for my thoughts. It is a visual touchstone for things I wish to remember: plans, stories, moments and moods; things I would be happy to be haunted by.

'The Theatre evolves as the rooms are rearranged. The pigeon atop the Theatre evokes a happy autumnal memory. Calm and peaceful, she lives in the light of her own star, which she carries beneath one wing: a wing fashioned from a dilapidated quilt donated by a friend. The phrase 'because she loved the shadows so' came to me as I stood at twilight watching the pigeons playing in the trees opposite my home. I had to stitch it. Later I realised what self-acceptance those words contain. Like the pigeon, not everyone relishes the limelight, and that is more than okay. So, she continues to lift my spirits long after that original moment.

'Now, in this post-pandemic lifetime, I am working in the wider world again, hosting workshops, sharing my love of hand stitching and the enjoyment and companionship that stitching together brings. I encourage people to recycle fabric: to use treasured scraps of clothing or domestic embroideries to personalise their stitching; to create totems and mementos that make themselves and others smile.

'A piece of hand stitching can look quite simple while containing multitudes. It can be as complex as the human heart of the person who made it.'

The Torn Umbrella

She stood,
Uncontrollably sombre,
Staring at the grey forlorn sky,
It seems to slowly engulf her,
Tainting her mood with its own.

She didn't realise how long she had been,
Standing there,
It had seemed like seconds,
But her feet were sore.

A storm has come,
Unable to move,
A brief blank expression,
Frames her face,
Time has worn down,
Her former grace.

Standing uncovered,
The storm slowly evolving above,
Detains her mind,
Slowly seeping away,
The thoughts behind,
Carrying her away.

Quick enough to stay,
She plays her last card,
The plastic umbrella that has
Become her guard.
Someone is near,
Yet she does not hear,
They stand close,
Staring at her fragile existence,
Reaching up to her umbrella,
Gently tearing particles
From its frame,
Helping the storm,
To gain.

Both stay in a stance,
But she does not like this unemployed
Gesture,
Fending for herself,
She lays a hand,
On the frame's shoulder,
Making it clear her distant view,
Never to ensue.

The person remains in silence,
Holding onto possibilities,
A determined character,
Willing to wait.

A tree stands near,
Time twisted all over its chest,
Even leading up to its arms,
These have bred to become many.

She stares at the twisted branches,
Of time,
Seeing the contradiction they behold,

She must make a choice,
To let in,

Or let go,
She must know.

Her skeleton's frame wears thin,
A quick decision must commence,

No protection is best,
She gets so wet,
The cloud's anger sustaining,
This watery flow,
It feels so good,
A setting free,
Now a victim of what might,
Be.

Time is all she needs to repair,
The umbrella must be torn,
No shelter for protection,
From the hurtful sentiments of rain,
Only them will she learn to trust,
What she loves and must.

No clouds or storms will envelop her,
No umbrellas to hide her
From the rain.
Only a new jacket,
With the option of a hood;
This way she can still see,
What is good,
But is never far from the protection,
And the affection she needs.

With this option of a hood,
Yet this time a vague uncertainty,
And a reluctance for it to be used.
Never again will a plastic protection
Be abused.

The form still beside her....

Yes sadness could grow,
Yet happiness may also sow.

AH 2004

Narrative Ten:
The Torn Umbrella

As an angst-ridden child, I wrote a poem about a girl who had got caught in the rain. It stayed in my secret, padlocked, *Beauty and the Beast* diary for years. Then one day – I don't know why – I drew it out. I imagined what the girl and the scene itself would look like. This naïve drawing turned into more of a children's book illustration in time, then I used it as the basis for an embroidered book cover, made for an art textiles exam I took years later, at eighteen.

I left it there. Then, spin on another few years with a few more skills learned, and I transposed a mature version of this scene into the print-making studio, making a dry-point etching that became one of my most recognised prints.

The title of this piece also became the title for my first solo exhibition, back in 2013. As I began to educate myself in print design, this same piece has been remastered on my own interior and fashion ranges, comprising wallpaper, cushions, silk scarves and lampshades. I think my time with this initial piece of prose, spanning around twenty-five years since its natural birth, is pretty much burnt out! I now feel that I can put it to bed; I no longer need to push the what-ifs.

Do you have an itch in your mind that you feel the urge to scratch?

Gone by

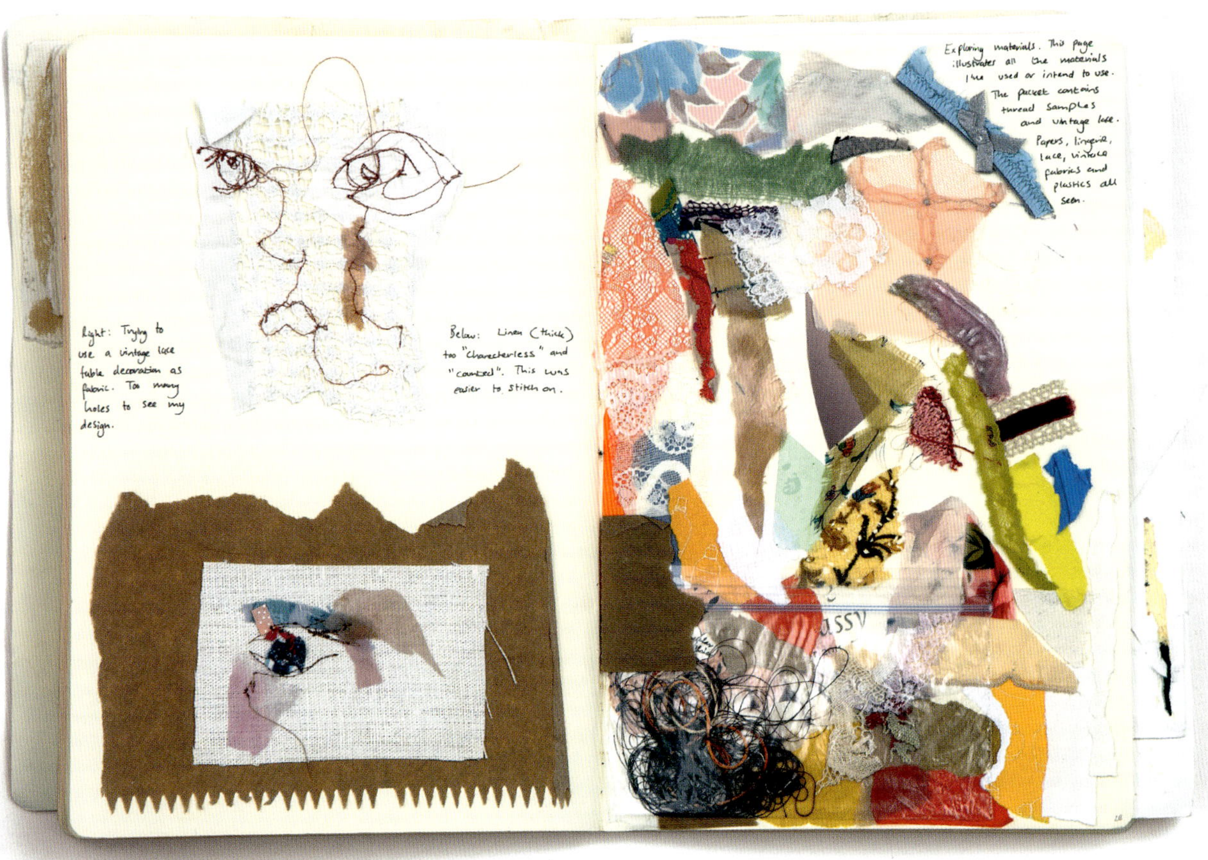

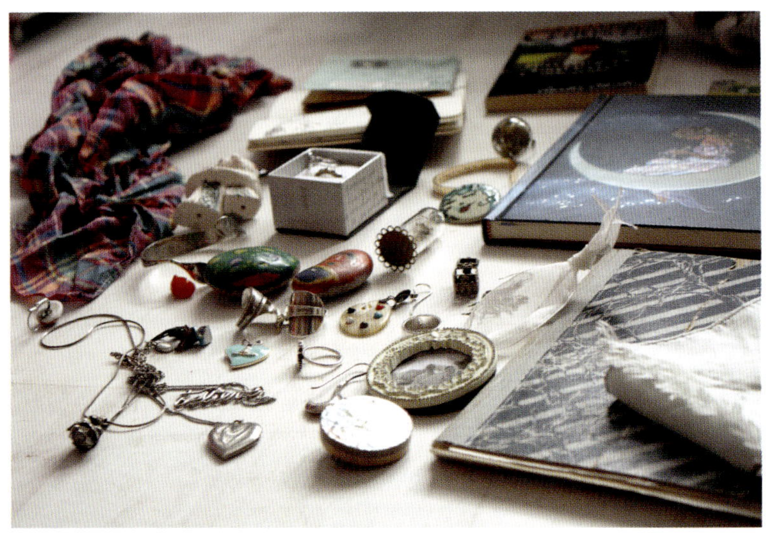

ABOVE: *Extract from* Stories My Grandmother Told Me *sketchbook (2019).*
RIGHT: *Collective archive findings, including mother's self-penned poetry book and emotionally charged imagery depicting hope (2021).*

Narrative Eleven:
The day of the British Museum visit

I often find inspiration, and interpretative immersive life lessons, via things unrelated to textiles. I am often surprised at what comes out of an experience.

My friend and I decided to have an art-based weekend in London. On the last day, we went to the British Museum. I decided to spend time in the Egyptian section, happy childhood memories tempting me in. Passing through the Egyptian and Mesopotamian sections, I paused by a rather feminine sculpture, affectionally named *The Last Woman Standing*. The historical context: King Ashur-bel-kala (who was the last king of the Middle Assyrian Empire and managed a rule of eighteen years) sent versions of this statue all around his kingdom as a rather expensive act of humanistic victimisation. Lovely, eh? Originally this piece was set up inside the temple of Ishtar and it is rather special as it's the only known Assyrian statue of a naked woman, as well as being the only one left from a few identical models.

Perhaps with an axe to grind, this king even paid attention to the small details; on each one – this and all the other naked ladies – was engraved a directive to all who came across her, that they should laugh. Apparently even the type of stone used was chosen to mock this sad lady. Personally, I think she is the last woman standing and has the last laugh. I see no king around – do you? And if I had this body, I wouldn't be complaining – would you?

How does this relate to the narrative and the character in the arts? What shape is the body? Are you attracted to hard sculpture, soft sculpture? Is it the story that makes you smile and inspires a drawing? Or maybe the title: *The Last Woman Standing* sounds like a real character. Could you make your own feminine character; a strong lady? Really, it is all down to how we use our experiences. A visit to a museum can be just that source of inspiration. Do we want to create something temporary? Or with a lasting future? These are all considerations we must weigh up in the pre-making stage of our works. Do we want an indelible tattoo or wash-off 'Billy Stamper' (ask your mother).

Percolate and filter, allow your brain time to consolidate and conclude key ideas that you wish to take on and run with. Do you have any familial historical connections to investigate? It may take a little research; however, the bounty of, often surprising, results can be inspiring artistically.

Be warned, it's like the monkey bars as a child...you just can't stem the determination to reach the next rung; so it is with the curiosity that your research will bring!

FEATURED ARTIST:

Joanna Barakat

The artist Joanna Barakat tells us:

'Palestinian embroidery became central to my art practice after I completed my painting *Heart Strings*, in which I depicted myself stitching a Palestinian motif on my skin. It was the first time I had hand-embroidered directly on a painting.

'This work reclaims and re-embodies my story as a diaspora Palestinian, with the embroidery representing a longing to return to my indigenous land. Through embroidery, I can finally speak a native Palestinian language fluently, instead of broken Arabic, which always left me feeling like an outsider.

'When I started researching the history of Palestinian embroidery, I became fascinated with how Palestinian farm and village women used embroidery as a storytelling device. Cross-stitch motifs hand-embroidered on a woman's dress communicated which village she came from, her marital status, wealth, beliefs, and natural environment.

After 1948, this personally made, localised form of self-expression transformed into a commodified and collective symbol of Palestinian identity. The preservation and celebration of Palestinian embroidery counters the narrative denying the existence of Palestinians, along with the cultural appropriation and erasure involved in the ethnic cleansing of Palestine and its native population.

'Another aspect of Palestinian embroidery that appealed to me is how it builds a sense of self within a community. In the past, a girl would learn to embroider from her mother along with other women in her family and neighbourhood, picking up life lessons along with the skill. It is still common practice for women to embroider together, creating a space for connection and healing. I am drawn to this energetic exchange between people and between the embroiderer and their work. Though initially drawn to Palestinian embroidery as a language, I've grown to love how it facilitates connection and community while creating opportunities for conversations and activism.'

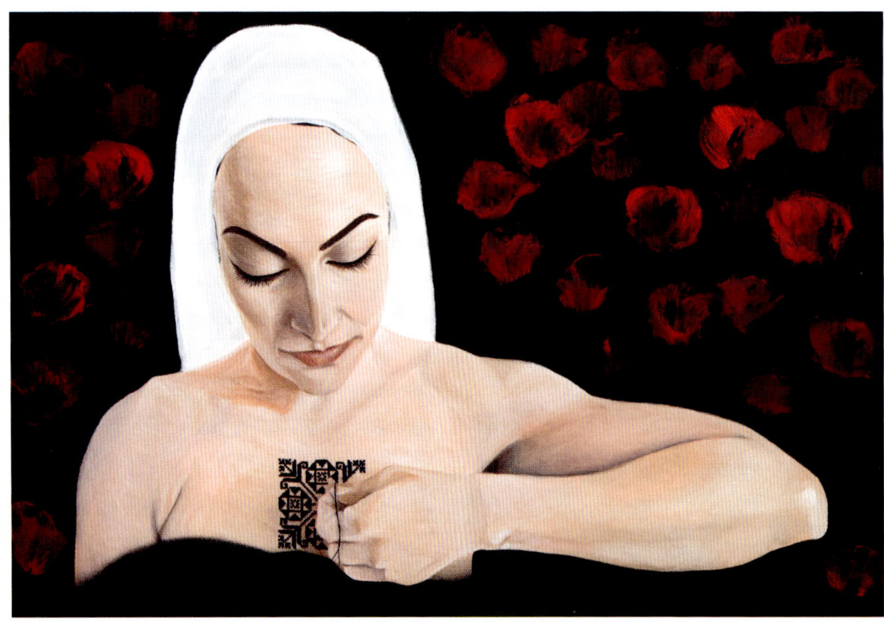

LEFT: Heart Strings *(Joanna Barakat, 2017). Acrylic, spray paint and cotton thread on canvas.*

Flying the nest

Escaping our homes for flights of our own fancy can be just the refresh we need. But how can it inspire us? I know from experience that it does not have to be when we are on that holiday that we suddenly have a lightbulb moment – it may be a long time afterwards. Whatever the case for you – it is the possibility which counts.

At eighteen, I got myself on a plane to my uncle and aunt's flat in Paris. I held grief within my heart, having just experienced my father's cardiac arrest (he is now my visual miracle). On that holiday I remember drawing and painting a lot, crying in the rain under the Eiffel Tower, mourning my way through Versailles and many arduous steps up and down the many flights to my uncle's flat every day, with their dog, dear, passed Lana, at my heels. (This early intervention via fur was a definite healing source which I have since tapped into much more, finally purchasing my own fur piece). I didn't have a clue how to stitch at the time, so I didn't spend my weeks in Paris with any fabrication in mind, but I was making art, the type I knew at the time, with no idea of its future.

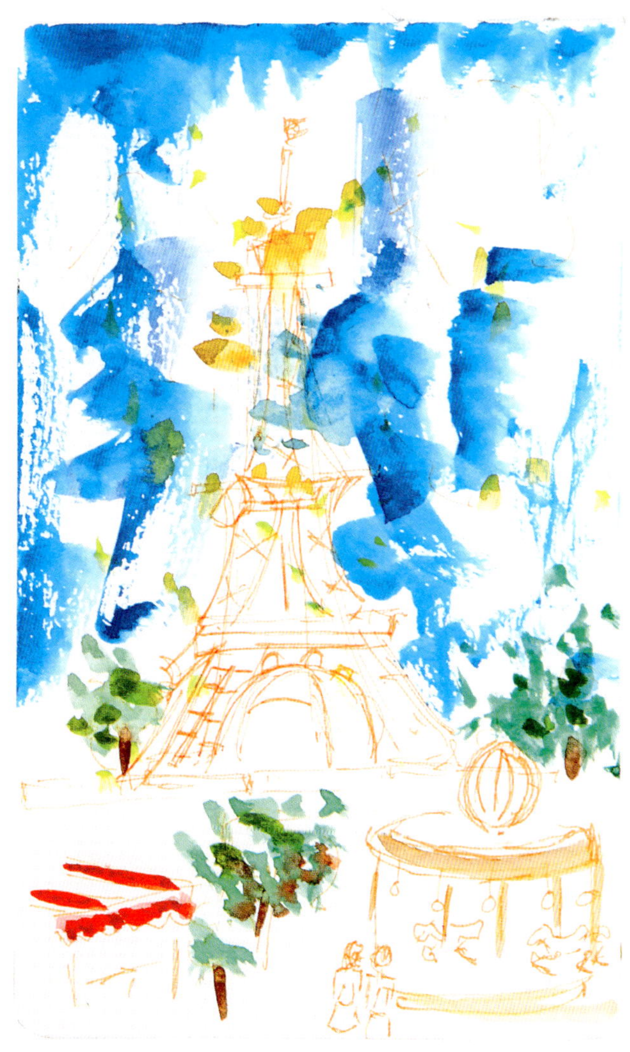

ABOVE: *Onsite Eiffel drawing (Ailish Henderson, 2017). A6.*

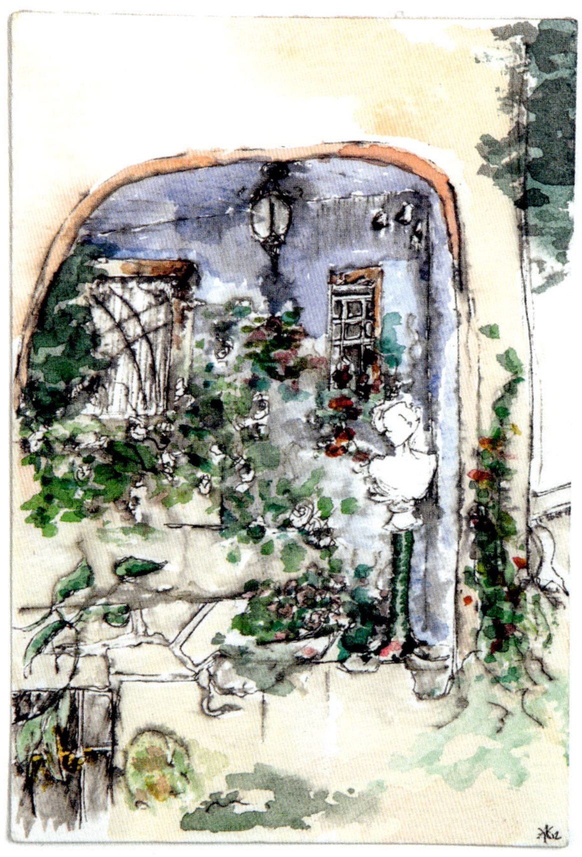

Narrative Twelve:
The Palace of Versailles

I have now visited this venue several times. Most visitors are taken by the luxurious interiors, the chandeliers, the grand appearance of the palace itself. Let's go, though, beyond the Palace and walk into the gardens...

At the bottom of the grounds, to the right, lies Marie Antoinette's playground, where she was allowed to 'play house', albeit on a lavish budget. It is a more compact closed-off area than the main palace, with its farm, towers and Disney-esque appeal. The subsequent imagery illustrates my version of this magical, fairy-tale setting. We begin with a photograph taken 'on location' and finish with a sculpture I was moved to create.

I wrote prose, I wrote poetry, I reflected on all the images I had taken, many selfies (not yet a thing then) and basically worked intuitively. I never questioned my place, my worth, I simply was.

So, what did this teach me? What can we learn from this example?

• Grief, loss and memories all fuel our art

• We then create art based on the above

Both lie in hand; we need the fuel to create the art. The sketches I made both in Paris at that time and many years afterwards have since inspired the *Stitched Collage Portraits* project, which you will also find in this book (see pages 52–55).

How can you relate this to your own life? Have you kept photographs from holidays? Have you kept travel documents you could add to a collage? Get them all out in front of you and consider how they could be used.

ABOVE LEFT: Gigi *(Original) (Ailish Henderson, 2011). Watercolour, inks.*

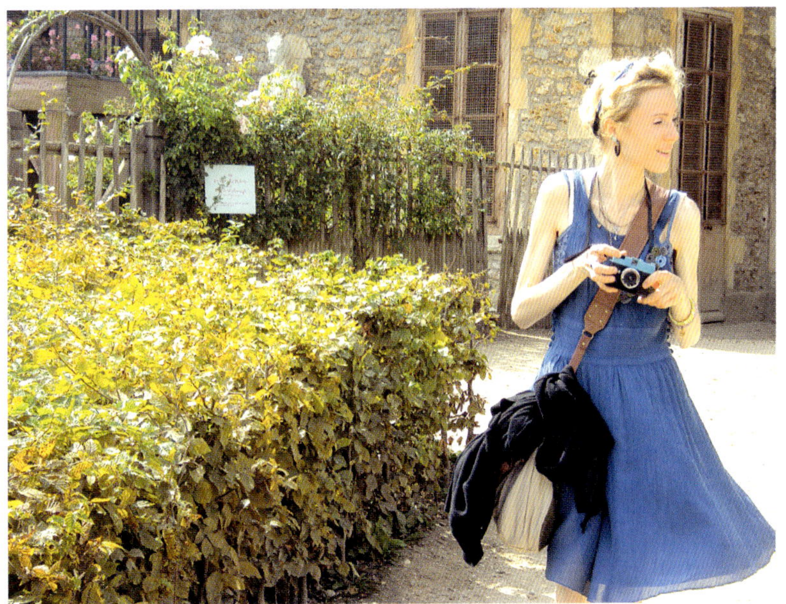

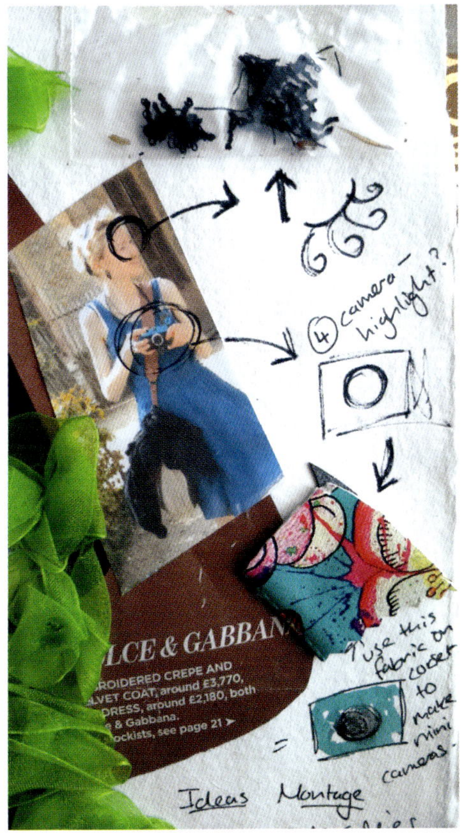

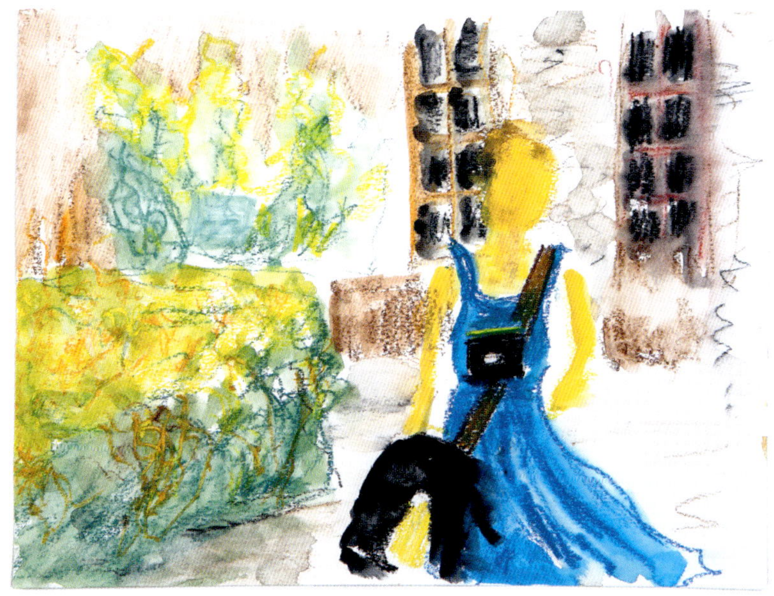

THIS PAGE: *From photograph to mixed-media collective trio (Ailish Henderson, 2018).*

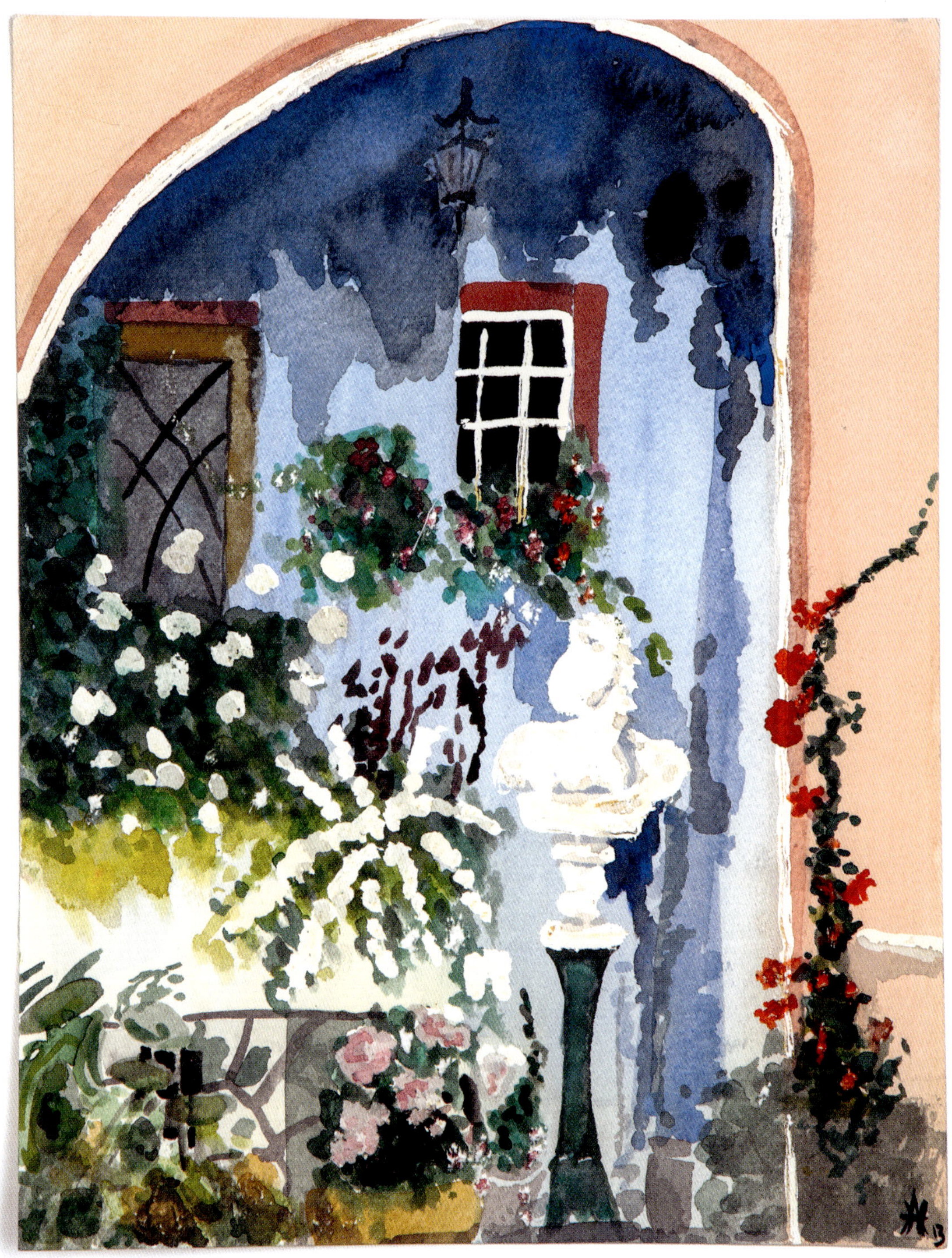

ABOVE: Gigi *(larger version) (Ailish Henderson, 2018). Watercolour.*

Narrative Thirteen:
Gigi's soirée

Who is Gigi? Although you will never meet her, you will become ever so slightly attached to her through my own imperfect retelling of the narrative, I know. It is a small, needlepoint mark on my mind, as I only met her once and now she is no longer in existence to vocalise her own story.

When I was a young artist, staying with my Parisian family who were keen to open up as many opportunities as possible to me, I was invited to a Sunday soirée at Gigi's. I was taken in by the location, its 'palace-in-miniature' form, with the busts so imperfect, ghostly white in contrast to this out-of-Paris leafy wonderland.

With my partial French and Gigi's 'probably-could-but-decided-not-to' English, I remember doing a lot of sitting and watching, rather than speaking. I left that to my proud aunt and uncle. Gigi was very much inside the arts scene, a lecturer at École Duperré, The Duperré School of Applied Arts. My aunt and uncle had met her by chance on the 1970s arts scene, where my aunt and uncle flourished, and they had formed a lifelong link of deep attachment. I took many photographs during this brief time. Those images have become the memory pool for much of my career; I still turn to them now.

I cannot tell you everything about Gigi. She led a vivid life, though not without its underlying personal loss; however, this never stopped her. As a teacher, artist and friend to even her own students, she quietly braved the inner pain and made it as whole as she could through her active participation in the arts; this was her life.

My recollections of being at Gigi's home include my uncle striving to explain to me that the Bresaola and other alien food groups were in fact edible and not there as some sort of still life or decoration. I was so nervous, unable to communicate or understand; were they discussing me? At one point, several homemade wines along, I remember being drowned in a cape; did I look cold? What impression was I giving, especially as I now looked like a Navajo lady?

This experience has brought me so much visual mind fuel that it has become an anchor to my developing practice. The subsequent image shows how I have been continually inspired by this once-in-a-lifetime insight into Gigi's world.

I have two sets of imagery from Gigi's soirée; my own, and those taken by my uncle, who was the observer in a different way. He could take the shots unobserved; the natural, unplanned, not-posed-for ones.

You too could create your own version of this by simply taking a camera with you when on a walk with a friend. Ask them to take a shot with your camera, of the same object as you have captured yourself.

Once home, reflect on the two shots. What did you see that your friend didn't? What was their focus point when taking the image? They may just capture a moment that mattered to you too; you simply didn't know it at the time.

The *healing* powers

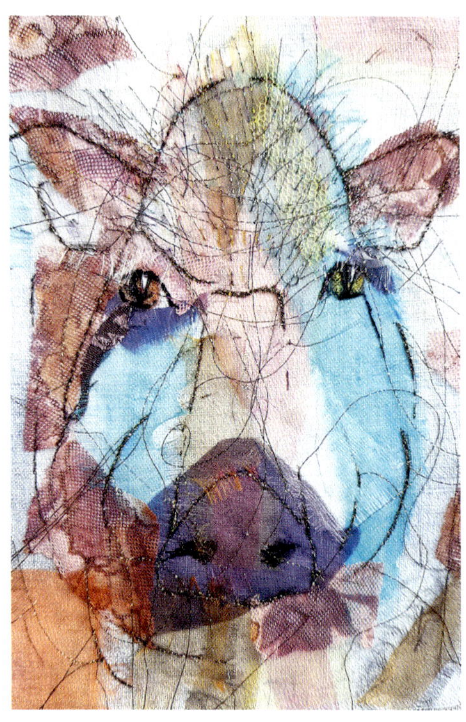

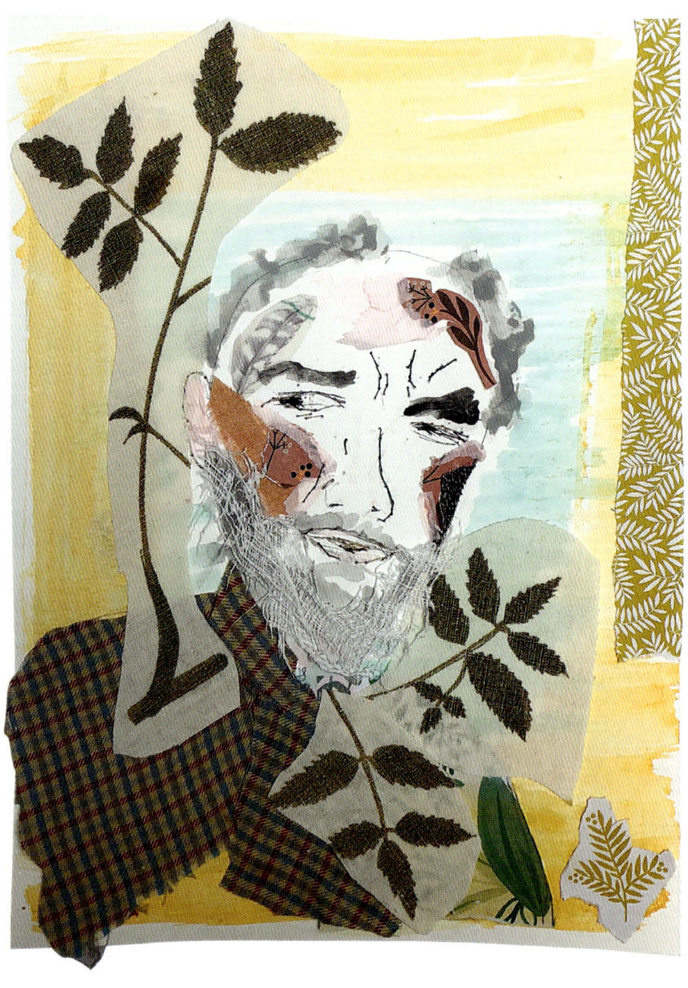

Where can your healing power come from?

This part of my book will cover nature, found locally and a little further afield. I may be preaching to many of you who are already aware of this natural medicine, yet the reminder may be worth a gander. We will glance upon three key areas:

• Walks within natural places

• Gardens and personal outdoor spaces

• Furry friends

ABOVE LEFT: Chacoan Peccary *(Pam Smyth, 2020). Mixed media.*
ABOVE RIGHT: My dad the environmentalist *(Mieke Lockefeer, 2020). Mixed media.*

TOP: 虎死留皮, 人死留名
When a Tiger Dies it Leaves Behind its Skin, When a Man Dies He Leaves Behind His Name *(Woo Jin Joo, 2021). Embroidery on an IKEA bag, 80 × 28 × 40 cm.*

BOTTOM: 十长生 Ten Symbols of Longevity *(Woo Jin Joo, 2021). Embroidery on an IKEA bag, 85 × 35 × 30 cm.*

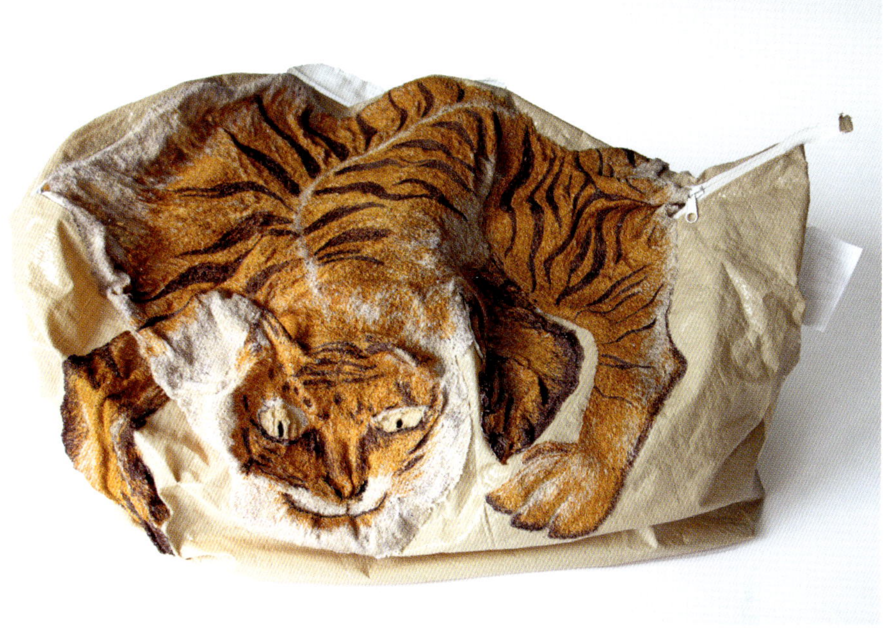

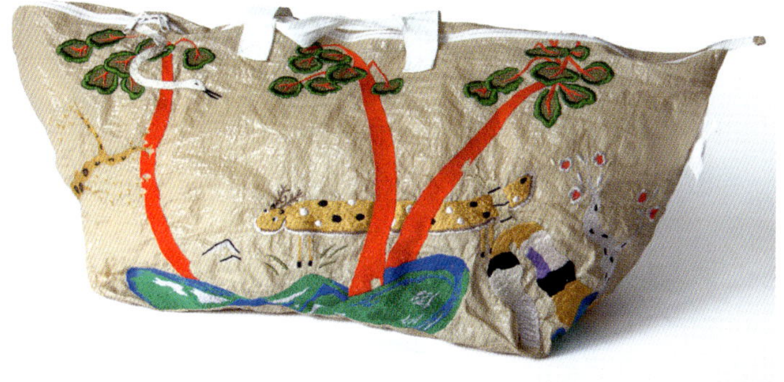

FEATURED ARTIST:
Woo Jin Joo

I now present to you the work of Woo Jin Joo, whose multidisciplinary practice takes aspects from traditional East Asian folklore, mythology and philosophy to explore ways of re-enchanting the stories of the objects and world around us through these lenses.

'When a tiger dies, it leaves behind its skin. When a man dies, he leaves behind his name' is a traditional Korean proverb that spurred this work. Guided by the title of the piece, this work provokes the question of what we are leaving behind as a generation, and as human beings. By embroidering a tiger onto an Ikea bag that is often considered valueless and disposable, this work is a reminder to be vigilant of the material legacy we are leaving behind.'

'The Ten Symbols of Longevity are a set of traditional Korean symbols that were traditionally used to wish for a person's long and prosperous life. By embroidering these cherished symbols onto an Ikea bag, which represents the fast, affordable, and disposable modern material culture, the work seeks to challenge our material hierarchy and value system.'

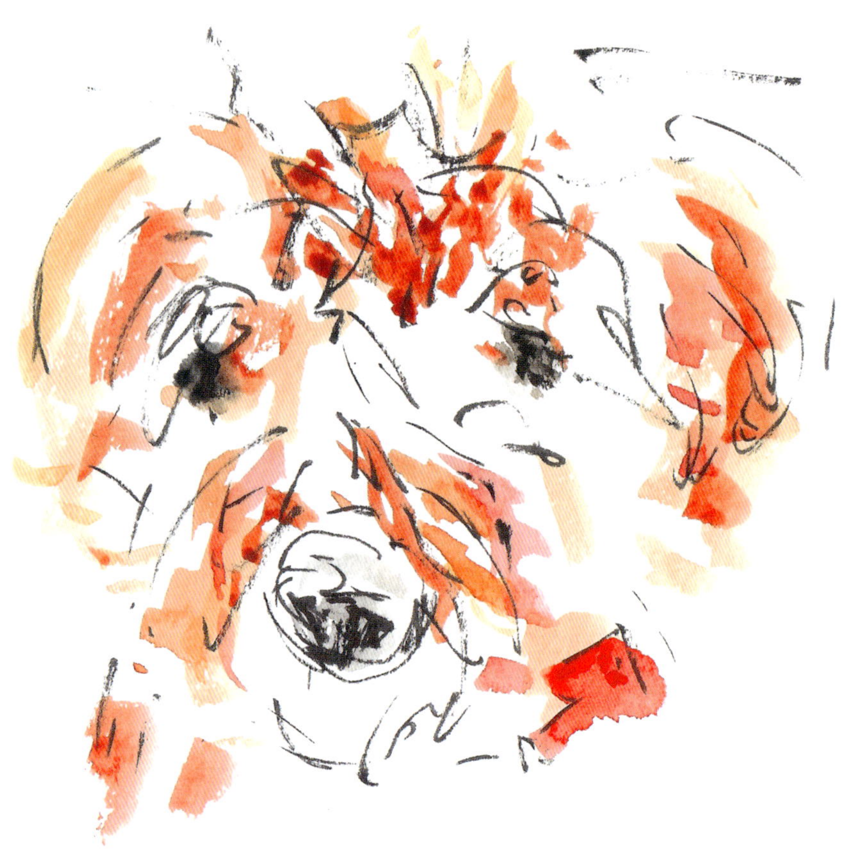

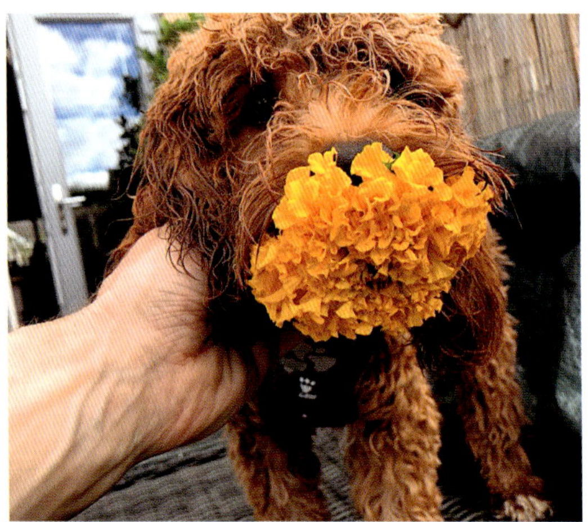

Narrative Fourteen:
He could heal the world if I let him off his lead

I didn't know what it was to love another so much until I met my furry man. I am not blinded; he is effectively time-limited, I accept, yet I know that he has been sent, not to try me, but to help me survive. He walks through life with me, yet he also has a nature so amicable and friendly that my whole village knows him more than they know me. Have you a similar piece of tamed nature? He is my everything.

Sometimes I get jealous on our wanderings because of how loving he is to everyone else. How often I get dragged along to the biscuit man's house or to the lady who lost her son, for him to do some healing unique to his kind. He would, I believe, at least try to heal the world, if only that leather strap that holds 'his grace' would slip just once from my pinkie finger grasp.

Narrative Fifteen:
Mr Pigeon and his lady love: a soothing 4 a.m. tale

I don't sleep; I never have. So, as I wander downstairs, no matter how considerate I am, my little fur man follows. On the kinder days, we look out or indeed sit out and watch the new resident in our garden, Mr Pigeon, and now, much to my delight, his lady love, which makes me even more awake and unable to sleep. Yes, readers, I admit that I make up stories about him and her and their goings-on. Isn't it wonderful to be able to appreciate the highs in what could be seen as an annoying habit; one that truthfully isn't the best for one's health?

Who is the lady love or the Mr Pigeon in your own life? We will all have a positive or negative story somewhere. Nature can be soothing, yet this does not have to be the genre of your own experience. No matter the time on the clock, being the observer of a beautiful natural scene can freeze our pasts and, whatever dialogues are going on in our heads, put us more in the moment. The cock of their heads; the fact that they land on the narrow bird-table rooftop (not the inner platform) and do their wonderful 'will I fall, won't I fall' wobble.

Personal experience

I will admit, pre-Covid, I always felt that there were too many 'must-dos' to achieve. It felt wrong to simply be and enjoy. The thought of leaving my home to have a walk or experience nature was akin to having a bath with Jo Malone candles and champagne and caviar on the side (although caviar sounds like a trauma, quite frankly). However, life circumstances altered and, moving swiftly on a few years, as of January 2020, I was holding a baby of my own – a baby of the furry kind: my Barney. He has walked with me ever since. He cut his teeth in lockdown, and we learned to cross the doorstep, be brave and battle the winds and rain together.

I learned a few key things. One was that being out and about doesn't guarantee immediate inspiration. There is walking without thought and walking with presence. Do you see what is under your feet? Clasp every moment, do not go out with your head cast down, look up at the sky. What colour is it today? Try to associate it with a watercolour palette; what colour do you deem it to be? Azure blue? Patient grey? One thing is for sure, it is not set to stay. Mud brown or mud grey? Seasons change, so what are they saying to you today?

'If you go down to the woods today, you're sure of a big surprise…'

I always thought that lyric was a little creepy, but maybe we all have our own happenstance in our own version of a wood. The question is, what is yours?

Garden ganders

How does your garden grow? I am sure, post-Covid, we now know the answer to that question. Before the lockdowns, I spent most of my hours either out, dressed for meetings, in a smart bodycon skirt and blouse, or in my studio. As my skirt became a dress or shorts, my mind also began to become more like the elastic on my waistbands. I think now the family regret all that coaxing, as the downstairs can at times look rather like my studio and, dare I say it, my upstairs studio currently hosts a thick layer of dust.

Once again, I am coming around slowly to the point, which is that the garden, and a good old gander within it, can be just the thing to inspire your textile art.

What can be found in a garden or outdoor space? Observing growth has become an obsession of mine. I need to see life; I need to know if the cosmoses are open or closed and if my courgette flower is big enough to pick yet, ready to stuff with a burst of ricotta. I turn to certain plants depending on my mood. If in need of centring, I make myself walk to the bottom of the garden, where my David Austin 'Ancient Mariner' rose boasts its pink glory. I grab the nearest face of a flowerhead and inhale. It is not a plant I look upon to make me smile, to make me happy, yet it fulfils a certain medicinal need. I live for my sweet peas and the 'what might be'.

To quote Audrey Hepburn:

'To plant a garden is to believe in tomorrow.'

Isn't that the best reason to continue?

A garden can be used in a variety of ways. We don't all have to be covered in soil or be the Monty Dons of this world, the garden can be so much more: a place to sit and work artistically, a place to observe, a place to build memories, which our art may then be founded upon. Or, like me, you could sit and paint what you see. Is that really a carrot you have grown? Can you laugh at its knobbly, not-supermarket-worthy, body? If it was to be translated into art, what could it be?

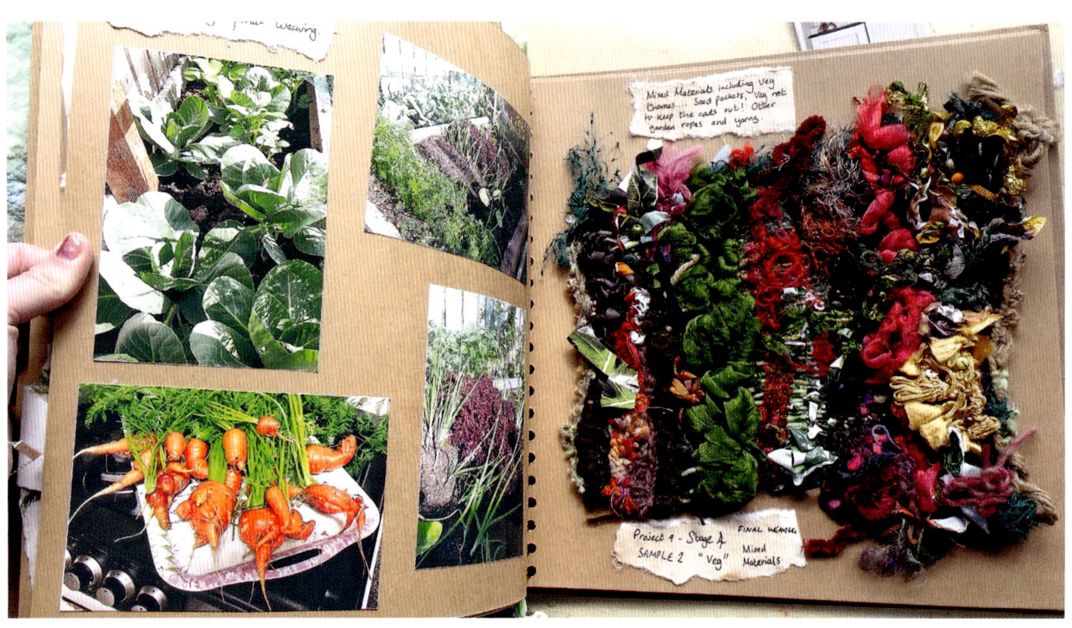

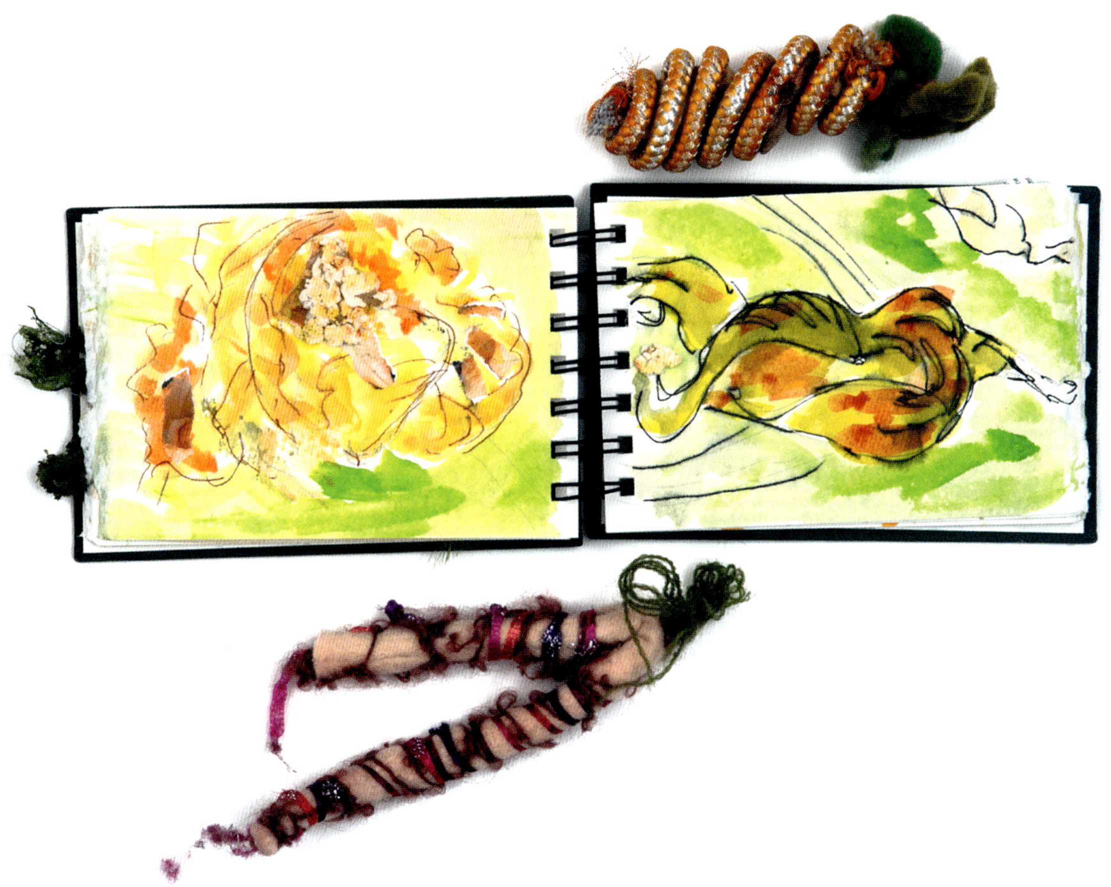

Narrative Sixteen:
Natural Introductions

As a child growing up on the Emerald Isle, a land divided in two both religiously and politically, my mother sought a kinder way for my fragile and sensitive soul. She would keep me at home and teach me about life herself, with one guiding rule: this was to be no airy-fairy alternative – this was *school*.

She led me down the curriculum line. There was no cheating the system, and this was the best one-to-one education I could have had. We lived near a wood and many a lunch break was spent with us becoming a duo of discovery. I was encouraged to notice the turning of the seasons, things like the acorns falling from their places and leaving space for winter's cold face. We collected leaves and carried them in our pockets along with wildflowers, all bound for the library of home tuition books, to be forgotten and found again months later, when they had a newer, flatter existence.

At the time, I just accepted this as life, I knew no other way. But it is these encounters with nature that have influenced much of my artistic practice. My mother is the reason why I keep asking, 'what if I...?'

Consider what your own background is. What was your own childhood like? We would all love to see it on paper (other materials are allowed!).

The Re-

There are many 're-' words that immediately suggest something positive:

- **Rewrite** **Revise** **Redraft** **Reset**

- **Rework** **Redo** **Recast**

And one I hold particularly dear:

REPAIR

Delving into the Oxford Dictionary, there are some key definitions I would like to present:

'the act of doing something to put something that is broken or damaged back into good condition or to make it work again'

'to do something to make a bad situation better'

These two key definitions convey my meaning of the word. To repair is not to induce perfection, it is to make something better or to return it to a condition where it can continue its life. As humans, this is what we hope for, both physically and mentally.

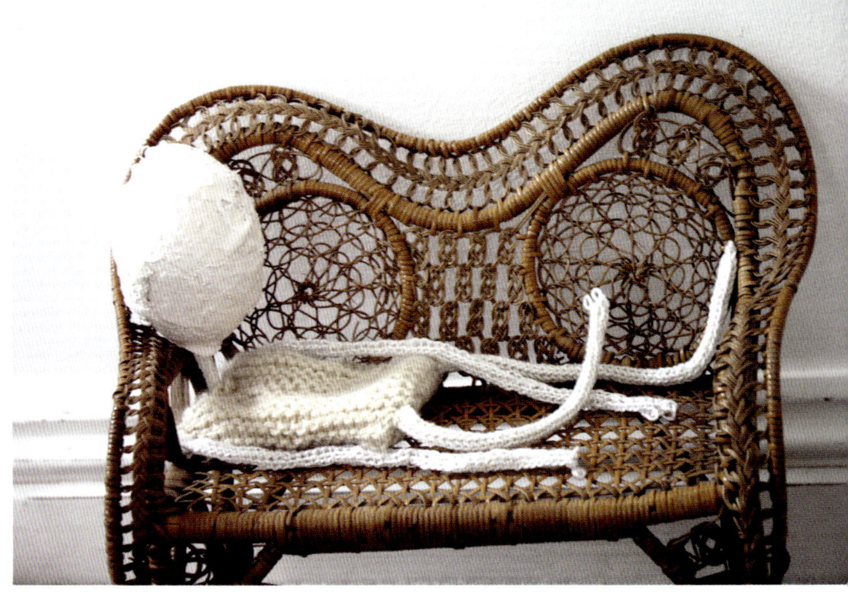

'Art is restoration: the idea is to repair the damages that are inflicted in life, to make something that is fragmented – which is what fear and anxiety do to a person – into something whole.'

Louise Bourgeois

At some point in our lives, we will all need to repair in some way. Having led a complete life in the arts, I can inform you, through much personal and audience-led research, that although art cannot create the perfect, it can and does repair.

ABOVE: I am just waiting, waiting *(Ailish Henderson, 2022). Miniaturised, humanised sculpture. Wool, silk, cashmere, Jesmonite, paint.*

FEATURED ARTIST:
Freddie Robins

Freddie Robins is an artist and Professor of Textiles at the Royal College of Art in London. Her studio practice focuses on the use of knitting as a medium to disrupt and subvert, exploiting the cultural preconceptions that continue to surround the activity.

'*I'm So Bloody Sad* is a sculptural work that I had been trying to resolve since 2007, eight years before it was first exhibited. It never felt right to me. Although I planned the piece, I struggled to accept it aesthetically. Conceptually, it felt too big a departure from work predating it. I simply couldn't come to terms with it until the exhibition title, *What Do I Need to Do to Make it OK?*, enabled me to reassess it. I didn't have to do anything to make it OK apart from wait.

'In her review of *What Do I Need to Do to Make it OK?* for the November/December 2015 issue of *Crafts* magazine, textile writer Jessica Hemmings used the term, "disarmingly confessional" in relation to the work. It was not intended to be disarming, although I do like that word. It is just a plain statement of fact. I can often find myself feeling so bloody sad. Don't we all suffer from overwhelming feelings of sadness every now and then? Isn't that part of the human condition that we have to come to terms with. When I was typing this I accidently typed "sad mess", which also seems appropriate.

'In *I'm So Bloody Sad*, the head of the figure falls heavily forward, weighted down by the knitting needles protruding from its crown. The elongated arms are trailing behind. Where the fingers should be are more needles. There are no facial features and the body is a simple rectangular block. The colour of the wool used is mundane and

ugly compared to the usual strong, attractive palette that I employ.

'There is no partner piece entitled *I'm So Bloody Happy*. Perhaps there should be, but I have always found happiness a banal emotion. Clinique produce a fragrance called 'Happy'. I love the smell of it but couldn't bear to wear it because of the name. I once had a student come to intern with me. Every morning she would greet me with the same question, "Are you happy?" Even if I was, this question was enough to wipe the smile from my face for the rest of the morning.

'I like to flatter myself with this quotation from *Garden of Eden* by Ernest Hemingway, "Happiness in intelligent people is the rarest thing I know".

'A quotation that is closer to my feelings is found in Haruki Murakami's 2002 novel *Kafka on the Shore*, "There's only one kind of happiness, but misfortune comes in all shapes and sizes."

'In Hemmings' review she goes on to say that the work "refuses to suggest recovery. Not mending, not repairing, and not saying that things can ever be made good again." That's right: although this work came good in the end, some things just can't be made OK.'

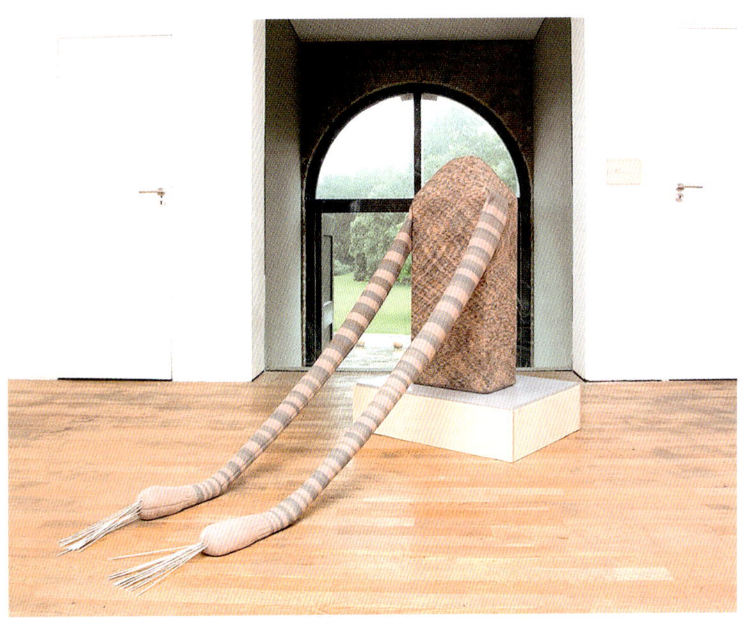

ABOVE: I'm so bloody sad, (Freddie Robins, 2007–2015). Machine knitted wool, foam block, sand, knitting needles, 98 × 40 × 210 cm. Pump House Gallery.

Karen Nicol

'I have worked in mixed media textiles for half a century. It is a part of my being and as such is my strength and psychological safe space. As well as providing everyday purpose and comfort, it has been my solace through some very hard times over the last ten years. Creating in the way that I do embraces so many restorative mental and physical aspects. The necessity to be open to constant visual research and stimulus to feed the diverse aspects of my work makes my brain fizz with joy. It wakes my mind

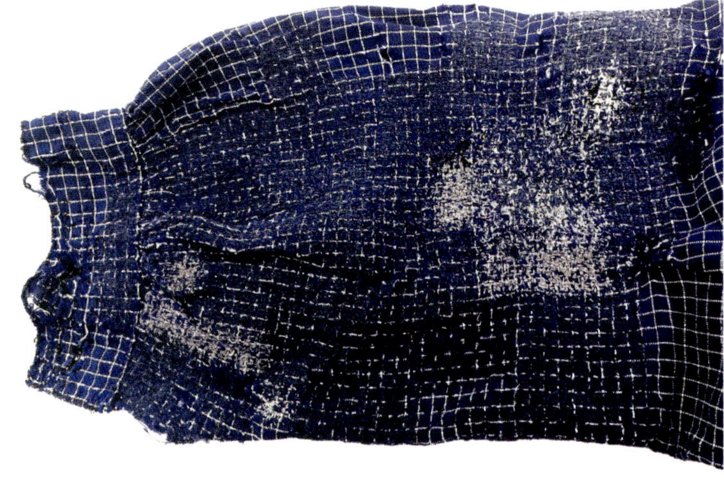

up facing the wonderful challenges of the medium in all the different sides of my career. Then, when the exciting nervous tension of creating something new bears fruit, the decisions have been made and I see that the piece is going to be okay, I feel palpable relief. Then the quiet, fulfilling labour brings me peace and comforting concentration.

'These large wall pieces saw me through lockdown in the COVID-19 pandemic, explaining the words of the loud, lonely voices in my head as I escaped the confines of the house to walk my dog. I was simply awestruck afresh by the beauty of nature in the quietness. The bright blue sky gloriously visible through the burgeoning plants recalled the Oscar Wilde quote about the man "who knows the price of everything and the value of nothing." Surely far truer today than when he penned it. I had to illustrate these thoughts.

'One of my most treasured possessions is a girl's darned dress. The mending beautifully tells the narrative of a girl's life in the past, the stitches revealing clues and maybe

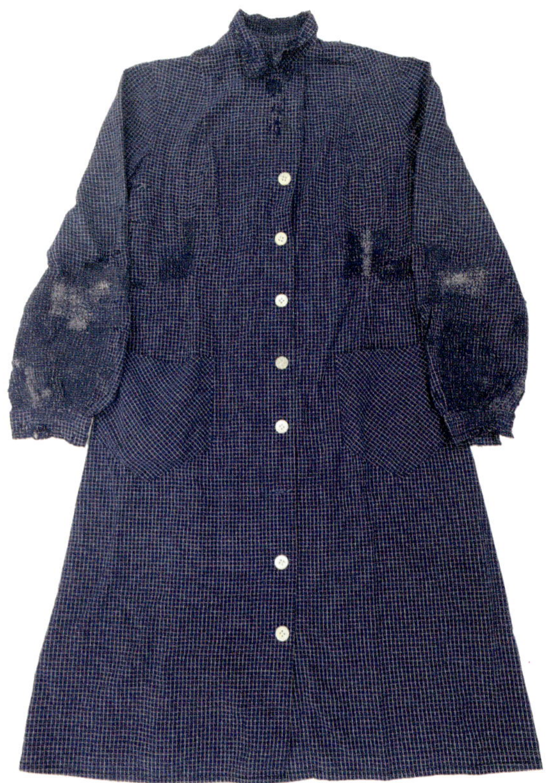

ABOVE: *Workwear made into art by happenstance (Karen Nicol, c.2013).*
TOP RIGHT: *Detail.*

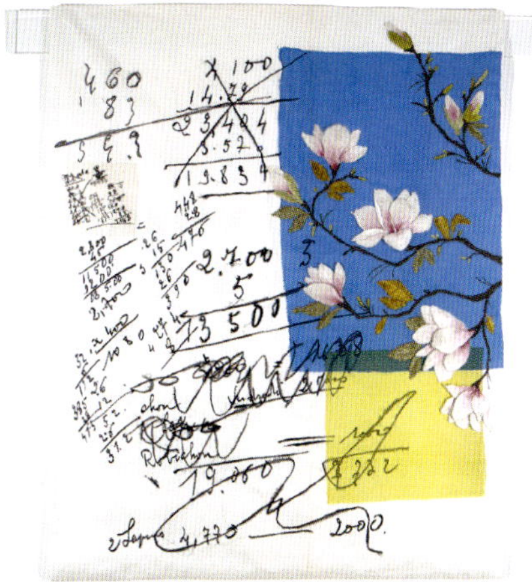
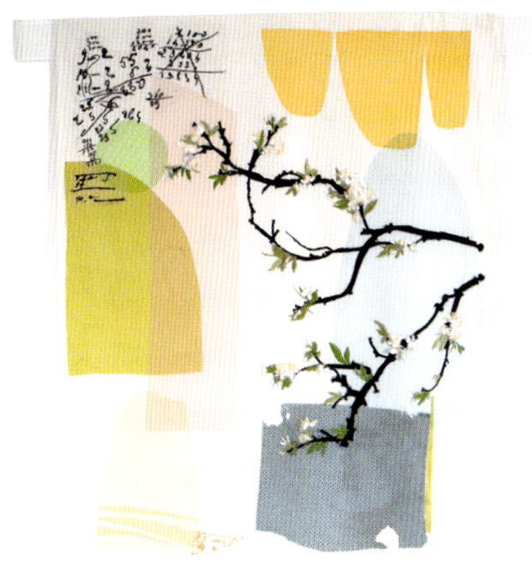
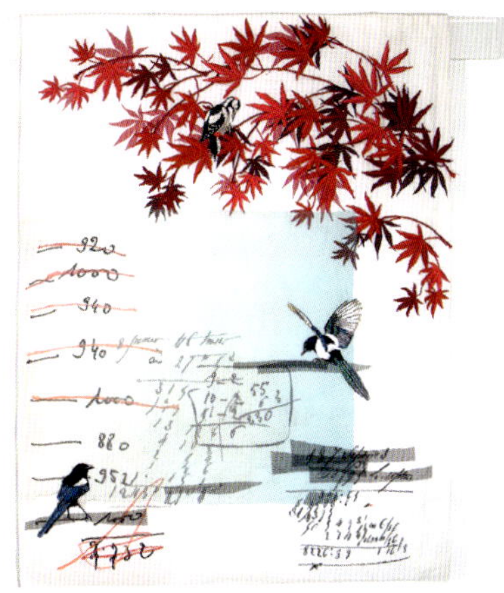
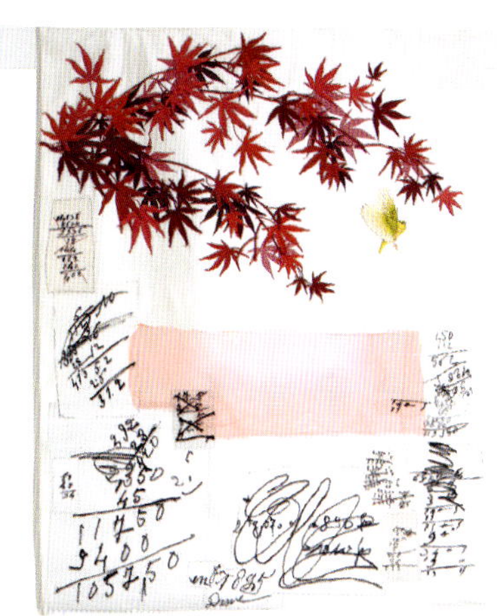
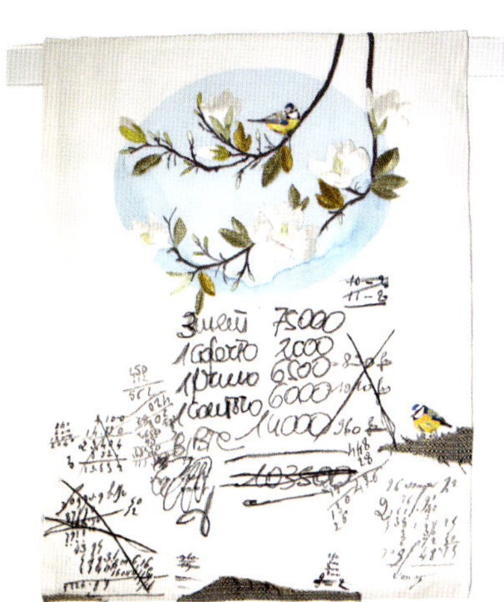
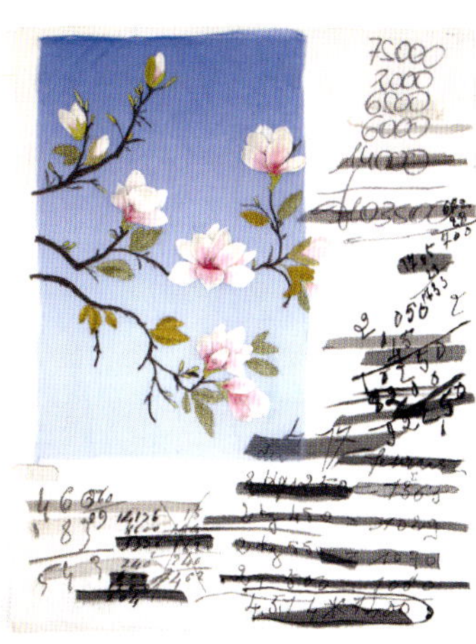

ABOVE: Value not the cost *(Karen Nicol, 2021). Individual art pieces (109 × 137cm).*

offering a glimpse into her story. The fact that this is hypothesis adds to the quiet drama of it. It's obviously an overall that has been worn daily. The neck, which she must have pinned closed every day, is tiny compared to the size of the dress, which makes you imagine it hanging off a thin young woman. She obviously sits in her job all day, her forearms and breasts rubbing against a surface, as these areas are heavily mended, and then the table protecting the front of the skirt where there are no darns. Likewise, one supposes she sits quite still as the bottom is just patched. Higher on the back of the garment she must have leant against something so her bra strap rubbed through.

'I imagine she worked in a factory. At the end of her day, she would go to her room and darn the dress where the fabric was wearing away, time after time…and so beautifully! On the sleeves she has almost tried to follow the checks of the weave, but it wasn't embellishment, it was pure necessity. The darning shows that her dress would then be hung on a hook ready to start again the next day. An amazing testament to a young woman's life and a delight that some stitches can tell such a story.'

The End (tying up the narrative)

I can only give you examples from my own life experience, honesty-led revelations to visually impart my narrative.

Let this book not be an end. I want your story, your tale, to go on, with further chapters – in all the variety of ways we have discussed.

This has been my interpretation so far. Yet with the final full stop there is still much left unwritten, yet to be experienced. An unseen comma should take its place, as really there is no end.

So, gather your thoughts, and begin a visual chapter of your own.

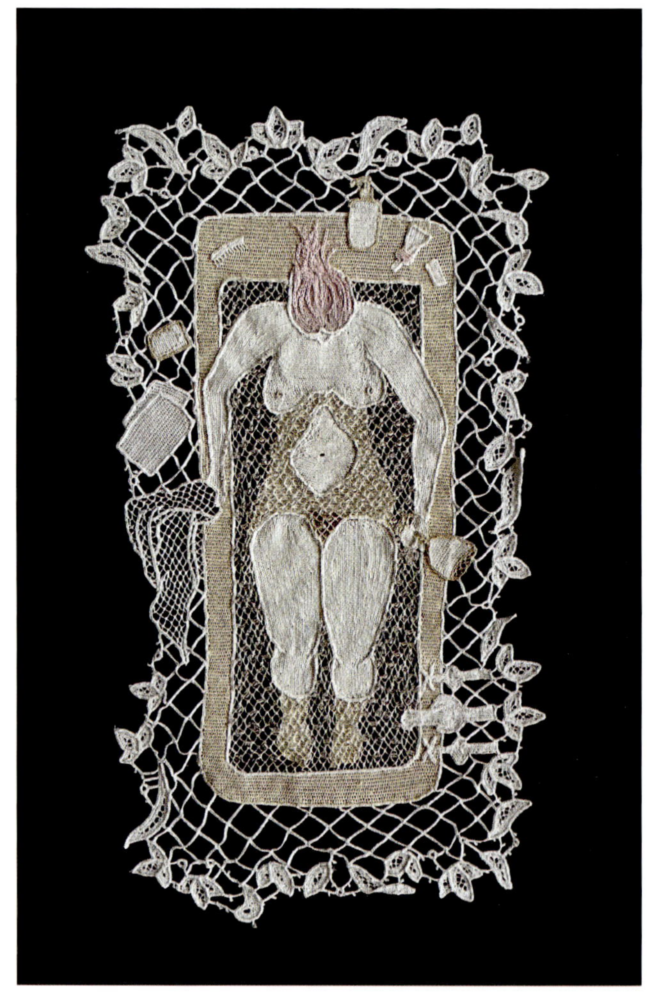

RIGHT: Pink Rinse *(Maggie Hensel-Brown, 2021). Needle lace made with silk thread, glass beads (13 × 23cm).*

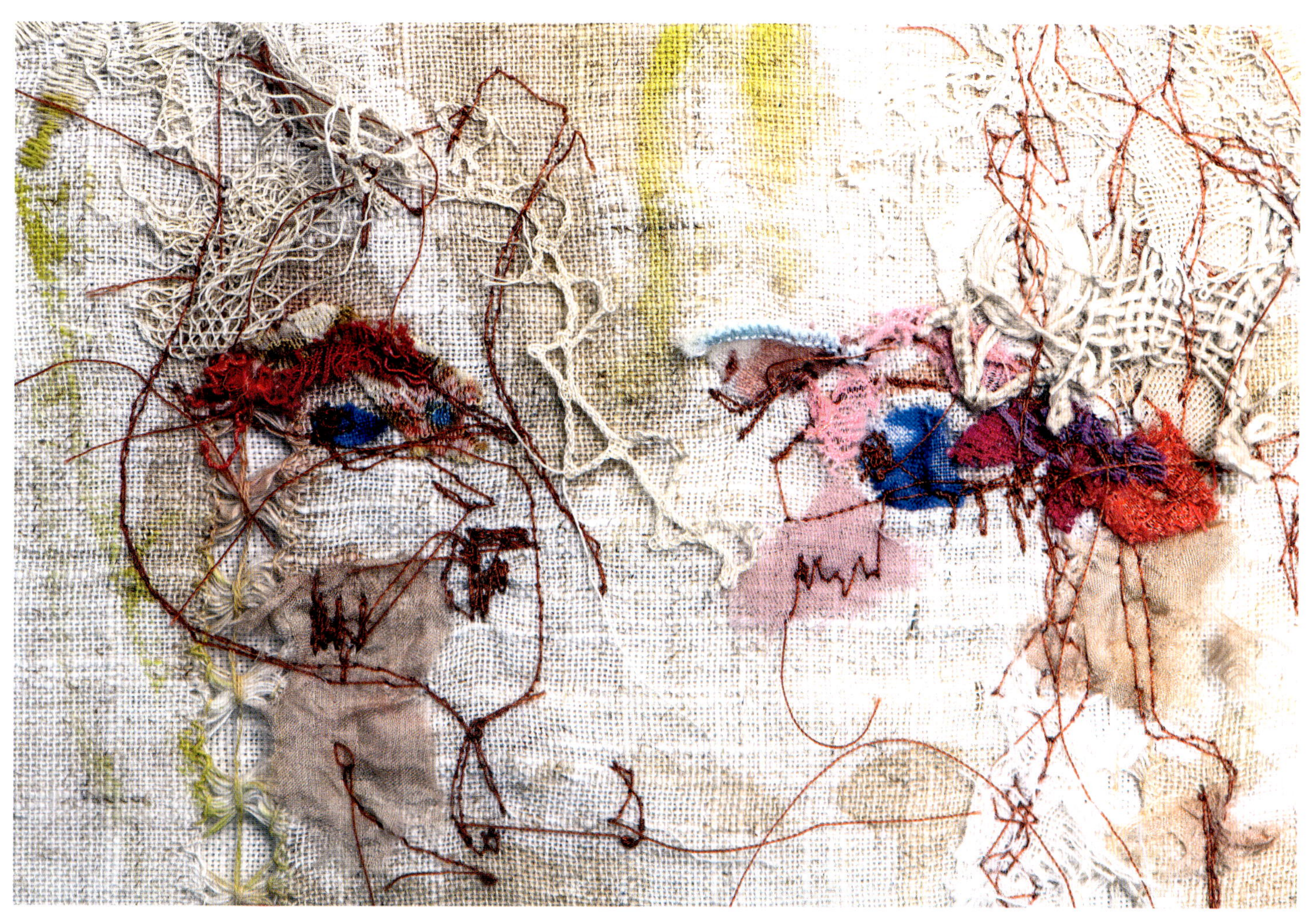

ABOVE: Lovelock bridge crossing *(Ailish Henderson, 2020). Ancestral cloth, poignant particles, thread.*

Featured artists

Joanna Barakat
www.joannabarakatart.com
Instagram: @joanna.barakat.art

Rosalind Byass
Instagram: @byass.rosalind

Linda Carswell
astitch4u@outlook.com

Daisy May Collingridge
www.daisycollingridge.com
Instagram: @daisy_collingridge

Jordan Cunliffe
www.jordancunliffe.co.uk
Instagram: @artisan_embroidery

Gaynor Devaney
www.gaynordevaney.co.uk
Instagram: @pompombelle

Jenni Dutton
www.jennidutton.com
Instagram: @jennidutton9342

Susan Forbes
Instagram: @mixedtextileartist

Caren Garfen
www.carengarfen.com
Instagram: @carengarfen

Maggie Hensel-Brown
www.maggiehenselbrown.com
Instagram: @maggiehenselbrown

Lise Howie
Instagram: @liseann31

Karen Hughes
Instagram:
@karenhughestextileart

Aran Illingworth
www.aran-i.com
Instagram: @aranillingworth

Angela James
Instagram: @9465angela

Woo Jin Joo
www.woojinstudio.com
Instagram: @woojinstudio

Michelle Kingdom
www.michellekingdom.com

Mieke Lockefeer
www.misswoolple.blogspot.com
Instagram: @mieke_lockefeer

Vicky Lockwood
Instagram: @vicky_lockwood_art

Karen Nicol
www.karennicol.com
Instagram: @karennicolstudio

Mandy Pattullo
www.mandypattullo.co.uk

Dr Sharon Peoples
www.sharon-peoples.com
Instagram: @SharonPeoplesStudio

Aiga Praulina
www.kripata.eu
Instagram: @lettin_in_nittel

Anne Richards
Instagram: @anne.e.richards

Freddie Robins
www.freddierobins.com

Pam Smyth
artintowords@gmail.com

Julia Triston
www.juilatriston.com

Gill Tyson
www.gilltyson.com

Wendy Ward
Instagram: @thatwendyward

Featured quotes

'Let's start at the very beginning, a very good place to start'
Lyrics from 'Do-Re-Mi', written by Oscar Hammerstein, featured in the film *The Sound of Music* (1965)

Sketchbook: 'a book of sheets of paper for drawing on'
Oxford Advanced Learner's Dictionary

Narrative: '... a spoken or written account of connected events; a story'
Oxford Languages

'My shadow's the only one that walks beside me. My shallow heart's the only thing that's beating. Sometimes, I wish someone out there will find me'
'Boulevard of Broken Dreams', Green Day

'The things that make me different, are the things that make me ME'
Winnie the Pooh by A.A. Milne

'To plant a garden is to believe in tomorrow.'
Audrey Hepburn

Repair: 'The act of doing something to put something that is broken or damaged back into good condition or to make it work again'
Oxford Dictionary

Repair: 'To do something to make a bad situation better'
Oxford Dictionary

'Art is restoration: the idea is to repair the damages that are inflicted in life, to make something that is fragmented – which is what fear and anxiety do to a person – into something whole'
Louise Bourgeois

'How lucky I am to have something that makes saying goodbye so hard'
Winnie the Pooh by A.A. Milne

'I don't feel very much like Pooh today,' said Pooh. 'There there,' said Piglet. 'I'll bring you tea and honey until you do.'
Winnie the Pooh by A.A. Milne

Picture credits

Sourcing materials

I would love to tell you that I have a certain list to proffer of go-to suppliers for all your magpie finds and the ingredients you require for all the 'could do' offerings in this book. But honestly, I find most of my own materials by chance.

I am kindly gifted many vintage textiles. I reuse a lot of my own family's heirlooms, and the rest I purchase at local and further afield textile and art venues, such as shows and galleries.

Many of you may find the internet to be a place for purchasing. If possible, I strive to stay away from the usual famous haunts, preferring to support independent retailers.

See also my ideas for Inspirational places.

Inspirational places

I will of course, have missed many places out from this list. I have not mentioned the Knitting and Stitching Show, or the other textile art shows, for example; I have concentrated on the personal places where I find peace and the strength to create.

Alhambra Palace, Spain
alhambra.org
Settling moments with narrow waters and silence as my song. I visited with my mother and father in the months after my mother had received positive news post-operation, having undergone a reoccurrence of breast cancer. I saw how it settled her; the tinkle of the streams was soothing to her soul. At age thirteen, I found myself sketching simply for the sake of it, no future set – looking back,

I was cutting my art-teeth as it were.... little did I know where it would lead me! One day I will reunite myself with this place – who knows what it will spark off this time.

The Biscuit Factory, Newcastle Upon Tyne
thebiscuitfactory.com
This has a gallery and café. I often teach one-off classes and courses here in a variety of textile-related subjects. It is light and airy and the café does a sublime oat milk flat white, which fuels the pencil on the page.

The British Museum, London
britishmuseum.org
I got lost here as a child (found by my hair-pulling-out parents, flouncing on the floor

with my pencil and pad, making a modern masterpiece). In later years, I have dragged various companions here.

Chester's By the River, Ambleside, Cumbria
chestersbytheriver.co.uk
A mixed gallery and shop, where you can rifle through the candles and pottery to locate the sketchbooks and ribbons.

Cook House, Newcastle Upon Tyne
cookhouse.org
You may wonder why I mention a restaurant. Ask any of my friends; they humour me as I napkin-draw my way through our socialising, observing the wildflower table displays.

Details Art Materials, Newcastle Upon Tyne
details.co.uk
Great for the handmade paper I favour as well as many other painting and drawing implements. There is a shortage of local shops like this now, so this offering is worth saving.

Dovecot Studios, Edinburgh
dovecotstudios.com
They offer constantly changing exhibitions and an events calendar of workshops and markets with a textile art edge. At heart, this is a world-known tapestry studio; tours are available.

Heaton Cooper Studio, Grasmere, the Lake District
heatoncooper.co.uk
I would recommend an in-person visit as their shop and café are sublime.

Louvre, Paris, France
louvre.fr
At the risk of reminiscing about all the locations where I was lost and found as a child, this one is pretty cliché. Where was Ailish? At the *Mona Lisa*, of course. Maybe it was this early insight into the great master that led me to produce a never-to-be-repeated pattern, exhibited and bought by the Kelvingrove Art Gallery, Glasgow, for the 2019 exhibition *Leonardo Da Vinci: A Life in Drawing*.

Lowther Castle and Gardens, Cumbria
lowthercastle.org
The rose garden has inspired many of my own digitally printed patterns.

Musee de l'Orangerie, Paris, France
musee-orangerie.fr
I can't help myself, I cry every time I visit this museum. The greatness of the works of Monet, gigantism in the visual; I feel small here, but not in a negative way.

Musee d'Orsay, Paris, France
musee-orsay.fr
A smorgasbord of masters with the ability to source champagne and good cheese. You could never be melancholy here.

The National Gallery of Modern and Contemporary Art, Rome
museopertutti.org
If I only have time for one gallery when in Italy, I go here. It has all the masters under one roof.

The National Trust (various locations throughout the UK)
nationaltrust.org.uk
I am a die-hard National Trust lover. It is my 'colour green', as it were. I am a self-confessed bashed-in Barbour wearer, Mr B at my side. I find the vegetable gardens of Gibside (in the northeast) to be draw-worthy. The dolls' houses at Wallington (in the northeast) are thought-provoking.

Look around Beatrix Potter's home in the Lake District to feel at a level with the natural habitat (rabbits bounce everywhere) or fluster over the roses in season at Acorn Bank, Penrith.

Palace of Versailles, Paris, France
en.chateauversailles.fr/
Moments matter. It was within the lower sections of the estate, stepping away from the main shadows of the place itself, where I made my most enlightening decisions regarding my degree practice. Inspired by the cumbersome outfits worn by past royals, in opposition to the flora and fauna and levity that this part of the grounds provides, I later produced a corset and subsidiary work.

RE, Corbridge, UK
re-foundobjects.com
You just don't know. That's why I go! The founders of RE seem to know about the art of surprise. From garden sinks to French soaps, what will you discover for your own art studio?

Rijksmuseum, Amsterdam
rijksmuseum.nl
The home of many grand masters.

The Royal Academy of Arts, London
royalacademy.org.uk
I recommend planning a visit when there is a show on that attracts your attention. Personally, I make the Summer Show an annual treat. This is also where I created a one-off Royal Academy design of a digitally printed scarf. A run of one hundred were made exclusively for this shop and became a part of their permanent collection. All gone now, I'm afraid!

Stedelijk Museum, Amsterdam, Netherlands
stedelijk.nl
Its modern art may shock you or go completely over your head, but at some point, in the future, you WILL remember it. I remember being very inspired by one artist who designed all their paintings (portraits) to be painted and hung on their back sides, so the canvas rims acted as a frame without the frame, as it were.

Tynemouth Markets, UK
tynemouthmarkets.co.uk
This place is a problem! Don't take a phone or a credit card, a budget is safer in cash form. With vintage textiles and artist-studio-worthy drawers and tables, it is a market of two halves, inside a working metro train station. Cross the bridge and on the way you will see an art gallery that is the bridge itself.

Van Gogh Museum, Amsterdam, Netherlands
vangoghmuseum.nl
I feel his story. I wish I could have had just one hour in the company of this man. A painter who felt too much – yet who can judge? He is proof that through pain one can produce a masterpiece – or many, in his case.

Victoria and Albert Museum, London
vam.ac.uk
I have spent many afternoons pounding the floors of touring exhibitions here. One that seems most brightly lit within my mind's eye was Alexander McQueen. I still have all the on-site drawings and paintings I produced on the day of my visit.

Index

Appreciations
and loves

First, I want to thank my earth makers: my duo of parents who walk through my life with me, binding me and bolstering my soul.

Thank you, Daddy, for the almond milk and honey nights and the muted love, visual in all its details woven into my DNA, the dishwasher remodelling, and the silent sweep, sweep, sweep, removing the latest breakage – not careless – but because I cared too much.

Mum, your 'narrative line' has been my constant evidence of hope and a real life 'Shouldn't have been but was'. Faith, 3 a.m....I won't even bother to start. You never gave up (oh, and you taught me to read and write, so that was helpful!) So, thank you, Mum, for everything.

I dedicated this book first and foremost to my Narg, my grandmother who has now become a 'comma'. I finish my book, by thanking her again, dear Narg. You know what I mean when I tell you that, in my imagination, I have already painted your door green. Thank you for giving me the strength to continue your sentence line. As a favoured writer of mine once stated: 'How lucky I am to have something that makes saying goodbye so hard' (*Winnie the Pooh* by A.A. Milne).

May I also thank my bolsters and prodders, those who have taken over my Narg's voice in the pursuit to ignite my hands to type and finish this book. Scared to name names here: my 'should-have-been S', Vitamin 'E', 'G', oh and Momma G.

There are a few special people in my life, and I am so thankful for their Piglet care. In the words of A.A. Milne, the moments where I don't feel quite like 'Pooh today' – their answer? 'I will bring you tea and cake till you do'. Quiet love.

Thank you to my featured artists: you have all been so patient with my emails!

Finally, the team at Batsford. I will admit to you now that I am still surprised that you took me on without more proof that I could pull this off. Let's just say I have surprised myself!